THE FREUD/JUNG LETTERS

THE CORRESPONDENCE
BETWEEN SIGMUND FREUD AND C. G. JUNG

Edited by William McGuire

TRANSLATED BY RALPH MANHEIM AND R. F. C. HULL
ABRIDGED BY ALAN McGLASHAN

PENGUIN BOOKS

PENGUIN BOOKS

Published by the Penguin Group
Penguin Books Ltd, 27 Wrights Lane, London W8 5TZ, England
Viking Penguin, a division of Penguin Books USA Inc.
375 Hudson Street, New York, New York 10014, USA
Penguin Books Australia Ltd, Ringwood, Victoria, Australia
Penguin Books Canada Ltd, 2801 John Street, Markham, Ontario, Canada L3R 1B4
Penguin Books (NZ) Ltd, 182–190 Wairau Road, Auckland 10, New Zealand

Penguin Books Ltd, Registered Offices: Harmondsworth, Middlesex, England

First published in Great Britain by The Hogarth Press and
Routledge & Kegan Paul 1974
This abridged edition published in Picador by Pan Books 1979
Published in Penguin Books 1991
10 9 8 7 6 5 4 3 2 1

Copyright © Sigmund Freud Copyrights Ltd and
Erbengemeinschaft Prof. Dr C. G. Jung, 1974
Preface copyright © Alan McGlashan, 1979
All rights reserved

Printed in England by Clays Ltd, St Ives plc

began simply as a method of treating neurotic patients by investigating their minds, but it quickly grew into an accumulation of knowledge about the workings of the mind in general, whether sick or healthy. Freud was thus able to demonstrate the normal development of the sexual instinct in childhood and, largely on the basis of an examination of dreams, arrived at his fundamental discovery of the unconscious forces that influence our everyday thoughts and actions. Freud's ideas have shaped not only many specialist disciplines but the whole intellectual climate of the last half-century.

The Swiss psychiatrist C. G. Jung, born in 1875, began his professional career at the Burghölzli Hospital in Zurich, where he was the first to apply psychoanalytic ideas to the study of schizophrenia. He collaborated with Freud from 1906 to 1913 but parted with him when their differences could no longer be reconciled. Jung opposed Freud's theory of a sexual basis for neurosis and went on to found his own school of 'Analytical Psychology'. Jung, in his method of therapy, emphasized normal and healthy psychology; he considered that symptoms were disturbances of normal processes and not entities themselves. His major contribution to the study of the psyche was his impressive hypothesis of the existence in every human being of what he called the collective unconscious – a hitherto disregarded psychic level at which all the strange imaginings of the human mind, the myths, legends, dreams and fantasies

took on a new and luminous meaning. He saw these phenomena as the innumerably repeated imprint of certain basic
human situations, and the figures appearing in them as
archetypes. His influence has been felt in many fields outside
psychiatry, in both the arts and the sciences. C. G. Jung died
in 1961.

William McGuire was executive editor of the *Collected Works
of C. G. Jung* and associate editor of the Bollingen Series
before his retirement from Princeton University Press.

Dr Alan McGlashan, M.C., war pilot and psychiatrist, is also
author of *The Savage and Beautiful Country* and *Gravity and
Levity*.

Contents

Preface

Napoleon once said – 'Mightier than an army with banners is an idea whose time has come.' This well describes the advance, against almost universal opposition, made by the ideas of Freud and Jung in the early stages of their brief partnership.

These two men began corresponding in April 1906. Eleven months later they met for the first time in Vienna, and according to Jung 'talked uninterruptedly for thirteen hours'. Thereafter, with occasional gaps due to illness or holidays, they wrote to each other every few days for the next seven years. The story of their mutual attraction, close collaboration and eventual estrangement is unfolded in a curiously direct and moving way by these letters.

The considerable correspondence which resulted – some 360 letters – has been collected and translated with copious footnotes, illustrations, and appendices in a large, scholarly hardback volume (*The Freud/Jung Letters*; edited by William McGuire; The Hogarth Press and Routledge & Kegan Paul, 1974)[1]. This standard edition is necessary reading for any serious student of psychiatry. The efforts made to ensure accuracy in the translation of the text, and the patient diplomacy employed to achieve permission to publish these historic letters, are fully set out in the Editor's Introduction, which has been included in full in the present book.

Inevitably in so frequent an exchange of letters, many are chiefly concerned with minor publishing problems and other organizational details of little interest to the general reader; and in places there are

[1] Originally published in the Bollingen Series by Princeton University Press, Princeton, New Jersey, USA, which also issued an unabridged paperback edition (1979). Another paperback edition has been published by Harvard University Press. The editor's corrections and additions in both paperback editions have been made available for the present abridgement.

highly technical discussions for the appreciation of which professional knowledge is required.

The aim of this abridged edition of the letters is to make available to the widest possible readership the core of the correspondence: the fateful encounter between these two world-renowned figures, and the courage with which they faced together the bitter hostility of the medical world of their day.

In the letters as here published can be traced the gradual transition from the intimate 'son-to-father' relationship of the beginning, through the slowly increasing frictions and divergencies of two powerful but fundamentally opposed minds, to the final break. Incidentally, Jung's wife, Emma, recognized as early as 1911 signs of the approaching estrangement, and included in this book are the letters which she wrote secretly to Freud in an unavailing attempt to reconcile the two men.

Apart from its intrinsic interest, the story as it unfolds in the letters has also the structure of a paradigm: a classic instance of the love-hate relationship acted out in countless homes between gifted sons and gifted fathers. The Freud-Jung split has been usually regarded as a great tragedy. But the point is arguable. It is possible to see it as a painful but highly fortunate event. This type of 'father-son' clash is one which is apt to call out the negative side of both contestants, alternating with exhausting efforts to reach mutual understanding. It was precisely their breaking with each other that put a stop to all this, and gave room for the eventual full flowering of personality and achievement in both men. If the break had not occurred, the continual adjustments each was constrained to make in order to accommodate to the other and so preserve the relationship, might have resulted in a still greater tragedy. It might have robbed the world of two magnificent and highly individualistic contributions to the understanding of the human psyche.

Alan McGlashan 1979

Introduction

These letters are the direct evidence of the intensely fruitful and finally tragic encounter of Freud and Jung. The quality of tragedy, however, resides only in the encounter, the drama of the letters themselves, moving forward in almost a classical way towards the foreshadowed catastrophe of conflict and dissension. It can scarcely be said that the career, the life, of either man was tragically altered, but rather that Freud and Jung each derived creative values from the inevitable break.

Unlike their courteous and appreciative references to one another's published work while they were collaborators, or anything that either one wrote about their relationship during the bitter aftermath, the letters bear the most acute witness to the complex interplay of these two unique personalities, so different yet so strongly attracted to one another. The dialogue inevitably tempts analytical and psychoanalytical interpretation, philosophical rumination over its beginnings and its effects and its 'meaning', and the weighing up of its aggressions, projections, magnanimities, shafts of wisdom, seminal particles, and whatever else could be put into the balance. A consideration of the correspondence along such lines, however, has been ruled out by the sons of the two principals, who, in concluding an agreement to publish the letters, prudently stipulated that they were to be treated 'like historical documents ... in order to guarantee impartiality'.

In the years just before the beginning of this century, Freud was in a state of what he more than once called 'splendid isolation'.[1] His

---

[1] For the details of this period of Freud's career, see Jones, I, ch XIV–XVI, and II, ch I–II; Freud, *The Origins of Psychoanalysis*; Ellenberger, *The Discovery of the Unconscious*, ch 7; and K. R. Eissler, *Sigmund Freud und die Wiener Universität* (Bern, 1966). (For explanation of abbreviated titles, see pp 39–40.)

career had been wracked by frustrations; he had not become a research scientist as he had once hoped to, and he had not become a University professor.[2] His collaboration with Josef Breuer had resulted in an important work, the *Studies on Hysteria* (1895; SE II), but afterwards the two became estranged. Freud had first used the term 'psychoanalysis' in an 1896 publication, and during the latter part of the decade he was elaborating the psychoanalytic technique. Entirely alone, he had embarked in 1897 on the self-analysis of his own unconscious, which led into the writing of *The Interpretation of Dreams* (published in late 1899 but dated 1900; SE IV–V). According to Ernest Jones's account, the book was inadequately reviewed and sold poorly. Nevertheless, it was a turning point in Freud's life. 'He regarded it both as his most significant scientific work, the foundation stone of his whole achievement, and as the work that brought him into the clear personally, giving him the strength to face a troubled life anew.'[3]

The year 1902 was marked by three further events of major consequence in Freud's career. Since 1887 he had been carrying on a correspondence and a close friendship with Wilhelm Fliess, an otolaryngologist of Berlin; the letters to Fliess, which have almost miraculously survived,[4] are a principal source of knowledge about the genesis of psychoanalysis. But in 1902 the correspondence and the friendship came to an end. Furthermore, very much through his own exertions, he was appointed to the equivalent of an associate professorship at Vienna University. Finally, in the autumn of that year, Freud inaugurated the 'Psychological Wednesday Evenings', at Wilhelm Stekel's suggestion, by inviting four of his acquaintances who were interested in psychoanalysis to meet for discussions in Freud's waiting room.[5]

[2] C. A. Schorske, 'Politics and Patricide in Freud's *Interpretation of Dreams*', *American Historical Review*, LXXVIII:2 (Apr 1973), 330f.

[3] Ibid, 330.

[4] Published in *The Origins of Psychoanalysis*.

[5] Jones, II, p 8/8. The original four – Wilhelm Stekel, Alfred Adler, Rudolf Reitler, Max Kahane – gradually increased to more than twenty and in April 1908 became the Vienna Psychoanalytic Society. The *Minutes* (see p 40) were recorded, beginning in 1906, by Otto Rank.

Freud's reputation and his contacts were spreading slowly beyond the confines of Vienna. He next wrote *The Psychopathology of Everyday Life* (1901; SE VI) and 'Fragment of an Analysis of a Case of Hysteria' (not published until 1905; SE VII); and then, also simultaneously, *Jokes and Their Relation to the Unconscious* (1905; SE VIII) and *Three Essays on the Theory of Sexuality* (1905; SE VII). It was the latter work, Jones has said, 'that brought the maximum of odium on Freud's name',[6] because of Freud's findings concerning the sexual instinct in childhood.

The first significant focus of interest in psychoanalysis outside Freud's immediate circle was at the Burghölzli Mental Hospital in Zürich. An austere block of buildings on heights overlooking the lake of Zürich, the Burghölzli had been established in 1860 as the cantonal asylum for the insane, and it served also as the psychiatric clinic of Zürich University. Under Auguste Forel, who became director in 1879, it acquired an international reputation for advanced treatment and research, which was carried forward by Eugen Bleuler, Forel's successor in 1898.

On 10 December 1900, Jung arrived at the Burghölzli to take up his first professional post, as an assistant physician. He had completed his medical studies at the University of Basel, his home town, and had received his diploma barely a fortnight before, on 27 November.[7] Despite the hospital's *avant-garde* reputation, Jung later described his work at the Burghölzli as 'a submission to the vow to believe only in what was probable, average, commonplace, barren of meaning, to renounce everything strange and significant, and reduce anything extraordinary to the banal. Henceforth there were only ... oppressively narrow horizons, and the unending desert of routine.'[8] Against this background, Jung's first experience of Freud must have been exciting in double measure. 'As early as 1900,' he wrote, 'I had read Freud's *The Interpretation of Dreams*. I had laid the book

[6] Jones, II, p 321/286.
[7] For Jung's years at the Burghölzli, see *Memories, Dreams, Reflections*, pp 111–13/113–15, and ch IV; and Ellenberger, ch 9. The dating of events in Jung's academic career has been confirmed by Mr Franz Jung.
[8] *Memories*, p 111/113.

aside, at the time, because I did not yet grasp it ... In 1903 I once more took [it] up ... and discovered how it all linked up with my own ideas.'[9] In an interview in 1957, Jung said that in 1900 Bleuler had asked him to give a report on *The Interpretation of Dreams* at a staff 'report evening'.[10]

Before Jung 'laid the book aside' in 1900 (or 1901), he had digested enough of Freud's 'dream investigations' to cite them for their relevance to his own experimental findings in his doctoral dissertation, published in 1902.[11] Most other publications of Jung's in the years 1902–1905[12] contain citations of Freud's work (though not of his sexual theories).

Jung spent the winter semester of 1902–1903 at the Salpêtrière, in Paris, attending Janet's lectures on theoretical psychopathology. On 14 February 1903, soon after returning to Zürich, he was married to Emma Rauschenbach, and they moved into a flat in the central building of the Burghölzli, upstairs from the flat in which the Bleuler family lived.[13] The resident staff of the hospital in Jung's day also included Karl Abraham, Franz Riklin, Max Eitingon, and Hermann Nunberg, and there were visitors from abroad – notably, A. A. Brill – who came for periods of observation and study.

[9] Ibid, pp 146f/144f.

[10] R. I. Evans, *Conversations with Carl Jung* (Princeton: Van Nostrand, 1964); also, as a corrected transcript, in CW 18. In Jung's posthumous papers a typescript was discovered, dated 25 Jan 1901, which constitutes a report not on *Die Traumdeutung* but on *Über den Traum* (= 'On Dreams', SE V), a summary of the former which Freud published in *Grenzfragen des Nerven- und Seelen-lebens*, ed L. Löwenfeld and H. Kurella (Wiesbaden, 1901). For Jung's report, see *Spring*, 1973, pp 171–79, and CW 18.

[11] *On the Psychology and Pathology of So-called Occult Phenomena* (CW 1). The MD degree was awarded to Jung by Zürich University on 17 July 1902.

[12] 'A Case of Hysterical Stupor in a Prisoner in Detention' (1902), 'On Simulated Insanity' (1903), 'On Hysterical Misreading' (1904), 'Cryptomnesia' (1905) – all in CW 1; the first four studies in word association (1904–5) and 'The Psychological Diagnosis of Evidence' (1905) – all in CW 2.

[13] Here Freud visited the Jungs for four days in Sept 1908 and was shown at least one of Jung's classic cases (*Memories*, pp 125ff/126). In June 1909, when the Jung family removed to their new house at Küsnacht, Jung resigned from the Burghölzli staff.

Introduction

Freud's first direct contact with the Burghölzli had apparently been a correspondence that he and Bleuler had opened in September 1904, which continued more or less sporadically until at least 1925.[14] In his autobiography Jung says that he himself 'first took up the cudgels for Freud at a congress in Munich where a lecturer discussed obsessional neuroses but studiously forbore to mention the name of Freud'.[15] In any event, Freud's 'Fragment of an Analysis of a Case of Hysteria' had appeared in 1905, and Jung lost no time in drawing on it in his paper 'Psychoanalysis and Association Experiments' (CW 2), prepared that year and published the next. Jung presented a case of obsessional neurosis that he had treated in June 1905 by subjecting the patient first to the association test and then to psychonanalysis – interviews of one and a half to two hours every other day for three weeks. Jung discharged the patient rather inconclusively, but in November she came back and presented herself as cured. In summarizing the case, Jung stated that the association test might be useful 'for facilitating and shortening Freud's psychoanalysis'.

That paper closed, or climaxed, the volume of *Diagnostic Association Studies*[16] that Jung sent to Freud in April 1906, thus setting in motion their correspondence. The book had the force of a direct message, for in the studies written by both Jung and Bleuler there were citations of Freud's work that amply demonstrated the accept-

14 Alexander and Selesnick, pp 6, 8. Dr Manfred Bleuler believes that there were contacts between his father and Freud even earlier, in the 1890s (personal communication). In fact, in 1896, E. Bleuler reviewed *Studien über Hysterie*; cf Jones, I, p 278/253. The letters from Freud to Bleuler in M Bleuler's possession are at present barred from publication.

15 *Memories*, p 148–147. The congress has not been identified, and there may be a confusion here with the Congress of South-West German Neurologists and Psychiatrists at Baden-Baden, 27 May 1906, at which Aschaffenburg attacked Freud's 'Fragment of an Analysis of a Case of Hysteria' and Jung took the floor to reply vigorously. Both Aschaffenburg's paper and Jung's reply (CW 4) were published in a Munich periodical – *Münchener medizinische Wochenschrift*, LIII:37 and 47 (Sept and Nov 1906).

16 The studies had already appeared singly in the *Journal für Psychologie und Neurologie* over the previous two years, but there is no evidence that Freud had seen them there.

ance psychoanalysis had found at the Burghölzli. The first actual letter was Freud's of 11 April 1906, a warm acknowledgement of the book, which, in his eagerness to read it, Freud had already bought. A reply from Jung was not required by courtesy, and there matters rested for nearly six months. In June Freud gave a lecture that contains his first published comments on Jung, the association experiments, and the theory of complexes.[17] During the summer, Jung completed his monograph on *The Psychology of Dementia Praecox*, for which he had been amassing material since 1903. The book is interlarded with citations and extended discussions of Freud's work, and in the foreword, which Jung dated July 1906, he made the following declarations:

Even a superficial glance at my work will show how much I am indebted to the brilliant discoveries of Freud. As Freud has not yet received the recognition and appreciation he deserves, but is still opposed even in the most authoritative circles, I hope I may be allowed to define my position towards him. My attention was drawn to Freud by the first book of his I happened to read, *The Interpretation of Dreams*, after which I also studied his other writings. I can assure you that in the beginning I naturally entertained all the objections that are customarily made against Freud in the literature. But, I told myself, Freud could be refuted only by one who has made repeated use of the psychoanalytic method and who really investigates as Freud does; that is, by one who has made a long and patient study of everyday life, hysteria, and dreams from Freud's point of view. He who does not or cannot do this should not pronounce judgement on Freud, else he acts like those notorious men of science who disdained to look through Galileo's telescope. Fairness to Freud, however, does not imply, as many fear, unqualified submission to a dogma; one can very well maintain an independent judgement. If I, for instance, acknowledge the complex mechanisms of dreams and hysteria, this does not mean that I attribute to the infantile sexual trauma the exclusive importance that Freud apparently does. Still less does it mean

[17] 'Psycho-Analysis and the Establishment of the Facts in Legal Proceedings', SE IX, pp 104, 106, where Freud refers to Jung's paper on the same subject, 'The Psychological Diagnosis of Evidence' (1905). Freud's paper also contained his first reference to Alfred Adler (p 105).

that I place sexuality so predominantly in the foreground, or that I grant
it the psychological universality which Freud, it seems, postulates in view
of the admittedly enormous role which sexuality plays in the psyche. As
for Freud's therapy, it is at best but one of several possible methods, and
perhaps does not always offer in practice what one expects from it in
theory. Nevertheless, all these things are the merest trifles compared with
the psychological principles whose discovery is Freud's greatest merit;
and to them the critics pay far too little attention. He who wishes to be
fair to Freud should take to heart the words of Erasmus:
'Unumquemque move lapidem, omnia experire, nihil intentatum
relinque.'[18]

Over the summer, Freud finished assembling the first volume of his
Short Papers on the Theory of the Neuroses, and he sent a copy to
Jung in October 1906. With Jung's letter of reply, the correspondence was under way in earnest – 'a most friendly and even intimate
exchange of both personal thoughts as well as scientific reflections
... for nearly seven years'.[19] When Jung's *Dementia Praecox* was
published in December, he sent one of the first copies to Freud, who
had expressed his eagerness to see it. Unfortunately, Freud's comments upon receiving that crucial book were made in a letter that is
one of the few missing in this collection.[20]

In his subsequent writings Freud unreservedly acknowledged the
services rendered to the spread of psychoanalysis by the Zürich
School, 'particularly by Bleuler and Jung'. Recounting the history of
the psychoanalytic movement in 1914, immediately after the break
with Jung, Freud stated, 'According to the evidence of a colleague[21]
who witnessed developments at the Burghölzli, it appears that
psychoanalysis awakened interest there very early. In Jung's work
on occult phenomena, published in 1902, there was already an allusion to my book on dream-interpretation. From 1903 or 1904, says

[18] CW 3, pp 3f. / 'Move every stone, try everything, leave nothing unattempted.'
   – Erasmus, *Adagia*, I.IV.xxx. The translation here is by Margaret Mann
   Phillips, to whom acknowledgement is gratefully made.
[19] Jones, II, p 35/30f.
[20] For a list of the missing items, see appendix 1, p 562, in the original edition.
[21] Karl Abraham. See *Freud/Abraham Letters*, 15 Jan '14, in which Abraham
   supplied information that Freud had requested.

my informant, psycho-analysis was in the forefront of interest.'[22] After describing his period of isolation and the gradual development in Vienna from 1902 onwards, Freud told how 'in 1907 the situation changed all at once and contrary to all expectations ... A communication from Bleuler had informed me before this that my works had been studied and made use of in the Burghölzli. In January 1907, the first member of the Zürich clinic came to Vienna – Dr Eitingon. Other visits followed, which led to an animated exchange of ideas. Finally, on the invitation of C. G. Jung ... a first meeting took place at Salzburg in the spring of 1908 ...'[23]

The account of the relationship of Freud and Jung from 1906 forward is, of course, contained in the letters in this volume – the gradual warming of mutual regard, confidence, and affection, the continual interchange of professional information and opinions, the rapidly elaborating business of the psychoanalytic movement, the intimate give-and-take of family news, the often acerb and witty observations on colleagues and adversaries, and at length the emergence of differences, disagreements, misunderstandings, injured feelings, and finally disruption and separation.

After Jung's letter of 20 April 1914 resigning from the presidency of the International Association, there is a long silence in the history of these letters.[24] Freud himself did not again engage in a holocaust of unwanted papers, as he had done in March 1908, when he took over an adjoining flat and rearranged his study (occurrences which, incidentally, are not mentioned in his letters to Jung). Into the file of Jung's letters to him he also placed some of the programmes of the congresses and Jung's circular letters to the presidents of the branch

[22] SE XIV, p 28.

[23] Ibid, p 26. Writing eleven years later, Freud gave a more succinct but slightly less exact account: '... my isolation gradually came to an end. To begin with, a small circle of pupils gathered round me in Vienna; and then, after 1906, came the news that the psychiatrists at Zürich, E. Bleuler, his assistant C. G. Jung, and others, were taking a lively interest in psycho-analysis. We got into personal touch with one another, and at Easter 1908 the friends of the young science met at Salzburg...' ('An Autobiographical Study', SE XX, p 48).

[24] Jung's letter of 1923 (359 J) is the sole exception.

societies, as well as several letters from Jung to Ferenczi, which apparently Ferenczi had turned over to Freud.[25] The letters Freud received from Emma Jung were kept separately. There is no evidence that he ever consulted the Jung file again, though he himself must have placed Jung's referral letter of 1923 in it. Freud's correspondence was filed chronologically in cabinets in his study at Berggasse 19. When the time approached for the Freuds to leave Vienna in 1938, Anna Freud and Marie Bonaparte went through Freud's papers and correspondence and burned some items that would have been dangerous if they had fallen into Nazi hands.[26] Then the remaining files of papers and letters – from Jones, Abraham, Eitingon, Pfister, Ferenczi, Lou Andreas-Salomé, Jung, Martha Bernays Freud – were labelled and shipped along with the family's other effects.[27] Professor and Mrs Freud and Anna boarded the departing train on 4 June 1938 and after a stop in Paris arrived at Dover on 6 June; they had been accorded diplomatic privileges, and none of the luggage was examined there or in London. The files of papers were stored away in the house at 20 Maresfield Gardens, which became the family's permanent home in the autumn of 1938, and where Freud died on 23 September 1939. There the letters rested, surviving another kind of holocaust – the air raids of the Second World War – and afterwards, amidst the concerns of the Freud family with the immediacies of life and profession, were seemingly forgotten.

Jung's letters from Freud lay undisturbed for nearly forty years. For a time he kept them in what he called his 'cache', a narrow safe set into the wall of an alcove adjoining his large study-library upstairs.[28] The 'cache', which was locked with a key that Jung carried

[25] Three of them are published in *Jung: Letters*, ed Adler, vol 1.
[26] Private communication from Miss Freud, who added, 'Otherwise what we performed were really works of rescue. There was too much accumulated material to take with us to London, and my father was all for throwing away much of it, whereas Princess Bonaparte . . . was all for preservation. Therefore she rescued things from waste-baskets which my father had thrown there.' The account given by Jones (III, p 238/233), of burning everything considered not worth preserving, is not quite exact.
[27] Private communication from Mrs E. L. Freud.
[28] Private communication from Aniela Jaffé.

in his pocket, also contained, among other valuables, the four fragments of a breadknife that had shattered when he was experimenting with occultism as a student.[29]

In all of his later writings, including his autobiography, Jung never referred to his correspondence with Freud.[30] Nor did Freud ever mention the correspondence in his writings afterwards, other than to allude in 'The History of the Psycho-Analytic Movement' (1914) to Jung's letter of 11 November 1912 (323 J). The existence of this valuable *Briefwechsel* was not generally known until the publication of volume II of Ernest Jones's *Life and Work of Sigmund Freud* in 1955. Around 1950 Jones had begun work on the biography, the first volume of which (1953) comes up to 1900. By 1952 he had started to prepare the second volume, and in February he wrote to Jung asking if he might see Freud's letters to him. Aniela Jaffé, who was at that time the secretary of the C. G. Jung Institute,[31] had been in analysis with Jung for several years. During an analytical interview in February, Jung asked her if she would read the Freud letters. She agreed, and Jung's secretary, Marie-Jeanne Schmid, brought the bundle of letters from the 'cache'. As Mrs Jaffé remembers it, 'I was more than excited; but then, after having read all the night, rather disappointed, because I had expected sentences of the deepest wisdom and psychological insight and met with a lot of politics and such, besides the most personal remarks. When I told this to Jung he was pleased, and I suppose his answer to Jones reflects it.'[32] Jung replied to Jones:

They are not particularly important. They chiefly contain remarks about publishers or the organization of the Psychoanalytical Society. And some others are too personal. As a matter of fact I don't care for their publication. On the whole they wouldn't be an important contribution to Freud's biography.[33]

A month later Jung entrusted the bundle of letters to Mrs Jaffé, and

29 Aniela Jaffé, *From the Life and Work of C. G. Jung*, tr R.F.C. Hull (1971), p 123. See also *Letters*, ed Adler, vol 1, 27 Nov '34, to J. B. Rhine.
30 He mentioned the letters in private correspondence late in life.
31 Established in 1948 in Zürich for training and research in analytical psychology. Courses are given in both English and German.
32 Private communication.
33 *Letters*, ed Adler, vol 2, 22 Feb '52, to Jones.

Introduction

she carried it to the director of the Jung Institute, C. A. Meier, MD,[34] with a covering letter (22 March 1952) in which Jung stated that he was handing over the letters to the Institute for safekeeping, his wish being that the collection be considered a possession that was not for sale. 'The letters have a certain historical value, after all,' he wrote, 'though their contents are unimportant.'

Meier replied to Jung, thanking him for the gift on behalf of the Curatorium of the Institute, and he added: 'It will interest you to learn that we have been asked by the Sigmund Freud Archives, Inc,[35] of New York, whether we could prepare photocopies of these letters, and we intend to ask them whether they would be in a position to reciprocate by providing photocopies of your letters to Freud. I'll be glad to keep you informed of this.'

The information that Meier received from K. R. Eissler, MD, the Secretary of the Archives, was abruptly disappointing: 'Unfortunately the letters which Professor Jung wrote to Professor Freud have not been preserved. As far as I know, Professor Freud destroyed his whole correspondence before leaving Vienna in 1938, and I assume that Professor Jung's letters were among those documents which were destroyed during those hectic days.'[36] Eissler told Meier that he would, with his permission, inquire of the Freud family in London. By the end of the year the Jung letters had not come to light, but the photostats of the Freud letters had been made and sent to New York, with the Jung Institute's proviso that they be kept confidential for one hundred years.

[34] Later, professor of psychology at the Federal Polytechnic ('ETH'), Zürich.
[35] The Sigmund Freud Archives was incorporated in New York in 1951 as a nonprofit, tax-exempt organization, its goal being the collection of all documents directly or indirectly related to the life and work of Freud; the archives entered into a formal agreement with the Library of Congress whereby the library becomes owner of the materials, which, if designated as restricted, are kept confidential for as long as the donor or archives and the library consider proper. The library's Freud collection, which includes the materials donated by the archives, comprises letters to and from Freud and his family, original manuscripts, official documents, photographs, and interviews with persons who had been in contact with Freud.
[36] Eissler to Meier, 4 June '52. This and other letters written by Dr Eissler are quoted with his kind permission.

In September 1953, Jung received Eissler at Küsnacht and granted him an interview for the Freud Archives. The transcript of the interview is under standard restriction until the year 2010. Jung also, on the occasion of Eissler's visit, donated various pieces of memorabilia to the archives.[37] Soon afterwards, with the permission of the Jung Institute, the Freud Archives arranged to have Freud's letters transcribed. In November, Jung was again asked if Jones could read the Freud letters, this time by Eissler on Jones's behalf. Jung replied directly to Jones:

Of course you have my permission to read Freud's letters, copies of which are in the Freud Archives in New York.

Your biographical material [in volume 1] is very interesting, although it would have been advisable to consult me for certain facts. For instance you got the story of Freud's fainting attack quite wrong. Also it was by no means the first one; he had such an attack before in 1909 previous to our departure for America in Bremen, and very much under the same psychological circumstances.[38]

Hoping you are going on to continue enjoying old age, I remain, etc.[39]

Jones thus was able to read Freud's letters to Jung, but the other side of the dialogue was assumed to have been lost. On 22 March 1954, however, Eissler wrote again to Meier: 'To my very great joy I can tell you that I have just been informed by Miss Anna Freud that the letters from Professor Jung to Professor Freud have been found. I am sure that Miss Freud will have no objection to sending copies, as she had originally agreed to this in case they should be found. I shall probably see her in London this summer and will discuss the matter.' Miss Freud has recalled, more recently, that

[37] Appendices 3 and 4 of the Hogarth Press/Routledge & Kegan Paul edition.
[38] Jones had written of the 1912 fainting attack in volume I (p 348/317), a copy of which Jung had received from his friend E. A. Bennet, of London, the month before. See Letters, ed Adler, vol 2, 21 Nov '53, to Bennet, for Jung's version of the event; also Memories, p 157/153. Jones referred briefly to the 1909 attack in volume II (pp 61/55, 165/146); Jung gives a fuller account in Memories, pp 156/152f.
[39] Letters, ed Adler, vol 2, 19 Dec '53.

during the war years all the various parcels of correspondence that had been brought from Vienna were safely stored in every possible place in both her house and her brother Ernst's house. It took some time to bring all the material together and catalogue it, and while this work was going on, the Jung letters were securely put away and in due course came to light.[40]

In the same letter, Eissler broached the question of whether the Jung Institute might be interested in a joint publication of the correspondence. Meier replied that the institute indeed would.

During a visit to New York in November 1954, Meier met Eissler, who gave him the photostats of Jung's letters, and the two talked over the idea of publication. Meier arranged to borrow the uncorrected transcript of the Freud letters, and when he got back to Zürich he read the entire exchange. Surely the first person to read all the letters on both sides, Meier wrote Eissler:

The first impression is really that of a shattering tragedy. And just for that reason I am completely in favour of publishing the whole thing. It is true that recently Jung thought it should wait until after his death; he didn't want to look at the letters at all, however. I'm therefore of the opinion that he could be persuaded to change his mind. I think not only that the world should learn something from this tragedy, but also that from this publication a great deal of nonsense that is current will finally be laid to rest, which can only be a good thing for clearing the atmosphere. More difficult than consideration for Freud and Jung, it seems to me, is consideration for other colleagues, who turn up frequently in the letters and to some extent are labelled with rather unflattering, spirited expressions ... Personally, I think we should give the world a brave piece of scientific objectivity for the common good.[41]

Eissler felt that as much as possible should be published, 'without causing any annoyance or detriment to the individuals mentioned'.[42] Transcripts of the entire correspondence should be prepared, he thought, and be read by the persons on whose decision the publication would depend. The work of transcribing the Jung letters

[40] Private communication from Anna Freud.
[41] Meier to Eissler, 14 Jan '55, quoted with Dr Meier's kind permission.
[42] Eissler to Meier, 18 Jan '55.

went ahead, and the institute in Zürich, dissatisfied with the New York transcript of the Freud letters, began to make its own transcript of them. Meier hoped that Miss Freud would then examine the authoritative texts and permit their publication.

In 1955, Jones published volume II of his life of Freud, dealing with the 'Years of Maturity', 1901–1919. He had had access to some five thousand letters from Freud's correspondence, the most valuable being those between Freud and Abraham, Ferenczi, Jung, and himself. It is not certain at what point he was able to read Jung's letters to Freud; in volume II there are only three direct citations of them, as against some fifty citations of Freud's letters to Jung, in addition to sixteen extended quotations in an appendix (though Jones refrained from quoting entire letters from this correspondence).[43] Upon the publication of the second volume, with its copious references to himself, Jung made no further comment on Jones's *Freud*, so far as it is known, in his published writings or letters.

During the summer of 1955, the painstaking work of transcribing both sides of the correspondence proceeded at the Jung Institute in Zürich. Then, on 1 October, Meier notified Eissler that he had had a discussion with Professor and Mrs Jung and that they did not yet agree to the publication of the letters. Jung wanted to see the letters first. Perhaps the letters could be edited by contemporaries of the two correspondents and published in the distant future, for the grandchildren's generation. But for the present nothing was definite until Jung saw the letters.[44]

Eissler replied sympathetically; he also had doubts about an unabridged publication. Many passages, he supposed, might need comments or they would not be understandable to future generations. But would people be willing to devote time to the work without seeing it realized during their lifetime?[45] Meier was wholeheartedly

---

[43] Volume III contains five citations of Freud's letters and one of Jung's. Volume II also contains several citations of Jung's letters to Jones, which have now disappeared.

[44] A. Jaffé, on behalf of Meier, to Eissler, 1 Oct '55.

[45] Eissler to Meier, 4 Oct '55.

for obtaining commentaries by contemporaries; Mrs Jaffé stood ready to help on the Zürich side; and Jung had indeed given his approval to the publication, but only after his death. However, Meier expected to discuss this further with Mrs Jung.[46] There was no doubt that the institute was truly authorized to publish the correspondence, in view of the statement Jung had made when he turned over the letters.[47] At the end of October, the institute sent Eissler the Zürich transcripts of both the Jung and the Freud letters, as well as the uncorrected New York transcript of the Freud letters.

Not until March 1956 was a working plan agreed upon among the Freud Archives, Anna Freud, and the Jung Institute: 'The transcript ... should be submitted for evaluation to the following five persons: Dr Anna Freud, and Drs Heinz Hartmann, Ernst Kris, Ernest Jones, and Hermann Nunberg. The plan is to obtain and preserve available information from informants who have particular knowledge about events and people who played a prominent role at the time when Professor Freud worked with Professor Jung. Since most of this information is probably of a personal nature, it is not intended to publish it. The idea is to have each of the informants provide the manuscript with footnotes, or a longer commentary, as the case may be. These additions to the manuscript would be kept strictly confidential at the Library of Congress for as many years as each of the informants may wish.'[48]

In August 1956, Meier notified Eissler that Jung had stipulated that his letters to Freud could be published, at the earliest, twenty years after his death, though Meier hoped that work on the commentaries could proceed anyway.[49] But no commentary or footnotes were ever produced. Kris died in 1957, Jones in 1958, and Nunberg and Hartmann in 1970. The photostats of the original letters and of the Zürich transcripts were deposited in the Library of Congress in 1958, labelled as follows: 'Confidential, not to be opened until twenty years after the death of Carl Jung with permission of the Jung Archives, Küsnacht, Zürich.'

[46] Meier to Eissler, 7 Oct '55.
[47] Meier to Eissler, 21 Oct '55. Mrs Jung died 27 Nov '55.
[48] Memorandum by Eissler, 20 Mar '56.
[49] Meier to Eissler, 3 Aug '56.

In 1956, Dr Gerhard Adler put to Jung the idea of publishing a general selection of his entire correspondence. Adler, originally of Berlin and after 1936 in England, was one of Jung's most prominent pupils. As he wrote, some years later, 'Originally the idea of such publication had come not from [Jung] himself but from friends who were aware of the unique literary and psychological value of Jung's correspondence. At first Jung had reacted against the whole notion, since he felt that the spontaneity and immediacy of his letters were not for the general public; but in his later years he changed his attitude . . .'[50] Responding to Adler's proposal, Jung immediately ruled out the inclusion of the Freud/Jung correspondence. In a letter of 24 May 1956 he wrote: 'Separate treatment of this correspondence is justified, because it touches in parts upon very personal problems, whereas the planned publication refers to scientific subjects. I consider it inopportune to expose the personal material so long as the waves of animosity are still running so high. At the date suggested by me Freud and I will be "historical personalities", and the necessary detachment from events will prevail by then.'[51]

In August 1957, Jung confirmed his agreement to the publication of a selection of his letters. In January 1958 he recommended that the work be entrusted to a committee composed of Mrs Jaffé, now his secretary, his daughter Marianne Niehus-Jung (an editor of the Swiss edition of the collected works), and Dr Adler, who was to act as the chairman and as the editor of the letters; and at the same time Jung stated that the Freud/Jung correspondence was to be published 'only after 1980'.[52]

The idea of publication of the Freud/Jung correspondence was broached again in the summer of 1958. It is not clear who succeeded in persuading Jung to change his mind so soon after he had pushed the project into the distant future. The impetus may have originated with the publisher Kurt Wolff, who before the Second World War

50 Adler, introduction to *Letters*, vol 1 (1973), p ix.
51 Ibid, pp xi–xii.
52 Letters to Bollingen Foundation, 19 Aug '57, and to John D. Barrett, 29 Jan '58, in the foundation archives. Marianne Niehus-Jung died in March 1965.

had had a distinguished career in Germany and Italy, and had founded the New York firm of Pantheon Books in the early 1940s. Pantheon had been chosen as publisher of Bollingen Series, a programme of the Bollingen Foundation, the keystone of which was the Collected Works of C. G. Jung. Kurt Wolff, who had known Jung for many years, had convinced him in 1956 that his autobiography should be written. This project grew into a collaboration between Jung and Aniela Jaffé; Mrs Jaffé wrote the greater part of it from interviews with Jung, and he wrote other parts in longhand.[53] Wolff was in Zürich during the summer of 1958 for editorial conferences. And in Europe during the same period were the editor and assistant editor of Bollingen Series, John D. Barrett and Vaun Gillmor, and Sir Herbert Read, a director of Routledge & Kegan Paul, the publishers of Jung's works in England. These three, with Jung, composed the 'Editorial Committee', which met once a year to review the progress of the collected works and plan the future programme.

The first document is a letter Jung wrote on 20 July 1958 to Eissler:

As you know, I have stipulated that my correspondence with Freud ought not to be published before thirty years[54] have elapsed after my death, but lately I have been asked from different sides to permit – inasmuch as I am competent – an earlier publication of the whole correspondence.

Such a change of my will[55] is not a simple matter. First of all I don't

[53] *Memories, Dreams, Reflections*, 'by C. G. Jung, recorded and edited by Aniela Jaffé', was published simultaneously in New York, London, and Zürich in 1963.

[54] On 12 Aug '60, Dr Franz N. Riklin, who had succeeded Meier as director of the Jung Institute, informed Eissler of a further proviso, namely that Jung now wished that no one be permitted to study the correspondence until thirty years after his death. He proposed that a protocol be made by both sides, stipulating this limitation, and Eissler referred him to Ernst Freud. Such a document has not been found.

[55] Jung's last will and testament contains no dispositions regarding the correspondence with Freud. He may have used the term 'will' here not in its legal meaning, but in the nontechnical sense of intention. (Information from Dr Hans Karrer and Mr Franz Jung.)

know how you feel about such a proposition, and secondly I could not permit an earlier publication without a necessary revision of my letters. My letters were never written with any thought that they might be broadcasted. As a matter of fact, many of them contain unchecked and highly objectionable materials, such as are produced in the course of an analysis, and shed a most one-sided and dubious light on a number of persons who I don't want to offend in any manner whatever. Such material enjoys the protection of the *secretum medici*. These people or their descendants are still alive.

I should be deeply obliged to you, if you would kindly inform me of your feelings in this matter, especially if you would agree with an earlier publication under strict observation of the rule of discretion and the risk of libel.[56]

Dr Eissler responded:

There are two aspects to the question you asked me regarding the publication of the letters Prof Freud and you exchanged: the legal aspect and my personal feeling about the whole matter. There can be no doubt that anything which might offend anyone who was under your treatment or a descendant of such persons should not be published. However, permission to publish at least the letters written by Freud does not depend on the Archives, since the Archives never acquired the copyright. This question has to be discussed with the Sigmund Freud Copyrights, Ltd, c/o Mr Ernst Freud . . . in London.

Since I consider it an indiscretion to read letters that have not been published, I made it my habit not to read the letters acquired by the Archives unless there is an objective necessity for doing so. Since this did not arise regarding your correspondence with Prof Freud I never took the liberty of reading the letters and cannot express an opinion about whether or not this correspondence should be published at this time. However, I recall the opinion of the late Dr Kris, the editor of the Freud/Fliess correspondence, who read the letters at the request of the Jung Archives[57] in Zürich. If I recall correctly, his opinion was that it would be worthwhile to publish at present those parts of the correspondence which contain strictly scientific problems such as the questions of narcissism and schizophrenia, which apparently came up quite frequently in your communications with Freud.

[56] *Letters*, ed Adler, vol 2.
[57] That is, the C. G. Jung Institute.

This is the only contribution I can make in answer to your letter of July 20th. The most important questions I think have to be straightened out between you and Ernst Freud.[58]

On 23 August, at his home at Küsnacht, Jung met with Barrett, Miss Gillmor, Read, and Wolff. Agreement to publish the Freud/Jung correspondence was reached – in principle. Wolff had read the entire correspondence and prepared a fifty-page summary; this presented the first conspectus of the letters and was testimony to the importance of publishing them.[59]

Shortly afterwards, Mrs Jaffé, Jung's secretary, wrote to John Barrett: 'Dr Jung said that he fully agreed with Dr Eissler's idea to "publish at present those parts of the correspondence which contain strictly scientific problems" and asked me to inform Dr F. Riklin, President of the C. G. Jung Institute, of this fact. (Dr Jung has given the Freud letters to the Institute as a donation.) Yesterday Dr Jung told me in a few words about your talk on Saturday, August 23rd, and added that he would very much like to reread or at least peruse the letters in question before giving his definite "placet".'[60]

Mrs Jaffé remembers that Jung did not look at the letters himself – in fact, to her knowledge he never showed any desire at any time to reread any of his correspondence with Freud – but asked another one of his pupils to go through them and to make recommendations. The consequence was the following letter from Jung to Barrett, one week later:

Re: publication of the Freud correspondence, I want to tell you that I have decided to do nothing further. The letters are too personal and contain too little generally interesting material, so that the great work which ought to be done, to draw something worthwhile from them, would be wasted time.

It was nice to see you again, and I am glad that I am able to spare you

58 Letter of 13 Aug '58 (copy in Bollingen Foundation archives).
59 Mrs Helen Wolff kindly gave access to her late husband's summary of the letters and confirmed other details in his diary.
60 A. Jaffé to J. D. Barrett, 27 Aug '58, in the Bollingen Foundation archives; quoted by permission of Mrs Jaffé.

a superfluous trouble. Thus the conditions remain as they have been
before, namely the publication of the correspondence is postponed *ad
calendas graecas*.[61]

The following year, the British writer John Freeman (later, Ambassa-
dor to the United States) conducted a filmed interview with Jung for
the British Broadcasting Corporation. He asked Jung, 'When are the
letters which you exchanged with Freud going to be published?'

Professor Jung 'Well, not during my lifetime.'
Freeman 'You would have no objection to their being published after
your lifetime?'
Professor Jung 'Oh, no, none at all.'
Freeman 'Because they are probably of great historical importance.'
Professor Jung 'I don't think so.'
Freeman 'Then why have you not published them so far?'
Professor Jung 'Because they were not important enough. I see no
particular importance in them.'[62]

Later, the pupil who had read the letters at Jung's request the previous summer happened to write to him quoting his striking remarks
about Christianity in the letter of 11 February 1910 (178 J), and Jung
replied (9 April 1959):

Best thanks for the quotation from that accursed correspondence. For
me it is an unfortunately inexpungeable reminder of the incredible folly
that filled the days of my youth. The journey from cloud-cuckoo-land
back to reality lasted a long time. In my case Pilgrim's Progress consisted
in my having to climb down a thousand ladders until I could reach out
my hand to the little clod of earth that I am.[63]

In the autumn of 1960, Ernst L. Freud brought out the *Letters of
Sigmund Freud*, a volume of selected letters that he had edited. By

[61] Letter of 5 Sept '58, in the Bollingen Foundation archives.
[62] Transcript published in *C. G. Jung Speaking* (1977). An abridged version, not
including this passage, is in *Face to Face*, ed Hugh Burnett (London, 1964),
pp 48–51.
[63] Quoted in a footnote to Jung's 11 Feb '10 letter to Freud in *Letters*, ed Adler,
vol 1, p 19.

agreement with the Jung Institute, he included seven of his father's letters to Jung (27, 38, 42, 45, 71, 129, 340, three of them with deletions).

An old friend of Jung's, meanwhile, had been writing a memoir of Jung as he had known him: this was Dr E. A. Bennet, a psychiatrist and analyst of London, whose book, *C. G. Jung*, was largely based on their conversations and correspondence that had continued up until a short time before Jung's death. In his chapter on Jung's relations with Freud, Bennet writes: 'More and more Freud came to rely on Jung and wrote him constantly, often every week. If Jung did not reply, he would get a telegram asking what had gone wrong. Jung has kept these letters, although he never intended to publish them; they are personal, mainly about current events, and in any case of no special importance or general interest.'[64] This estimate was based on what Dr Bennet had been told by Jung, who, furthermore, reviewed the book in manuscript.

Until the time of Jung's death, 6 June 1961, there was no further consideration of the correspondence with Freud and no change in Jung's wish that publication be postponed until long after his death. Editorial work had continued on *Memories, Dreams, Reflections*, and arrangements were made to publish in an appendix parts of three letters from Freud to Jung (139, 255, 260) dealing with occultism. Jung had expressly given his approval, and the permission of Ernst Freud was duly sought and granted.

In August 1961, shortly after Jung's death, there was another meeting in Zürich of Barrett, Miss Gillmor, and Read, this time with Mr and Mrs Walther Niehus-Jung, Franz Jung, Aniela Jaffé, Franz Riklin, and Max Rascher, Jung's Swiss publisher. The gathering carried on the tradition of the regular summer meetings to review the progress of the English-language publications of Jung's works. Jung had named Walther Niehus as his literary executor, and his wife Marianne Niehus-Jung had a principal role as an editor of the *Gesammelte Werke* and the selected letters. The main business of the 1961 meeting was indeed the selected letters, upon which intensive editorial work was now to begin. According to the minutes, 'It was

64 *C. G. Jung* (London and New York, 1961), p 39.

tentatively suggested that three volumes be prepared: (1) Freud correspondence, (2) letters concerning religion and theology, and (3) the balance of the scientific letters.' This revival of the Freud/Jung correspondence was countermanded as soon as all parties concerned were reminded of Jung's wish that the correspondence remain sealed until 1991. The selected letters were finally arranged chronologically, and Adler stated that 'I felt justified in publishing only a very few and quite uncontroversial letters of Jung's to Freud, eight in all', on the pattern of Ernst Freud's choice of seven of Freud's to Jung in the selection he edited.[65]

Earlier on, Freud's correspondence had begun to come out in several different collections. *The Origins of Psychoanalysis*, a volume of letters to Wilhelm Fliess and related papers, was published as early as 1950, and the selection by Ernst Freud, already mentioned, appeared in 1960. Then followed the exchanges of letters with Pfister (1963), Abraham (1965), Lou Andreas-Salomé (1966), and Arnold Zweig (1968).[66]

In the spring of 1969, Norman Franklin, chairman of Routledge & Kegan Paul, Jung's publishers in England, called on Ernst Freud at his home in London. Mr Freud pointed to a storage cabinet in his study and said it contained Jung's letters to his father, which the family were thinking of selling, along with the right to publish his father's letters to Jung. Mr Franklin wrote to Princeton University Press, as Jung's American publishers, conveying this news. The Princeton University Library, with whose staff the matter was discussed, was not in a position at that time to bid for the letters, which

[65] Adler, introduction to *Letters*, vol 1, p xii. The letters to Freud included in Adler's selection (also in Jaffé's, in the Swiss edition) are 138, 170, 178, 198, 224, 259, and 315, three with deletions. The translation is that of R.F.C. Hull, as in the present volume. The Swiss edition of Jung's *Briefe* appeared in three volumes in 1972–3 and the American–English edition in two volumes in 1973–4.

[66] In February 1965, Eissler wrote Riklin saying that he had heard that the Jung Institute would like to publish the Freud/Jung letters but believed that the Freud family were opposed, whereas he knew that the Sigmund Freud Copyrights had no objection. Riklin responded that the thirty-year embargo had to stand.

did not fall naturally into the university collections. But at the press
we were troubled at the thought of the letters being scattered or
perhaps disappearing into some restricted private collection.
Furthermore, though we were aware of Jung's embargo on publishing the letters, there was the faint hope that the embargo might
somehow be lifted. Accordingly, as executive editor of Jung's works
in English, I wrote to Ernst Freud on 23 May: 'If your family actually should be entertaining the idea of selling the Jung letters, I
would be most grateful if you gave me the opportunity to try to
arrange for their purchase in order to place them in the Jung archives
in Zürich.' At the same time, I wrote the Jung family, through the
legal counsel for the estate, Dr Hans Karrer, asking, 'Why shouldn't
the Freud and Jung families simply exchange their respective hold-
ings of the original letters?'

On 22 June, Ernst Freud replied, asking whether an offer could be
made for the Jung letters which his family could then consider. He
added, 'It is not correct that there exist any restrictions with regard
to the publication of the Freud letters – only Jung found it (unfortunately) necessary to withhold the right for thirty years after his
death. And although I have proof that in the last year of his life he
was willing to change this condition, the Jung Archives have been
unable to free them before this date. Clearly, it would be a pity to
publish only my father's letters alone.'

Shortly afterward, in Zürich, I took part in meetings with
members of the Jung family and their advisers. The consequence of
these discussions was a proposal that the Freud letters and Jung
letters be exchanged between the C. G. Jung Institute and the Freud
family. It was observed that Jung had given conflicting instructions
about restrictions on publication – for thirty years, for twenty, for
fifty, for one hundred, or until 1980. The family agreed that it would
be fortunate if the correspondence could be edited soon, while
persons survived who could contribute to an informed annotation.
The edited letters would then be put in safekeeping and published
only in 1980. I communicated these thoughts to Ernst Freud, who
replied on 2 August: 'We shall gladly agree to the exchange of the
originals. I have taken steps to get the declaration mentioned [that

Jung was willing to change the restrictions] but of course I am not certain how long this may take and whether I will be successful.[67] I share the opinion that an early editing of the letters would be fortunate ...' Henceforward, the two parties were in direct communication.

Dr Karrer wrote to me on 2 December 1969: 'My clients have taken a decision of considerable importance. They have come to the conclusion that this question must not be decided on the basis of the late Professor Jung's various and possibly contradictory statements, but in the light of the situation as it presents itself now. Under this angle, they attach overriding importance to the consideration that the publication should take place as long as persons are still available for the editorial work who had known Jung and Freud. Of course, it remains to be seen whether the Freud party shares this view.'

The Freud party did share that view. And, on 25 February 1970, Franz Jung flew from Zürich to London with the original Freud letters in his briefcase, and called on Ernst Freud in St John's Wood. Freud, who had been ill with a heart ailment, dressed and left his bedroom in honour of his guest. As he wrote me on 6 March, 'Mr Jung – whom I liked very much – visited me here, and we didn't only exchange our fathers' letters, but in the easiest and friendliest way agreed on plans for the early publication of the correspondence.' Both men were architects, and they readily found a mutual sympathy. Ernst Freud's letter went on: 'In order to guarantee impartiality, these letters will be printed like historical documents, that is to say without any comments whatsoever and absolutely complete, unless discretion concerning former patients or colleagues makes omissions unavoidable. The existing typescripts will once more be compared with the originals, necessary notes to explain names, book titles, quotations, etc, will be added.' Later, Franz Jung remarked, 'It was quite an historic moment. We decided that the letters should be given to publication while there are still people around who knew the personalities of the two men.'[68]

[67] This point was never clarified. (Mrs E. L. Freud kindly gave permission for publication of parts of her husband's letters.)

[68] Article by Henry Raymont, *New York Times*, 15 July 1970, p 41.

Introduction

Ernst Freud died suddenly on 7 April 1970, but the contractual arrangements for the publication were duly completed, and the news was made public in mid July. Shortly afterwards the original Freud letters were purchased from the Freud family by the Library of Congress, through funds provided by an anonymous benefactor, and they are now in the Manuscript Division of the library. The original Jung letters are in the C. G. Jung Institute at Zürich, and according to the terms of Jung's gift their sale is barred.

As explained heretofore, the transcripts of the letters were typewritten in 1955, and photocopies of these transcripts provide the text of the present volume. The transcripts were read against the holograph letters (or photocopies of them) once more by Anna Freud and her sister Mathilde Hollitscher and by Kurt Niehus-Jung, Professor Jung's son-in-law. On both sides, memoranda were prepared explaining abbreviations and noting handwritten corrections and slips of the pen by both writers.

Both translators – Ralph Manheim for the Freud letters, R.F.C. Hull for the Jung letters – worked from these prepared transcripts. During the course of the translating and editorial work, the transcripts were again checked against the holographs for problematical readings, sometimes with the assistance of other persons familiar with the handwriting.

In the present edition,[69] textual matters have not been presented in exhaustive detail, which would be distracting and tedious for most readers. The German edition of the letters, however, which is being published simultaneously (by S. Fischer Verlag, Frankfurt), is available to anyone who wants to study Freud's and Jung's original usages especially with respect to the salutations and valedictions of the letters. There are more diverse possibilities for these epistolary formulas in German than in English, and some of them if translated literally would sound stilted and odd. Variety and literality have been sacrificed for the sake of phrases that ring naturally in English. But the chief and most interesting forms and changes of forms have

[69] [The following seven paragraphs refer chiefly, but not entirely, to the original edition of *The Freud/Jung Letters*. – A.M.]

usually been mentioned in the notes. It will be seen that Freud, beginning with a formal expression such as *Sehr geehrter Herr Kollege* (literally, 'Very esteemed Mr Colleague'), came in time to the simple and warm *Lieber Freund*, which he used until the cooling of the relationship caused him to adopt *Lieber Herr Doktor.* Jung began formally with salutations on the order of *Sehr geehrter Herr Professor* and arrived rather slowly at *Lieber Herr Professor,* which he used almost to the end. The valedictions are even more varied; while literality here is, again, also impossible, they have been translated with strict consistency – for example, *Ihr ergebener,* though it allows of various English renderings, is always translated as 'Yours sincerely'.

The two writers, and particularly Freud, used many abbreviations, as was the custom in that day – it must certainly have expedited letter writing. In the interests of readability most of the abbreviated words have been spelled out, but certain abbreviations have been retained consistently because they are a characteristic part of the psychoanalytic vocabulary: 'ucs.' (unconscious), for *Ubw.* (*Unbewusstsein*); 'cs.' (consciousness), for *Bw.* (*Bewusstsein*); Greek psi-alpha (Ψ A) for *Psychoanalyse* (psycho-analysis). (Both letters, psi and alpha, of this Greek abbreviation are consistently capitalized in the present volume, though the writers' usage varied. Freud preferred capitals but often used lower case in adjectival forms. Jung preferred to write Ψ as a capital and α in lower case.) Some other abbreviations – of personal names, journal and book titles, and so on – are retained for flavour. The writers' placement of postscripts and interpolations has been indicated as faithfully as possible. Slips of the pen, cancellations, etc, have been indicated when they are of interest and can be given intelligibly in translation. Confusions of the pronominal forms *Sie/sie* and *Ihr/ihr* (you/they, your/their), etc, have in general been indicated, not only when they caused controversy between the writers but in the fairly frequent cases when they went unnoticed. Underlining has not been reproduced as italic when this device is used differently in German (as for personal names) than in English; underlining for emphasis is, however, usually indicated by italic. Book titles are italicized as they are normally in English.

Dates at the head of the letters, which the writers often gave in European number style, as 3.IV.10 or 3.4.10, have been standardized to the style '3 April 1910' (and, in the notes, '3 Apr '10'). The printed letterheads have also been somewhat simplified, as explained in the notes.

No letter that was in the two sets at the time they were transcribed in 1955 has been omitted from this edition, and (as indicated in the notes) a few more have since come to light. That the sets are intact is proved by the unbroken sequence of letter or page numbers pencilled by unknown hands on both sets of letters and visible on photocopies made earlier. The loss of some letters, cards, and telegrams (and enclosures, which were apparently not filed with the letters) is sometimes evident from context, and these are mentioned in the notes. It is not necessary to suppose these were suppressed by either recipient, as the surviving letters contain ample material that might have been considered suppressible. What is remarkable is that both sides of this correspondence have survived in nearly complete form.

Within the letters, there are deletions of two kinds: (1) The names of analysands whose cases are discussed are replaced by initials, beginning with 'A' for the first case mentioned. As the same initial is used consistently for an analysand, the references are coherent throughout the correspondence. This discretion, which was requested by both families, is in accordance with medical practice. (2) In Jung's letters, at the request of his family, a few passages have been omitted and replaced by: [...]. None of these refers to Freud, but to other personalities whose close relatives may survive.[70]

The system of numbering the letters has, of course, been devised for the present edition.[71] As explained in its annotation, item number 199a F was found (or rather, refound) after the numbers had been established. Thus the total number of items in the exchange is 360: 164 from Freud, 196 from Jung; and, in addition, 7 from Emma Jung. While slightly different totals are given by Ernest Jones (171, Freud; 197, Jung: in vol II, preface) and by Gerhard Adler (167,

[70] [In the Picador edition, abridgements are indicated by: ... – A.M.]
[71] [In the Picador edition, the letter numbers are retained even though some letters have been omitted. – A.M.]

Freud; 196, Jung: in vol I, introduction), the discrepancies result
from later finds and different ways of counting fragments.

As for the annotations, they are documentary and explanatory in
the spirit of Ernst Freud's and Franz Jung's agreement, but both
families have assented to the inclusion of notes that cite parallel and
related publications and events, textual details, and cross references;
passages of editorial comment that bridge discontinuities in the
letters (usually because Freud and Jung met and therefore did not
write); and illustrations, facsimiles, and documentary appendixes.
Occasional gaps in the information are regretted.

William McGuire, November 1973

Acknowledgements

Anna Freud devoted a great many hours to reading the translation, giving advice that only she could give, supplying many pieces of information, and with her sister Mrs Mathilde Hollitscher, correcting and working over the transcript of the Freud letters. She offered warm encouragement throughout. The late Ernst Freud, a prime mover of the project, Mrs Lucie Freud, and Mark Paterson, managing director of Sigmund Freud Copyrights, Ltd, were notably helpful.

Mr Kurt Niehus-Jung, acting for the Jung Estate, carefully corrected and worked over the transcript of the Jung letters and supplied special information and prudent advice. Mr Franz Jung kindly answered numerous questions and generously assembled much of the illustrative material. Mrs Lilly Jung was also most helpful. Dr Hans Karrer, legal counsel for the Jung Estate, was cooperative and encouraging beyond any obligation.

Dr Kurt R. Eissler, secretary of the Sigmund Freud Archives, Inc, and an authority on the history of the psychoanalytic movement, aided and fostered the work at every stage. The late Dr Otto Isakower, who had promised his assistance and counsel, contributed good advice before his death.

I am indebted to Aniela Jaffé and Dr Gerhard Adler for the example of their editions of the selected letters of Jung, for the occasional use of data from their notes, and for their freely given advice and support. Mrs Jaffé answered countless questions about Jung's life and writings and advised most constructively on textual problems. Jolande Jacobi generously gave valued background information.

Professional persons of long and clear memory, who gave infor-

mation and confirmation, included Grant Allan, Dr Roberto
Assagioli, Dr E. A. Bennet, Dr Grete L. Bibring, Dr W. Binswanger,
Professor Manfred Bleuler, Edmund Brill, Dr Violet S. de Laszlo, Dr
Helene Deutsch, Dr Oskar Diethelm, Dr Muriel Gardiner, Dr Clara
Geroe, Dr Imre Hermann, Mrs Ernest Jones, Dr Maurits Katan, Mrs
Tina Keller, Dr Lawrence S. Kubie, Dr Jeanne Lamplde Groot, Dr
C. A. Meier, Dr Henry A. Murray, Emil Oberholzer, Dr Paul Parin,
Professor Jean Piaget, Mrs Emmy Sachs, and Dr Jenny Waelder
Hall . . .

In tracing the history of the letters, I have been obliged not only to
Mrs Jaffé, Dr Eissler, Mr Jung, Miss Freud, and Dr Meier, but also
to the former president, vice-president, and secretary of Bollingen
Foundation, John D. Barrett, Vaun Gillmor, and Mary Curtis Ritter,
and to Helen Wolff.

The translators and the editor are indebted to the following for
advice on special problems of translation: Professor Ralph Freed-
man, Dr James Hillman, Professor Victor Lange, Professor Albert
Marckwardt, Professor William Moulton, Dr Willibald Nagler,
Richard Winston, and Professor Theodore Ziolkowski . . .

I am deeply grateful to all my colleagues at Princeton University
Press for their expertise, cooperation, and patience, and a most
heartening spirit of enthusiasm over the publication.

The translators – R.F.C. Hull, the official translator of Jung's
works and a sensitive and wise authority on Jungian thought and
terminology, and Ralph Manheim, one of the most versatile, experienced, and graceful of translators – coordinated their texts in the
most congenial way, though working far apart. Both made
significant contributions to the annotation.

Wolfgang Sauerlander was a true coadjutor. He produced a rich
fund of information for the notes, particularly on subjects in
German literature and history. The index is his work, and he has
edited the German edition of the present publication and translated
the editorial apparatus for it: thus he has had a double vantage point
from which he could survey the notes and translation and make
suggestions for reconciling and trueing-up countless details. His
long experience as a consultant on translation, editorial dis-

ciplinarian, and organizer of learned books has enabled him to make a pervasive and indispensable contribution.

Paula and Mary McGuire have helped inestimably.

W. M.

For permission to quote translations of Nietzsche and Goethe, grateful acknowledgement is made to Penguin Books, and for brief quotations from *Memories, Dreams, Reflections*, by C. G. Jung, edited by Aniela Jaffé, to Pantheon Books, New York, and Routledge & Kegan Paul and William Collins, London.

Abbreviations

Principal bibliographical references

Alexander and Selesnick = Franz Alexander and Seldon T. Selesnick, 'Freud-Bleuler Correspondence', *Archives of General Psychiatry* (New York), XII:1 (Jan 1965), 1ff.

CW = The Collected Works of C. G. Jung. Edited by Gerhard Adler, Michael Fordham, and Herbert Read; William McGuire, Executive Editor; translated by R.F.C. Hull. New York and Princeton (Bollingen Series XX) and London, 1953–79. 20 vols. For list, see appendix.

Freud/Abraham Letters = A Psycho-Analytic Dialogue; The Letters of Sigmund Freud and Karl Abraham 1907–1926. Edited by Hilda C. Abraham and Ernst L. Freud; translated by Bernard Marsh and Hilda C. Abraham. London and New York, 1965.

Freud, *Letters = Letters of Sigmund Freud*. Selected and edited by Ernst L. Freud; translated by Tania and James Stern. London and New York, 1960.

Freud, *The Origins of Psychoanalysis: Letters to Fliess = The Origins of Psycho-Analysis: Letters to Wilhelm Fliess, Drafts and Notes: 1897–1902*, by Sigmund Freud, edited by Marie Bonaparte, Anna Freud, Ernst Kris; authorized translation by Eric Mosbacher and James Strachey. New York and London, 1954.

Jones = Ernest Jones, *Sigmund Freud: Life and Work*. London and New York, 1953, 1955, 1957. 3 vols. (The editions are differently paginated, therefore double page references are given, first to the London edn.)

Jung, *Letters* = *C. G. Jung: Letters*, selected and edited by Gerhard Adler in collaboration with Aniela Jaffé. 2 vols. Princeton (Bollingen Series XCV) and London, 1973, 1974.

Jung, *Memories* = *Memories, Dreams, Reflections by C. G. Jung*, recorded and edited by Aniela Jaffé; translated by Richard and Clara Winston. New York and London, 1963. (The editions are differently paginated, therefore double page references are given, first to the New York edn.)

Minutes = *Minutes of the Vienna Psychoanalytic Society*. Edited by Herman Nunberg and Ernst Federn; translated by M. Nunberg. New York, 1962–74. (I: 1906–8; II: 1908–10; III–IV: 1910–15).

Putnam and Psychoanalysis = *James Jackson Putnam and Psychoanalysis; Letters between Putnam and Sigmund Freud, Ernest Jones, William James, Sandor Ferenczi, and Morton Prince, 1877–1917*, edited by Nathan G. Hale, Jr. Cambridge, Mass, 1971.

SE = The Standard Edition of the Complete Psychological Works of Sigmund Freud. Translated under the general editorship of James Strachey, in collaboration with Anna Freud, assisted by Alix Strachey and Alan Tyson. London and New York, 1953–74. 24 vols. For list, see appendix.

Zentralblatt = *Zentralblatt für Psychoanalyse; Medizinische Monatsschrift für Seelenkunde*. Wiesbaden, 1911–13.

Textual Abbreviations

$$cs. = conscious(ness)$$
$$D. pr., Dem. pr. = dementia praecox$$
$$\psi = psyche, psycho-$$
$$\psi A = psychoanalysis, psychoanaly-$$
$$\psi N = psychoneurosis$$
$$ucs. = unconscious$$

The Letters
1906–1914

Sigmund Freud
Freiburg (Příbor), Moravia   *London*
6 May 1856   23 September 1939

Carl Gustav Jung
Kesswil, Thurgau   *Küsnacht*
26 July 1875   6 June 1961

1F

Dear colleague,   11 April 1906, Vienna IX. Berggasse 19
Many thanks for sending me your *Diagnostic Association Studies*,
which in my impatience I had already acquired. Of course your latest
paper, 'Psychoanalysis and Association Experiments', pleased me
most, because in it you argue on the strength of your own experience
that everything I have said about the hitherto unexplored fields
of our discipline is true. I am confident that you will often be in a
position to back me up, but I shall also gladly accept correction.

Yours sincerely, DR FREUD

2J

Dear Professor Freud,   Burghölzli-Zürich, 5 October 1906
Please accept my sincerest thanks for the present you kindly sent me.
This collection of your various short papers should be most welcome
to anyone who wishes to familiarize himself quickly and thoroughly
with your mode of thought. It is to be hoped that your scientific
following will continue to increase in the future in spite of the attacks
which Aschaffenburg,[1] amid the plaudits of the pundits, has made
on your theory – one might almost say on you personally. The dis-
tressing thing about these attacks is that in my opinion
Aschaffenburg fastens on externals, whereas the merits of your
theory are to be found in the psychological realm of which modern
psychiatrists and psychologists have somewhat too scanty a grasp.
Recently I conducted a lively correspondence with Aschaffenburg
about your theory and espoused this standpoint, with which you,
Professor, may not be entirely in agreement. What I can appreciate,
and what has helped us here in our psychopathological work, are
your psychological views, whereas I am still pretty far from under-

[1] Gustav Aschaffenburg, German psychiatrist, later in the USA.

standing the therapy and the genesis of hysteria because our material on hysteria is rather meagre. That is to say your therapy seems to be to depend not merely on the affects released by abreaction but also on certain personal rapports, and it seems to me that though the genesis of hysteria is predominantly, it is not exclusively, sexual. I take the same view of your sexual theory. Harping exclusively on these delicate theoretical questions, Aschaffenburg forgets the essential thing, your psychology, from which psychiatry will one day be sure to reap inexhaustible rewards. I hope to send you soon a little book of mine, in which I approach dementia praecox and its psychology from your standpoint. In it I have also published the case that first drew Bleuler's[2] attention to the existence of your principles, though at that time with vigorous resistance on his part. But as you know, Bleuler is now completely converted.

With many thanks,

Very truly yours, C. G. JUNG

3F

Dear colleague,   7 October 1906, Vienna, IX. Berggasse 19
Your letter gave me great pleasure. I am especially gratified to learn that you have converted Bleuler. Your writings have long led me to suspect that your appreciation of my psychology does not extend to all my views on hysteria and the problem of sexuality, but I venture to hope that in the course of the years you will come much closer to

[2] Paul Eugen Bleuler (1857–1939), professor of psychiatry at the University of Zürich, director of the Burghölzli Hospital. In 1898, after 12 years as director of the Rheinau (Cant. Zürich) asylum, succeeded Forel at Burghölzli, serving as head until 1927. One of the great pioneers of psychiatry, he revised the entire concept of dementia praecox, renaming it schizophrenia; made major contributions, working under the direct impact of the psychoanalytic method, to the understanding of autism and ambivalence. He may actually have been receptive to Freud's ideas as early as 1901, when he had Jung report to the Burghölzli staff on Freudian dream-interpretation. He was a lifelong advocate of alcoholic abstinence.

me than you now think possible. On the strength of your splendid analysis of a case of obsessional neurosis, you more than anyone must know how consummately the sexual factor hides and, once discovered, how helpful it can be to our understanding and therapy. I continue to hope that this aspect of my investigations will prove to be the most significant.

For reasons of principle, but also because of his personal unpleasantness, I shall not answer Aschaffenburg's attack. It goes without saying that my judgement of it would be rather more severe than yours. I find nothing but inanities in his paper, apart from an enviable ignorance of the matters he is passing judgement on. He is still taking up arms against the hypnotic method that was abandoned ten years ago and he shows no understanding whatever of the simplest symbolism ... the importance of which any student of linguistics or folklore could impress on him if he is unwilling to take my word for it. Like so many of our pundits, he is motivated chiefly by an inclination to repress sexuality, that troublesome factor so unwelcome in good society. Here we have two warring worlds, and to all who live in the real world it will soon be obvious to all which is on the decline and which on the ascendant. Even so, I know I have a long struggle ahead of me, and in view of my age (50) I hardly expect to see the end of it. But my followers will, I hope, and I also venture to hope that all those who are able to overcome their own inner resistance to the truth will wish to count themselves among my followers and will cast off the last vestiges of pusillanimity in their thinking. Aschaffenburg is otherwise unknown to me, but this paper gives me a very low opinion of him.

I am eagerly awaiting your forthcoming book on Dem. praecox. I must own that whenever a work such as yours or Bleuler's appears it gives me the great and to me indispensable satisfaction of knowing that the hard work of a lifetime has not been entirely in vain.

Yours very sincerely, DR FREUD

My 'transference' ought completely to fill the gap in the mechanism of cure (your 'personal rapport').

4J

Dear Professor Freud,   Burghölzli-Zürich, 23 October 1906
By the same post I am taking the liberty of sending you another
offprint containing some more researches on psychoanalysis. I don't
think you will find that the 'sexual' standpoint I have adopted is too
reserved. The critics will come down on it accordingly.

As you have noticed, it is possible that my reservations about your
far-reaching views are due to lack of experience. But don't you think
that a number of borderline phenomena might be considered more
appropriately in terms of the other basic drive, *hunger*: for instance,
eating, sucking (predominantly hunger), kissing (predominantly sexuality)? Two complexes existing at the same time are always bound
to coalesce psychologically, so that one of them invariably contains
constellated aspects of the other. Perhaps you mean no more than
this; in that case I have misunderstood you and would be entirely of
your opinion. Even so, however, one feels alarmed by the positivism
of your presentation.

At the risk of boring you, I must abreact my most recent experience. I am currently treating an hysteric with your method. Difficult
case, a twenty-year-old Russian girl student, ill for six years.

First trauma between the 3rd and 4th year. Saw her father spank-
ing her older brother on the bare bottom. Powerful impression.
Couldn't help thinking afterwards that she had defecated on her
father's hand. From the 4th to 7th year conclusive attempts to defecate on her own feet, in the following manner: she sat on the floor
with one foot beneath her, pressed her heel against her anus and
tried to defecate and at the same time to prevent defecation. Often
retained the stool for two weeks in this way! Has no idea how she hit
upon this peculiar business; says it was completely instinctive, and
accompanied by blissfully shuddersome feelings. Later this phenomenon was superseded by vigorous masturbation.

I should be extremely grateful if you would tell me in a few words
what you think of this story.

Very truly yours, C. G. JUNG

5F

Dear colleague, 27 October 1906, Vienna, IX. Berggasse 19
Many thanks for the new analysis. You certainly did not show too
much reserve, and the 'transference', the chief proof that the drive
underlying the whole process is sexual in nature, seems to have
become very clear to you. As to criticism, let us wait until the critics
have acquired some experience of their own before attaching any
importance to it.

I have no theoretical objection to according equal importance to
the other basic drive, if only it would assert itself unmistakably in the
psychoneuroses. What we see of it in hysteria and obsessional neuroses can easily be explained by the anastomoses existing between
them, that is, by the impairment of the sexual component of the
alimentary drive. But I own that these are knotty questions that still
require thorough investigation. For the present I content myself with
pointing out what is glaringly evident, that is, the role of sexuality. It
is possible that later on we shall find elsewhere, in melancholia or in
the psychoses, what we fail to find in hysteria and obsessional neurosis.

I am glad to hear that your Russian girl is a student; uneducated
persons are at present too inaccessible for our purposes. The defecation story is nice and suggests numerous analogies. Perhaps you
remember my contention in my *Theory of Sexuality* that even
infants derive pleasure from the retention of faeces. The third to
fourth year is the most significant period for those sexual activities
which later belong to the pathogenic ones (*ibid*). The sight of a
brother being spanked arouses a memory trace from the first to
second year, or a fantasy transposed into that period. It is not unusual for babies to soil the hands of those who are carrying them.
Why should that not have happened in her case? And this awakens a
memory of her father's caresses during her infancy. Infantile fixation
of the libido on the father – the typical choice of object; anal autoerotism. The position she has chosen can be broken down into its
components, for it seems to have still other factors added to it.

Which factors? It must be possible, by the symptoms and even by the character, to recognize anal excitation as a motivation. Such people often show typical combinations of character traits. They are extremely neat, stingy and obstinate, traits which are in a manner of speaking the sublimations of anal erotism. Cases like this based on repressed perversion can be analysed very satisfactorily.

You see that you have not bored me in the least. I am delighted with your letters.

Sincerest regards,

Yours, DR FREUD

7J

Dear Professor Freud,   Burghölzli-Zürich, 4 December 1906
First of all I must tell you how sincerely grateful I am to you for not taking offence at some of the passages in my 'apologia'. If I allowed myself certain reservations it was not in order to criticize your theory but a matter of policy, as you will surely have noticed. As you rightly say, I leave our opponents a line of retreat, with the conscious purpose of not making recantation too difficult for them. Even so things will be difficult enough. If one attacked an opponent as he really deserves, it would merely result in a disastrous dissension which could have only unfavourable consequences. Even as it is, people find my criticism too harsh. If I confine myself to advocating the bare minimum, this is simply because I can advocate only as much as I myself have unquestionably experienced and that, in comparison with your experience, is naturally very little. I am only beginning to understand many of your formulations and several of them are still beyond me, which does not mean by a long shot that I think you are wrong. I have gradually learnt to be cautious even in disbelief.

I have seen *ad nauseam* that the opposition is rooted in affect and I also know that no amount of reason can prevail against it.

If I appear to underestimate the therapeutic results of psychanalysis[3] I do so only out of diplomatic considerations, with the following reflections in mind:

1 Most uneducated hysterics are unsuitable for psychanalysis. I have had some bad experiences here. Occasionally hypnosis gets better results.

2 The more psychanalysis becomes known, the more will incompetent doctors dabble in it and naturally make a mess of it. This will then be blamed on you and your theory . . .

For these reasons I consider it more cautious not to put too much emphasis on therapeutic results; if we do, there may be a rapid accumulation of material showing the therapeutic results in a thoroughly bad light, thus damaging the theory as well.

Personally I am enthusiastic about your therapy and well able to appreciate its signal merits. Altogether, your theory has already brought us the very greatest increase in knowledge and opened up a new era with endless perspectives.

Yours very sincerely, JUNG

8F

Dear colleague,　　　6 December 1906, Vienna, IX. Berggasse 19
I am sure you will draw your conclusions from this 'acceleration of reaction-time'[4] and guess that your last letter has given me great pleasure, which is far from being an auxiliary hypothesis. It did indeed seem to me that you had modified your opinions with the purposive idea of pedagogic effect, and I am very glad to see them as they are, freed from such distortion.

As you know, I suffer all the torments that can afflict an 'innovator'; not the least of these is the unavoidable necessity of passing, among my own supporters, as the incorrigibly self-righteous crank or fanatic that in reality I am not. Left alone for so long with my ideas, I have come, understandably enough, to rely more and more on my own decisions. In the last fifteen years I have been increasingly

[3] German *Psychanalyse*, a form in earlier use, preferred by the Zürich group.
[4] Allusion to one of Jung's association studies, on reaction-time.

immersed in preoccupations that have become monotonously exclusive. (At present I am devoting ten hours a day to psychotherapy.) This has given me a kind of resistance to being urged to accept opinions that differ from my own. But I have always been aware of my fallibility and I have turned the material over and over in my mind for fear of becoming too settled in my ideas. You yourself once remarked that this flexibility of mine indicated a process of development.

I can subscribe without reservation to your remarks on therapy. I have had the same experience and have been reluctant for the same reasons to say any more in public than that 'this method is more fruitful than any other.' I should not even claim that every case of hysteria can be cured by it, let alone all the states that go by that name. Attaching no importance to frequency of cure, I have often treated cases verging on the psychotic or delusional (delusions of reference, fear of blushing, etc), and in so doing learned at least that the same mechanisms go far beyond the limits of hysteria and obsessional neurosis. It is not possible to explain anything to a hostile public; accordingly I have kept certain things that might be said concerning the limits of the therapy and its mechanism to myself, or spoken of them in a way that is intelligible only to the initiate. You are probably aware that our cures are brought about through the fixation of the libido prevailing in the unconscious (transference), and that this transference is most readily obtained in hysteria. Transference provides the impulse necessary for understanding and translating the language of the ucs.; where it is lacking, the patient does not make the effort or does not listen when we submit our translation to him. Essentially, one might say, the cure is effected by love. And actually transference provides the most cogent, indeed, the only unassailable proof that neuroses are determined by the individual's love life.

I am delighted with your promises to trust me for the present in matters where your experience does not yet enable you to make up your own mind – though of course only until it does enable you to do so. Even though I look at myself very critically, I believe I deserve such trust, but I ask it of very few persons . . .

Yours cordially, DR FREUD

9J

Dear Professor Freud,   Burghölzli-Zürich, 29 December 1906
I am sincerely sorry that I of all people must be such a nuisance to you. I understand perfectly that you cannot be anything but dissatisfied with my book since it treats your researches too ruthlessly. I am perfectly well aware of this. The principle uppermost in my mind while writing it was: consideration for the academic German public. If we don't take the trouble to present this seven-headed monster with everything tastefully served up on a silver salver, it won't bite, as we have seen on countless occasions before. It is therefore entirely in the interests of our cause to give heed to all those factors which are likely to whet its appetite. For the time being, unfortunately, these include a certain reserve and the hint of an independent judgement regarding your researches. It was this that determined the general tenor of my book. Specific corrections of your views derive from the fact that we do not see eye to eye on certain points. This may be because I. my material is totally different from yours. I am working under enormously difficult conditions mostly with uneducated insane patients, and on top of that with the uncommonly tricky material of Dementia praecox. II. my upbringing, my milieu, and my scientific premises are in any case utterly different from your own. III. my experience compared with yours is extremely small. IV. both in quantity and quality of psychanalytic talent the balance is distinctly in your favour. V. the lack of personal contact with you, that regrettable defect in my preparatory training, must weigh heavily in the scales. For all these reasons I regard the views in my book as altogether provisional and in effect merely introductory. Hence I am extraordinarily grateful to you for any kind of criticism, even if it does not sound at all sweet, for what I miss is opposition, by which I naturally mean justified opposition. I greatly regret that your interesting letter broke off so abruptly.

You have put your finger on the weak points in my dream analysis. I do in fact know the dream material and the dream thoughts much better than I have said. I know the dreamer intimately:

he is myself. The 'failure of the rich marriage' refers to something essential that is undoubtedly contained in the dream, though not in the way you think. My wife[5] is rich. For various reasons I was turned down when I first proposed; later I was accepted, and I married. I am happy with my wife in every way (not merely from optimism), though of course this does nothing to prevent such dreams. So there has been no sexual failure, more likely a social one. The rationalistic explanation, 'sexual restraint', is, as I have said, merely a convenient screen pushed into the foreground and hiding an illegitimate sexual wish that had better not see the light of day. One determinant of the little rider, who in my analysis at first evokes the idea of my chief, is the wish for a boy (we have two girls). My chief is wholly conditioned by the fact that he has two boys. I have been unable to discover an infantile root anywhere. I also have the feeling that the 'package' has not been sufficiently clarified. But I am at a loss for an interpretation. Although the dream has not been analysed completely, I still thought I could use it as an example of dream symbolism. The analysis and use of one's own dreams is a ticklish business at best; one succumbs again and again to the inhibitions emanating from the dream no matter how objective one believes oneself to be.

... But you should not imagine that I am frenetically set on differentiating myself from you by the greatest possible divergence of opinion. I speak of things as I understand them and as I believe is right. Any differentiation would come far too late anyway, since the leading lights in psychiatry have already given me up for lost. It is enough for them to read in a report that I have championed your standpoint. Aschaffenburg's paper has whipped up a storm of protest against you. Faced with these fearsome difficulties there is probably no alternative but the *dosis refracta*[6] and another form of medication.

Very sincerely yours, JUNG.

5 Emma Jung, née Rauschenbach (1882–1955).
6 = *refracta dosi*, 'in repeated and divided doses'.

11F

Dear colleague,   1 January 1907

You are quite mistaken in supposing that I was not enthusiastic
about your book on dementia praecox. Abandon the idea at once.
The very fact that I offered criticism ought to convince you. If my
feelings had been different, I should have summoned up enough diplomacy to hide them. For it would have been most unwise to offend
you, the ablest helper to have joined me thus far. In reality I regard
your essay on D. pr. as the richest and most significant contribution
to my labours that has ever come to my attention, and among my
students in Vienna, who have the perhaps questionable advantage
over you of personal contact with me, I know of only one who might
be regarded as your equal in understanding, and of none who is able
and willing to do so much for the cause as you . . .

If I may be pardoned an attempt to influence you, I should like to
suggest that you pay less attention to the opposition that confronts
us both and not to let it affect your writings so much. The 'leading
lights' of psychiatry really don't amount to much; the future belongs
to us and our views, and the younger men – everywhere most
likely – side actively with us. I see this in Vienna, where, as you
know, I am systematically ignored by my colleagues and periodically
annihilated by some hack, but where my lectures nevertheless draw
forty attentive listeners, coming from every faculty. Now that you,
Bleuler, and to a certain extent Löwenfeld[7] have won me a hearing among the readers of the scientific literature, the movement in
favour of our new ideas will continue irresistibly despite all the
efforts of the moribund authorities. I believe it would be good policy
for us to share the work in accordance with our characters and posi-
tions, that you along with your chief should try to mediate, while I go
on playing the intransigent dogmatist who expects the public to swallow the bitter pill uncoated. But I beg of you, don't sacrifice everything essential for the sake of paedagogic tact and affability, and
don't deviate too far from me when you are really so close to me, for

[7] Leopold Löwenfeld, Munich psychiatrist, friendly to Freud's ideas.

if you do, we may one day be played off against one another. In my secret heart I am convinced that in our special circumstances the utmost frankness is the best diplomacy. My inclination is to treat those colleagues who offer resistance exactly as we treat patients in the same situation ...

Best wishes for the New Year. May we continue to work together and allow no misunderstanding to arise between us.

Most sincerely, DR FREUD

12J

Dear Professor Freud, Burghölzli-Zürich, 8 January 1907
I am sorry I have been so long in answering your last, exceedingly friendly and detailed letter ...

You may very well be right when you counsel me to practise more 'therapy' on our opponents, but I am still young, and now and then one has one's quirks in the matter of recognition and scientific standing. Working in a university clinic, one has to give a great many considerations their due which in private life one would prefer to ignore. But in this respect you may rest assured: I shall never abandon any portion of your theory that is essential to me, as I am far too committed to it.

I am now firmly resolved to come to Vienna during my spring holiday (April), in order to enjoy the long-desired pleasure of a personal conversation with you. I have an awful lot to abreact.

Concerning the question of 'toxins', you have again put your finger on a weak spot. Originally I wanted to leave material causes entirely out of my 'psychology'. But because I feared misunderstandings owing to the notorious dimwittedness of the esteemed public, I had at least to mention the 'toxin'. I was acquainted with your view that sexuality may play a role here. Also, I find it a thoroughly congenial idea that a so-called 'inner' endocrine secretion may be the cause of these disturbances, and that perhaps the *sex glands* are the makers of the toxins. But I have no proof of this, so I dropped the conjecture. Moreover it seems to me at present that the latter hypothesis is more applicable to *epilepsy*, where the sexual-religious complex holds a central place.

As to your conception of 'paranoia', I can see in it only a difference of nomenclature. With 'Dementia' praecox one should on no account think first of imbecility (though that can *also* happen!), but rather of a *complex-delirium* with fixations. Paranoia is built up exactly like Dementia praecox, except that the fixation is restricted to a few associations; with few exceptions, clarity of concepts remains unimpaired. There are, however, numerous fluid transitions to what we call D.pr.[8] D.pr. is a most unfortunate term! From your standpoint my D.pr. case could just as well be described as paranoia, which was in fact done in former times . . .

Recently I read with satisfaction that Löwenfeld has resolutely come over to our side, at least so far as the anxiety neuroses are concerned. In Germany his voice will carry further than mine. Perhaps your triumphal entry will begin sooner than we think.

I still owe you an explanation of the term 'habitual hysteric'. It is yet another makeshift. I have been struck by the fact that there are hysterics who live in perpetual conflict with their complexes, exhibiting violent excitement, fluctuations of mood, and wild changes of symptoms. In my limited experience these cases warrant a favourable prognosis. They have a component within them that resists subjugation by the pathogenic complex. On the other hand there are hysterics who live at peace with their symptoms, having not only *habituated* themselves to the symptom but also exploiting it for all kinds of symptomatic actions and chicaneries, and who batten parasitically on the sympathy of everyone in their environment. These are prognostically bad cases who also struggle against analysis with extreme obstinacy. They are the ones I call 'habitual hysterics'. Perhaps you will see what I mean from this sketchy description. Of course it is only a very crass and superficial classification, but it has been helpful to me in my work so far. Perhaps you can open my eyes

[8] 'Dementia praecox', introduced by Kraepelin (see 44J, note), was the term preferred by the Swiss psychiatrists. It has largely been replaced by the term coined by Bleuler, 'schizophrenia'.

in this respect as well. Countless uneducated hysterics (especially the hospital parasites) come into this category.

With most cordial wishes for the New Year and my warmest thanks.

Yours very sincerely, JUNG

The Jungs in Vienna

Jung and his wife Emma visited Freud on Sunday 3 March. They were accompanied by Ludwig Binswanger (1881–1966), Jung's pupil, later founder of existential analysis. The Jungs stayed for five or six days altogether, and Jung attended the 6 March meeting of the Swiss Branch Society of the International Psychoanalytic Association.

17J

Dear Professor Freud,   Burghölzli-Zürich, 31 March 1907
You will doubtless have drawn your own conclusions from the prolongation of my reaction-time. Up till now I had a strong resistance to writing because until recently the complexes aroused in Vienna were still in an uproar. Only now have things settled down a bit, so that I hope to be able to write you a more or less sensible letter.

The most difficult item, your broadened conception of sexuality, has now been assimilated up to a point and tried out in a number of actual cases. In general I see that you are right ... It has however become quite clear to me that the expression 'libido' and, in general, all the terms (no doubt justified in themselves) that have been carried over into the broadened conception of sexuality are open to misunderstanding, or at least are not of didactic value. They actually evoke emotional inhibitions which make any kind of teaching impossible ... Is it not conceivable, in view of the limited conception of sexuality that prevails nowadays, that the sexual terminology should be reserved only for the most extreme forms of your 'libido', and that a less offensive collective term should be established for *all* the libidinal manifestations? Herr Rank[9] is another who simply takes the broadened conception of sexuality for granted, in such a way that even I, who have been studying your thought intensively for more than four years, have difficulty in understanding this conception. The public Herr Rank writes for won't understand it at all ... I am no longer plagued by doubts as to the rightness of your theory. The last shreds were dispelled by my stay in Vienna, which for me was an event of the first importance. Binswanger will already have told you of the tremendous impression you made on me. I shall say no more about it, but I hope my work for your cause will show you the depths of my gratitude and veneration. I hope and even dream that we may welcome you in Zürich next summer or autumn. A visit from you would be seventh heaven for me personally; the few hours I was permitted to spend with you were all too fleeting.

Riklin[10] has promised to send you his piece on fairytales as soon as it is finished, though that will not be for some time yet ...

My wife and I thank you, your wife, and all your family most cordially for the kind reception you gave us.

Yours gratefully, JUNG

[9] Otto Rank (1884–1939), born Rosenfeld, changed his name because of conflict with his father. 1906–15, secretary of the Vienna Psychoanalytic Society (the so-called 'Wednesday Evenings'). In the early 1920s he dissented from psychoanalysis.

[10] Franz Riklin (1878–1938), psychiatrist at the Burghölzli 1902–4, during which time he collaborated with Jung on the word-association tests; 1904, they published jointly a study of 'The Associations of Normal Subjects' (CW 2). 1905–10, at the cantonal hospital, Rheinau (Cant. Zürich). Riklin was married to a cousin of Jung's. He remained with Jung after his dissension from Freud but was not actively concerned with analysis.

18F

I am choosing different paper because I don't wish to feel cramped in speaking to you. Your visit was most delightful and gratifying; I should like to repeat in writing various things that I confided to you by word of mouth, in particular, that you have inspired me with confidence for the future, that I now realize that I am as replaceable as everyone else and that I could hope for no one better than yourself, as I have come to know you, to continue and complete my work. I am sure you will not abandon the work, you have gone into it too deeply and seen for yourself how exciting, how far-reaching, and how beautiful our subject is.

Of course I am thinking of a return visit to Zürich, on which occasion I hope you will demonstrate your famous Dem. praecox case, but I doubt if it will be very soon. At the moment I am also troubled by the uncertainty of our relations with your chief. His recent defence of our position in the *Münchener medizinische Wochenschrift* made me think he could be relied on, but now you tell me of a very serious swing in the other direction, which like myself you probably interpret as a reaction to the conviction you took home with you. How the 'personal complex' casts its shadow on all purely logical thought!

... I appreciate your motives in trying to sweeten the sour apple, but I do not think you will be successful. Even if we call the ucs. 'psychoid', it will still be the ucs., and even if we do not call the driving force in the broadened conception of sexuality 'libido', it will still be libido, and in every inference we draw from it we shall come back to the very thing from which we were trying to divert attention with our nomenclature. We cannot avoid resistances, why not face up to them from the start? In my opinion attack is the best form of defence. Perhaps you are underestimating the intensity of these resistances if you hope to disarm them with small concessions. We are being asked neither more nor less than to abjure our belief in the sexual drive. The only answer is to profess it openly ...

My wife was very pleased with your wife's letter. It is the host, not the guest, who owes thanks for the honour and the pleasure. Unfortunately she cannot answer now, because she is suffering from (benign) iridocyclitis, resulting from an upset stomach.

Looking forward to your answer,

Yours cordially, DR FREUD

19J

Dear Professor Freud,   Burghölzli-Zürich, 11 April 1907
Many thanks for your long and exceedingly friendly letter! I only fear that you overestimate me and my powers. With your help I have come to see pretty deeply into things, but I am still far from seeing them *clearly*. Nevertheless I have the feeling of having made considerable inner progress since I got to know you personally; it seems to me that one can never quite understand your science unless one knows you in the flesh. Where so much still remains dark to us outsiders only faith can help; but the best and most effective faith is knowledge of your personality. Hence my visit to Vienna was a genuine confirmation ...

You will be interested to hear that I have been asked to report on 'Modern Theories of Hysteria' at this year's international congress in Amsterdam. My opposite number is Aschaffenburg! I shall naturally confine myself entirely to your theory. I feel in my bones that the discussion will be pretty depressing. A. wrote to me recently; he still hasn't understood anything.

I have just finished Rank's book. There seem to be some very good ideas in it though I haven't understood everything by any means. Later I'll read it through again.

Bleuler has now accepted seventy per cent of the libido theory after I demonstrated it to him with a few cases. His resistance is directed chiefly to the word itself. His negative shillyshallying seems to have been temporarily occasioned by my visit to Vienna. For a very long time Bleuler was a frosty old bachelor who must have done a lot of repressing in his life; hence his unconscious has become very well filled and influential. All the same, you have a staunch supporter in him, even though sundry *restrictions mentales* will put in an appearance from time to time. Once Bleuler is on to something he knows is right he will never let it go. He possesses the Swiss national virtues to a fault.

I shall be extremely grateful for your thoughts on D. pr., as indeed for any suggestions on your part.

Of course you are right about 'libido', but my faith in the efficacy of sweeteners is deep rooted – for the present.

Bezzola[11] is a confounded fusspot who has to compensate for a highly disagreeable position in life and thinks he can get rich on the crumbs that fall from the master's table. A hoarder of details with no clear overall vision, but otherwise a decent fellow still in the grim clutches of the unconscious. I found his paper infuriating.

My wife and I have heard with deep regret of your wife's illness and with all our hearts wish her a speedy recovery.

With best regards and gratefully yours, JUNG

26J

Dear Professor Freud,   Burghölzli-Zürich, 24 May 1907
Your *Gradiva*[12] is magnificent. I gulped it at one go. The clear exposition is beguiling, and I think one would have to be struck by the gods with sevenfold blindness not to see things now as they really are. But the hidebound psychiatrists and psychologists are capable of anything! I shouldn't wonder if all the idiotic commonplaces that have been levelled at you before are trotted out again from the academic side. Often I have to transport myself back to the time before the reformation of my psychological thinking to re-experience the charges that were laid against you. I simply can't understand them any more. My thinking in those days seems to me not only intellectually wrong and defective but, what is worse, morally inferior, since

[11] Dumeng Bezzola, Swiss psychiatrist.
[12] Freud's study of a novel by W. Jensen.

it now looks like an immense dishonesty towards myself. So you may be absolutely right when you seek the cause of our opponents' resistance in affects, especially sexual affects. I am just dying to know what the sexual complex of the public will have to say about your *Gradiva*, which in this respect is wholly innocuous. It would irritate me most of all if they treated it with benevolent patronage. What does Jensen himself say about it? Please tell me sometime what kind of literary reviews you get . . .

Lately I've been having unpleasant arguments with Bezzola . . . The bad thing in all this is that Bezzola, in his benighted blindness, is antagonistic to you and has already started telling lies about me. You discerned his character better than I did – a small [. . .] soul. Opposition and dissension in one's own camp are the very worst thing . . .

Ever sincerely yours, JUNG

27F

Dear colleague,   26 May 1907

Many thanks for your praise of *Gradiva*. You wouldn't believe how few people have managed to say anything of the kind; yours is just about the first friendly word I have heard on this subject (No, I must not be unfair to your cousin (?) Riklin). This time I knew that my work deserved praise; this little book was written on sunny days and I myself derived great pleasure from it. True, it says nothing that is new to us, but I believe it enables us to enjoy our riches. Of course I do not expect it to open the eyes of our hidebound opponents; I long ago stopped paying attention to those people, and it is because I have so little hope of converting the specialists that, as you have noticed, I have taken only a half-hearted interest in your galvanometric experiments, for which you have now punished me. To tell the truth, a statement such as yours means more to me than the approval of a whole medical congress; for one thing it makes the approval of future congresses a certainty . . .

What Jensen himself says? He has been really charming. In his first letter he expressed his pleasure, etc, and said that in all essential points my analysis corresponded to the intention of his story. Of course he was not speaking of our theory, the old gentleman seems incapable of entering into any other ideas than his own poetic ones. The agreement, he believes, must probably be laid to poetic intuition and perhaps in part to his early medical studies. In a second letter I was indiscreet and asked him about the subjective element in the work, where the material came from, where his own person entered in, etc. He then informed me that the ancient relief actually exists, that he possesses a reproduction of it from Nanny in Munich, but has never seen the original. It was he himself who conceived the fantasy that the relief represented a woman of Pompeii; it was also he who liked to dream in the noonday heat of Pompeii and has once fallen into an almost visionary state while doing so. Apart from that, he has no idea where the material came from; the beginning suddenly came to him while he was working on another story. He put everything else aside and started to write it down. He never hesitated, it all came to him ready and complete, and he finished the story at one stretch. This suggests that the analysis, if continued, would lead through his childhood to his most intimate erotic experience. In other words, the whole thing is another egocentric fantasy . . .

Thank you very much for the two bombshells from the enemy camp. I am not tempted to keep them for more than a few days, only until I am able to read them without affect. What are they, after all, but emotional drivel? . . . Envy is evident in every line of Isserlin's[13] paper, some of it is just too absurd, and the whole thing is a display of ignorance.

But all the same, don't worry, everything will work out all right. You will live to see the day, though I may not. As we know, others before us have had to wait for the world to understand what they were saying; I feel certain that you will not be all alone at the Amsterdam congress. Every time we are ridiculed, I became more convinced than ever that we are in possession of a great idea. In the obituary you will some day write for me, don't forget to bear witness

13 Max Isserlin, Munich neurologist, adversary of psychoanalysis.

that I was never so much as ruffled by all the opposition.

I hope your chief will recover soon and that your work load will then be reduced. I miss your letters very much when the interruptions are too long.

Yours cordially, DR FREUD

J28

Dear Professor Freud,   Burghölzli-Zürich, 30 May 1907
Unfortunately I can send only a short answer today to your very friendly letter as all my time is taken up with the affairs of the clinic.

Thanks above all for the news about Jensen. It is roughly what one would have expected. Putting it down at his age to his medical studies is splendid and suspiciously arteriosclerotic. In my entourage *Gradiva* is being read with delight. The women understand you by far the best and usually at once. Only the 'psychologically' educated have blinkers before their eyes.

I would gladly write something for your *Papers*. The idea is very attractive. Only I don't know *what*. It would have to be something worthwhile. The *Zukunft* article and its like are not good enough; Harden wrung it out of me. I would never have written it of my own accord. At the moment I am particularly keen on experimental studies, but I'm afraid they are hardly suitable for a wider circle of readers. Still, it is not beyond the bounds of possibility that Dementia praecox will send up something good from its inexhaustible depths. The snag is that I am so swamped with the affairs of the clinic that I can scarcely find the necessary time for my own work. It is impossible for me to immerse myself in the material at present. Any systematic working up of Dementia praecox is equally impossible as it demands unlimited time. I am therefore planning to change my position so as to have more free time to devote myself entirely to scientific work. My plan, which has Bleuler's vigorous support, is to affiliate to the clinic a laboratory for psychology, as a more or less independent institute of which I would be appointed director. Then I would be independent, freed from the shackles of the clinic, and able at last to work as I want. Once in this position, I would try to get the chair for psychiatry separated from the running of the clinic. The two together are too much and hamper any useful scientific activity. By taking such a step I would of course be abandoning my clinical career, but the damage would not be so great. I would have the material anyway. And I can imagine that I would get sufficient satisfaction from scientific work alone. As I have seen from my recent dreams, this change has its – for you – transparent 'meta-psychological-sexual' background, holding out the promise of pleasurable feelings galore. Anyone who knows your science has veritably eaten of the tree of paradise and become clairvoyant.

More news soon.

With sincerest regards, JUNG

32F

Dear colleague,   14 June 1907, Vienna IX. Berggasse 19
... Of course you have hit the nail on the head with what you say about your ambulatory cases. What with their habits and mode of life, reality is too close to those women to allow them to believe in fantasies. If I had based my theories on the statements of servant girls, they would all be negative. And such behaviour fits in with other sexual peculiarities of that class; well informed persons assure me that these girls are much less diffident about engaging in coitus than about being seen naked. Fortunately for our therapy, we have previously learned so much from other cases that we can tell these persons their story without having to wait for their contribution. They are willing to confirm what we tell them, but one can learn nothing from them ...

I am glad to see from your plan to visit Paris and London that your period of overwork is past. I wish you an interesting Paris complex, but I should not like to see it repress your Vienna complex. Our difficulties with the French are probably due chiefly to the national character; it has always been hard to import things into France. Janet[14] has a good mind, but he started out without sexuality and now he can go no further; and in science there is no going back. But you are sure to hear much that is interesting.

With kind regards,

Yours sincerely, DR FREUD

33J

Dear Professor Freud, Burghölzli-Zürich, 28 June 1907
... I see from your kind gift that your *Psychopathology of Everyday Life* has gone into a second edition – this gives me sincere pleasure. It is good that you have considerably expanded the text – the more examples the better. I hope you will soon be able to manage a new edition of *The Interpretation of Dreams* as well; it sometimes seems to me that your prophecy that you will have won through in ten years is being fulfilled. There are stirrings on all sides. You too will have received the book by Otto Gross;[15] I certainly don't cotton on to his idea that you are to be merely the mason working on the unfinished edifice of Wernicke's system. Nevertheless this demonstration that *all* the lines are converging upon you is very gratifying. Apart from that there are all sorts of oddities in Gross's book, though at bottom he has an excellent mind. I am eager to hear what you think ...

My experience on the trip was *pauvre*. I had a talk with Janet and was very disappointed. He has only the most primitive knowledge of Dem. pr. Of the latest happenings, including you, he understands nothing at all. He is stuck in his groove and is, be it said in passing,

[14] Pierre Janet (1859–1947), eminent French neurologist, one of the first to recognize the unconscious, though he was hostile to psychoanalysis. Jung studied with him in 1902–3.
[15] Austrian neurologist (1877–1919), sympathetic to psychoanalysis; later psychotic and a patient of Jung's. He led a turbulent life and died in dire straits.

merely an intellect but not a personality, a hollow *causeur* and a typical mediocre bourgeois. Déjerine's[16] grand *traitement par isolement* at the Salpêtrière is a very bad *blague*. It all struck me as unspeakably childish, not least the lofty haze that befogs all heads in such a clinic. These people are fifty years behind the times. It got on my nerves so much that I gave up the idea of going to London, where far, far less is to be expected. Instead, I devoted myself to the castles of the Loire . . .

With best regards,

Ever sincerely yours, JUNG

34F

Dear colleague,   1 July 1907, Vienna, IX. Berggasse 19
I was very glad to hear that you are back at work at Burghölzli and am delighted with your impressions of your trip. You can imagine that I should have been very sorry if your Vienna complex had been obliged to share the available cathexis with a Paris complex. Luckily, as you tell me, nothing of the sort happened, you gained the impression that the days of the great Charcot[17] are past and that the new life of psychiatry is with us, between Zürich and Vienna. So we have emerged safe and sound from a first danger.

In your last letter you bring up an unusual number of 'business' matters that call for a reply. You are right, the business is doing well. It remains of course to be seen whether it will take ten years and whether I can wait that long. The trend is clearly upwards. Our adversaries' activity can only be sterile; each one lets out a blast and claims to have crushed me (and now you as well); and that is all. There his activity ends. Whereas those who join us are able to report on the results of their work; after which they continue to work and

16 Joseph Déjerine, director of the Salpêtrière, an insane asylum in Paris, where Janet taught.
17 Jean-Martin Charcot (1825–1893), French neurologist, with whom Freud studied in 1885–60.

report again. Quite understandably, each one of us works in his own way and perhaps contributes his own specific distortion to the understanding of our still unfinished task . . .

Dr Stekel,[18] whom you know and whose forte is not ordinarily his critical faculty, has sent me a work on anxiety cases, written at the request of the *Berliner Klinik* (!). I persuaded him to consider these cases of 'anxiety hysteria' side by side with 'conversion hysteria'. I mean to do a theoretical defence of this procedure one of these days and recommend it to you in the meantime. It would enable us to include the phobias.

With kind regards,

Yours, DR FREUD

35J

Dear Professor Freud,   Burghölzli-Zürich, 6 July 1907

Would you mind my boring you with some personal experiences? I would like to tell you an instructive story about something that happened to me in Paris. There I met a German-American woman who made a pleasant impression on me – a Mrs St., aged about thirty-five. We were together at a party for a few hours and talked about landscapes and other indifferent matters. We were offered black coffee. She declined, saying that she couldn't tolerate a mouthful of black coffee, even a sip made her feel bad the next day. I answered that this

---

[18] Wilhelm Stekel (1868–1940), one of the four original members of the Wednesday Evening Society (forerunner of the Vienna Psychoanalytic Society), and earlier in analysis with Freud; considered a brilliant writer and an intuitive psychoanalyst. He was editor (at first with Alfred Adler) of the *Zentralblatt*, which he continued for a year after he separated from Freud in 1911. Later in London, where he took his own life. / Alfred Adler (1870–1937), since 1902 also a member of the Wednesday Evening Society; he was the first president of the Vienna Psychoanalytic Society, and the first of Freud's important followers to secede, in 1911, when he founded 'Individual Psychology'. After 1926, he spent much of his time in the USA and settled there in 1935. Died May 1937 at Aberdeen, Scotland, during a lecture tour.

was a nervous symptom; it was merely that she couldn't tolerate black coffee at home, but when she found herself 'in different circumstances', she would surely tolerate it much better. Scarcely had this unfortunate phrase left my mouth than I felt enormously embarrassed, but rapidly discovered that – luckily – it had 'slipped by' her. I must remark that I knew absolutely nothing about this lady's history. Soon afterwards another lady suggested we should all say a number – such numbers were always significant. Mrs St. said '3'. An acquaintance of hers cried out: 'Naturally, you, your husband, and your dog.' Mrs St. retorted: 'Oh no, I was thinking all good things come in threes!' From which I concluded that her marriage was barren. Mrs St. had lapsed into silence but suddenly said to me out of the blue: 'In my dreams my father always appears to me so wonderfully transfigured.' I found out that her father is a doctor. A few days later she gave me, despite my protests, a magnificent engraving. *Sapient sat*! My wife, who knows a thing or two, said recently: 'I am going to write a psychotherapeutic handbook for gentlemen.'

... For the time being Dem. pr. is having an enforced rest. July 14 I must go to Lausanne for three weeks on military service.[19] Afterwards my chief will be away for a month. Then once again I shall have the whole clinic on my shoulders. So the outlook is bad. Binswanger's paper will come out soon, I hope. You will then see that you too have absorbed the secrets of the galvanometer. Your associations are indeed excellent!

With best regards,

Ever sincerely yours, JUNG

Anxiety neurosis and anxiety hysteria
are still wrapped in obscurity for me –
unfortunately – from lack of experience.

---

[19] Military service is compulsory in Switzerland. In 1895, Jung had first served with the infantry, and in 1901 he became an officer in the medical corps. From 1908 he was a captain, and from 1914 commander of a unit, until he retired in 1930. Two weeks of service were obligatory each year.

36F

Dear colleague,   10 July 1907, Vienna IX. Berggasse 19
I am writing to you – briefly and in haste – in order to catch you
before you leave and wish you a period of rest from mental effort. It
will do you good.

The many charming 'trifles' in your last letter remind me that I too
am at the end of my year's work. On the fourteenth I am leaving for:

> Lavarone in *Val Sugana*
> South Tyrol

Hotel du Lac

I should not like to be without news of you all this time – I shall not
be coming back until the end of September – your letters have
become a necessity for me. So I shall keep you informed of my
movements. I hope to be in Sicily when you are reading your paper
in Amsterdam. In spite of all the distractions, a part of my thoughts
will be with you there. I hope you will gain the recognition you
desire and deserve; it means a great deal to me too.

I am already corresponding with Dr Abraham.[20] I have every
reason to be deeply concerned with his work. What is he like? His
letter and article have predisposed me very much in his favour. I am
expecting to receive your cousin Riklin's manuscript any day. It
seems to me that I have come across a nest of especially fine and able
men, or am I letting my personal satisfaction becloud my judgement?

Only today I received a letter from a student in Lausanne who
wishes to speak about my work at a scientific gathering at Docent
Sternberg's house. Things are getting very lively in Switzerland.

My hearty greetings. And don't, during the long holiday, forget

Cordially yours, DR FREUD

[20] Karl Abraham (1877–1925), Berlin psychiatrist, on the Burghölzli staff 1904–7;
founded the Berlin Psychoanalytic Society and remained close to Freud.

37J

Dear Professor Freud,   Burghölzli-Zürich, 12 August 1907
Please excuse my long silence. The three weeks of military service
left me not a single moment for myself. We were at it from 5 in the
morning till 8 in the evening; evenings I was always dog tired. When
I got back home, the chores at the clinic had piled into mountains
and on top of that Prof Bleuler and the first assistant went on holiday. So I have more than enough to keep me busy. Just to make the
cup brim over, the secretariat of the Amsterdam congress began cla-
mouring for my manuscript which did not yet exist. I had to throw
myself head over heels into working up my lecture. It's a hard nut!
The most difficult feat of all is to leach out the wealth of your ideas,
boil down the essence, and finally bring off the master wizard's trick
of producing something homogeneous. To me it seems all but impossible to water the product down so as to make it more or less pal-
atable to the ignorant public. Just now I am working on the latest
development of your views– the detailed introduction of sexuality
into the psychology of hysteria. Often I want to give up in sheer
despair. But in the end I console myself with the thought that none of
this will be understood by ninety-nine per cent of the public anyhow,
so that in this part of my lecture I can say pretty much what I want.
It won't be understood either way. It is only a demonstration, a
confirmation, of the fact that in the year 1907 someone officially said
something positive about Freud's theory of hysteria at an international congress. I am becoming more and more convinced that
you are right when you attribute the not wanting to understand only
to ill will. One makes all sorts of discoveries in this respect. America
is on the move. In the last three weeks six Americans, one Russian,
one Italian, and one Hungarian have been here. No Germans!

As soon as I have finished my lecture, this child of sorrow, I hope
to be able to write you again.

Again apologies for the long pause,

Ever sincerely yours, JUNG

38F

Dear colleague,   Hotel Wolkenstein in St Christina, Gröden
My personality was impoverished by the interruption in our correspondence. Fortunately that has now come to an end. Though I
myself am wandering lazily about the world with my family, I know
that you are working again and that your letters will carry me back
to what for both of us has become the centre of interest.

Don't despair; I presume it was only a phrase that cropped up in
your letter. It doesn't matter whether we are understood by the
official figures of the moment. Among the nameless masses hidden
behind them there are plenty of individuals who *want* to understand
and who at a given moment suddenly step forward; I have had that
experience time and time again. Your lecture in Amsterdam will be a
milestone in history and after all it is largely for history that we
work. What you call the hysterical element in your personality, your
need to impress and influence people, the very quality that so emi-
nently equips you to be a teacher and guide, will come into its own
even if you make no concessions to the current fashions in opinion. And when you have injected your own personal leaven into
the fermenting mass of my ideas in still more generous measure,
there will be no further difference between your achievement and
mine.

I am not well enough to risk the trip to Sicily we had planned for
September, because at this time the scirocco is said to blow without
let up. Consequently I don't know exactly where I shall be in the
next few weeks. Until the end of August I shall stay here, hiking in
the mountains and picking edelweiss; I shall not be returning to
Vienna before the end of September . . .

I don't believe that Germany will show any sympathy for our
work until some bigwig has solemnly given his stamp of approval.
The simplest way might be to arouse the interest of Kaiser Wilhelm –
who of course understands everything. Have you any connections
in those quarters? I haven't. Perhaps Harden, the editor of *Die*

Zukunft,[21] will sniff out the psychiatry of the future in your work. As you see, this place puts me in a jocular mood. I hope your enforced holiday has done you as much good as I am expecting from my intentional rest.

Ever cordially yours, DR FREUD

39J

Dear Professor Freud,   Burghölzli-Zürich, 19 August 1907
As usual you have hit the nail on the head with your accusation that my ambition is the agent provocateur of my fits of despair. But this I must say in my own defence: it is my honest enthusiasm for the truth that impels me to find some way of presenting your teachings that would best bring about a breakthrough. Otherwise my unconditional devotion to the defence and propagation of your ideas, as well as my equally unconditional veneration of your personality, would be bound to appear in an extremely peculiar light – something I would gladly avoid even though the element of self-interest could be denied only by the very obtuse. All the same I have unpleasant presentiments, for it is no small thing to be defending *such* a position before *such* a public. I have now finished my lecture and see that I have taken the general stance which you deem the best: intransigence. If one wants to be honest one can't do anything else. Luckily I have just brought an analysis of hysteria in an uneducated person to a successful conclusion and this has given me heart.

In one of your earlier letters you asked for my views about Dr Abraham. I admit at once that I am 'jealous' of him because he corresponds with you. (Forgive me this candour, however tasteless it may seem!) There are no objections to A. Only, he isn't quite my type. For instance, I once suggested that he collaborate on my writings, but he declined. Now he pricks up his ears whenever Bleuler and I talk about what we are investigating, etc. He then comes up

21 Jung had published an essay in this Berlin weekly edited by Maximilian Harden.

with a publication. Of all our assistants he is the one who always holds a little aloof from the main work and then suddenly steps into the limelight with a publication, as a loner. Not only I but the other assistants too have found this rather unpleasant. He is intelligent but not original, highly adaptable, but totally lacking in psychological empathy, for which reason he is usually very unpopular with the patients. I would ask you to subtract a personal touch of venom from this judgement. Apart from these cavilings A. is an agreeable associate, very industrious and much concerned with all the bureaucratic affairs of the clinic, which nobody can say of me. A little drop of venom may derive from that source too, for in this respect my chief has long since reached the pinnacle of perfection.

I would now like to ask you for an explanation: do you regard sexuality as the mother of all feelings? Isn't sexuality for you merely one component of the personality (albeit the most important), and isn't the sexual complex therefore the most important and most frequent component in the clinical picture of hysteria? Are there not hysterical symptoms which, though co-determined by the sexual complex, are predominantly conditioned by a sublimation or by a non-sexual complex (profession, job, etc)?

Certainly in my small experience I have seen *only* sexual complexes and shall say so explicitly in Amsterdam.

With kindest regards,

Yours very sincerely, JUNG

40F

Hotel Annenheim und Seehof am Ossiacher See (Kärnten),
Dear colleague, Annenheim, 27 August 1907
You will forgive me for addressing you more formally in an open postcard.[22] Well, your letter was charming and once again showed me more of you than I could have learned from a whole dissertation. At the beginning you found yourself face to face with a

[22] (Missing.)

serious matter and seemed frightened at the contrast. I should be very sorry if you imagined for one moment that I really doubted you in any way. But then you pulled yourself together and took the only attitude one can take when confronting one's + + + unconscious,[23] to wit, one of humour, and yours turned out delightfully.

I was predisposed in Abraham's favour by the fact that he attacks the sexual problem head on; consequently I was glad to provide him with what material I had. Your picture of his character seems so apt that I am inclined to accept it without further examination. Nothing objectionable, yet something that precludes intimacy. You make him out to be something of an 'uninspired plodder', which is bound to clash with your open, winning nature. It would be interesting to discover the private circumstances at the source of this reserve, the secret wound to his pride, or the thorn of poverty or wretchedness, unhappy childhood, etc. By the way, is he a descendant of his eponym?

As for your question, a ream of this paper would not suffice for an answer. Not that I know so much, but there are so many equally valid possibilities. For the present I do not believe that anyone is justified in saying that sexuality is the mother of all feelings. Along with the poet, we know of two instinctual sources. Sexuality is one of them ...

I am so out of touch with everything that I don't even known the date of the Amsterdam congress. But I shall hear from you before that. I shall be here until September 10th.

Most cordially yours, DR FREUD

[23] Three crosses were chalked on the inside of doors in Austrian peasant houses to ward off danger.

42F

Hotel Annenheim und Seehof am Ossiacher See (Kärnten),

Dear colleague,   Annenheim, 2 September 1907

I know you are now in Amsterdam, just before or after your perilous
lecture, engaged in the defence of my cause, and it strikes me as
almost cowardly that I should meanwhile be looking for mushrooms
in the woods or bathing in this peaceful Carinthian lake instead of
fighting for my own cause or at least standing by your side. I take
comfort by telling myself that it is better for the cause this way, that
you as the other, the second, will be spared at least a part of the
opposition that would have been in store for me, that for me to say
the same thing over and over would be mere useless repetition, and
that you are better fitted for propaganda, for I have always felt that
there is something about my personality, my ideas and manner of
speaking, that people find strange and repellent, whereas all hearts
open to you. If a healthy man like you regards himself as a hysterical
type, I can only claim for myself the 'obsessional' type, each speci-
men of which vegetates in a sealed-off world of his own.

Whether you have been or will be lucky or unlucky, I do not
know; but now of all times I wish I were with you, taking pleasure in
no longer being alone and, if you are in need of encouragement,
telling you about my long years of honourable but painful solitude,
which began after I cast my first glance into the new world, about the
indifference and incomprehension of my closest friends, about the
terrifying moments when I myself thought I had gone astray and was
wondering how I might still make my misled life useful to my family,
about my slowly growing conviction, which fastened itself to the interpretation of dreams as to a rock in a stormy sea, and about the
serene certainty which finally took possession of me and bade me
wait until a voice from the unknown multitude should answer mine.
That voice was yours; for I know now that Bleuler also came to me
through you. Thank you for that, and don't let anything shake your
confidence, you will witness our triumph and share in it.

I am glad to say that I can no longer claim too much of your
sympathy for my ailing state. I made my entry into the climacteric

years with a rather stubborn case of dyspepsia (after influenza), but in these wonderful weeks of rest it has reduced itself to an occasional gentle reminder.

I made up my mind long ago to visit you in Zürich. But I see it as a Christmas or Easter excursion. Then I shall come straight from my work, stimulated and teeming with problems, not in my present almost somnolent state, with all my cathexes discharged. I too feel the need of chatting with you for a few hours.

With kind regards (and wishes!),

Yours, DR FREUD

43J

Hôtel de l'Europe,
Amsterdam, 4 September 1907

Dear Professor Freud,

Just a couple of words in haste by way of abreaction. I spoke this morning but unfortunately couldn't quite finish my lecture as I would have exceeded the time limit of half an hour, which wasn't allowed. What a gang of cut-throats we have here! Their resistance really is rooted in affect. Aschaffenburg made two slips of the tongue in his lecture ('facts' instead of 'no facts'), which shows that unconsciously he is already strongly infected. Hence his furious attack. Typical that in conversation he never tries to learn anything but goes all out to prove to me what a frightful mistake we are making. He won't listen to any of our arguments. I have compiled a pretty dossier of his negative affects. All the rest of them are cowards, each hanging on to the coat tails of the fatter man in front. The discussion is tomorrow. I shall say as little as possible, for every word sacrificed to this kind of opposition is a waste of time. A ghastly crowd, reeking of vanity, Janet the worst of the lot. I am glad you have never been caught in the bedlam of such a mutual admiration society. I constantly feel the urgent need of a bath. What a morass of nonsense and stupidity! But in spite of everything I have the impression that the ferment is working. However, we still need a few highly intelligent and dynamic men capable of creating the right atmosphere – I mean in Germany. We in Switzerland are a little too far from the centre. Once again I have seen that if one is to serve the cause one must stick to the most elementary things. What people *don't* know surpasses the imagination, and what they don't *want* to know is simply unbelievable. Aschaffenburg has been treating a case of obsessional neurosis and when she wanted to talk about sexual complexes he forbade her to speak of them – therefore Freudian theory is moonshine! A. announced this in public (with a moral undertone of course), puffing out his chest.

How can one discuss anything with these people?

With best regards,

Ever sincerely yours, JUNG

44J

Dear Professor Freud,   Burghölzli-Zürich, 11 September 1907
I got back from Amsterdam yesterday evening and am now in a better position to view my experiences at the congress in the proper perspective. Before I try to describe the subsequent developments I want to thank you heartily for your letter, which came just at the right moment; it did me good to feel that I was fighting not only for an important discovery but for a great and honourable man as well. Whether the facts are recognized slowly or quickly, or are attacked or not, leaves me pretty cold; but pouring unadulterated sewage over everything that isn't approved of is disgusting. *One* thing that has filled me up to the neck at this congress is a contempt bordering on nausea for the genus *Homo sapiens*.

As I told you, my lecture was, most unfortunately, broken off prematurely and the discussion took place only the following day, although there were no valid reasons for the postponement. The first to take the floor was Bezzola, to 'protest' against you, against me, and against the sexual theory of hysteria (moral undertone!). An hour beforehand I had tried in a public conversation to come to a friendly understanding with him – impossible. He begrudges you your books and your income; it's enough to make one die of laughter or burst a blood vessel. Nothing but furious, insensate affect against you and me.

Then Alt of Uchtspringe proclaimed a reign of terror against you, he'd never refer any patient of his to a doctor of the Freudian persuasion – unscrupulous, filthy people, etc. Huge applause and congratulation of the speaker by Prof Ziehen, Berlin. Then came Sachs of Breslau, who only uttered a couple of stupendous asininities that don't bear repeating; again roars of applause. Janet couldn't help letting it drop that he had already heard your name. He knows absolutely nothing about your theory but is convinced that it's all rubbish. Heilbronner of Utrecht found only the association experiments, the 'cornerstone of your theory', worth mentioning. Everything I had brought forward as proof was a fake – to say nothing of what Freud may have done. Aschaffenburg was not present at the discussion so I didn't wind up the debate. Before this, Frank of Zürich spoke up for you energetically, as did Gross of Graz, who in the psychology section went very thoroughly into the significance of your theory so far as it touches upon the secondary function. It is a pity that G. is such a psychopath; he has a very intelligent head on him and with his *Secondary Function* has influenced the psychologists. I had a long talk with him and saw that he is a keen supporter of your ideas. After the discussion Geheimrat Binswanger, Jena, told me that Aschaffenburg, before his lecture, had said to him that he (B). *ought to help him in the discussion!*[24] In my last letter, you remember, I told you about A.'s slips of the tongue. The other one, as I discovered afterwards, was 'Breuer and *I*'[25] instead of 'Breuer and *Freud*'. All this fits in very nicely with my diagnosis. His absence

[24] Of the neurologists mentioned in this paragraph, only two merit comment: Ludwig Frank, follower of A. H. Forel, and Otto Binswanger, director of the psychiatric clinic at Jena, uncle of Ludwig Binswanger.
[25] Jose Breuer, Austrian physician, co-author with Freud of *Studies on Hysteria* (1895).

the following day was due to a court case that couldn't be postponed. Had he been present I would definitely have given him some more of the truth. The others I found too dumb.

Now for a great surprise: among the English contingent there was a young man from London, Dr Jones[26] (a Celt from Wales!), who knows your writings very well and does psychanalytical work himself. He will probably visit you later. He is very intelligent and could do a lot of good.

Oppenheim and Binswanger maintain a position of benevolent neutrality although both show signs of sexual opposition. In spite of the – at present – overwhelming opposition I still have the comforting certainty that your ideas are infiltrating from all sides, slowly but surely, because they won't let anyone go once he has assimilated them.

Janet is a vain old buffer, though a good observer. But everything he says and does now is sterile. The rest of the proceedings at the congress were, as usual, futile. Once again I discovered to my satisfaction that without your ideas psychiatry will inevitaby go to the dogs, as has already happened with Kraepelin.[27] Anatomy and attempts at classification are still the rule – sidelines that lead nowhere.

I hope your health will soon be fully restored. In the circumstances I naturally dare not insist on my wishes but would be very glad if I might hope to see you again in the Christmas holidays.

Perhaps I may take this opportunity to express a long cherished and contantly repressed wish: I would dearly like to have a photograph of you, not as you used to look but as you did when I first got to know you. I expressed this wish to your wife when we were in

---

[26] Ernest Jones (1879–1958), later one of Freud's staunchest disciples; a co-founder of the American Psychoanalytic Association in 1911 (he had taken a post at the University of Toronto in 1908) and the London Psycho-Analytical Society in 1913; after 1913, he organized the 'Committee' (see below, comment following 321 J). Author of *Sigmund Freud: Life and Work* (1953–1957), in the preparation of which he had access to the present correspondence, with Professor Jung's permission.

[27] Emil Kraepelin, Munich psychiatrist, whose classification of psychotic states was authoritative.

Vienna, but it seems to have been forgotten. Would you have the great kindness to grant this wish of mine sometime? I would be ever so grateful because again and again I feel the want of your picture.

With best regards and wishes,

Yours very sincerely, JUNG

45F

Dear colleague,   Rome, 19 September 1907

On my arrival here I found your letter about the further developments at the congress. It has not depressed me and I am glad to see that you are not depressed either. On you, I believe, this experience will have an excellent effect, at least of the kind that I like best. As for me, my respect for our cause has increased. I was beginning to think: 'What, already gaining recognition after scarcely ten years? There must be something wrong with it.' Now I can believe in it again. But you see that your tactics have been unrealistic. Those people don't want to be enlightened. That is why they are incapable right now of understanding the simplest things. If some day they want to understand, you'll see, nothing will be too complicated for them. Until then, there is nothing for it but to go on working and to argue as little as possible. What can we say after all? To this one: you're an idiot! To that one: you're a scoundrel! And fortunately these are convictions one does not express. Besides, we know that they are poor devils, who on the one hand are afraid of giving offence, because that might jeopardize their careers, and on the other hand are paralysed by fear of their own repressed material. We must wait until they die out or gradually shrink to a minority. All the young fresh blood, after all, is on our side . . .

But Aschaffenburg, whom you have seen through so brilliantly (see above my slip: 'am' instead of 'are'), is obviously the chief scoundrel, because he is intelligent and ought to know better. We must remember that. You are quite right in stressing the absolute sterility of our opponents, who can do no better than exhaust themselves with one outburst of abuse or identical repetitions, whereas we are able to forge ahead, and so can all those who join us. The Celt who surprised you is certainly not the only one; before the year is out we shall hear of unexpected supporters, and you will acquire others at your flourishing school.

Now for my *Ceterum censeo*.[28] Let's go ahead with our journal. People will abuse us, buy it and read it. Some day you will remember the years of struggle as the best. But please, don't make too much of me. I am too human to deserve it. Your desire to have a picture of me encourages me to make a similar request that will undoubtedly be easier to meet. In the last fifteen years I have never willingly sat for a photographer, because I am too vain to countenance my physical deterioration. Two years ago I was obliged (by the regulations) to have my picture taken for the hygiene exhibition, but I so detest the picture that I won't lift a finger to let you have it. At about the same time my boys took a picture of me; it is much better, not at all artificial. If you like, I shall find a print for you when I get back to Vienna. The best and most flattering of all is probably the medallion that C. F. Schwerdtner made for my fiftieth birthday. Just say the word and I shall have it sent to you.

Here in Rome I am leading a solitary existence, deep in day-dreams. I don't intend to return home until the last of the month. My address is *Hotel Milano*. At the beginning of the holidays I put science far away from me, and now I should like to get back to normal and produce something. This incomparable city is the right place for it. Though my main work probably lies behind me, I should like to keep up with you and the younger men as long as I can.

Eitingon,[29] whom I met in Florence, is now here and will probably visit me soon to give me detailed impressions of Amsterdam. He seems to have taken up with some woman again. Such practice is a deterrent from theory. When I have totally overcome my libido (in

---

[28] Cato the Elder (234–149 BC) ended all his speeches in the Roman Senate with the phrase *Ceterum censeo Carthaginem esse delendam* ('Also, I think Carthage must be destroyed').

[29] Max Eitingon (1881–1943), then on the Burghölzli staff; later prominent in the psychoanalytic movement and founder of the Palestine Psychoanalytic Society.

the common sense), I shall undertake to write a 'Love-life of Man-kind'.

In anticipation of your reply, with kind regards,

Yours very sincerely, DR FREUD

46J

Dear Professor Freud,   Burghölzli-Zürich, 25 September 1907
I'm afraid my answer is again a little late; most of the time I have been in bed with acute gastroenteritis. I'm still pretty run down.

I should be most grateful if you could let me have the picture your sons took of you. May I also ask you to let me know where I can get the medallion? I should like to buy one.

Here we have now founded a Freudian Society of Physicians which will hold its first meeting next Friday. We are counting on about twelve people. The subject for discussion is naturally case material ...

Dr Gross tells me that he puts a quick stop to the transference by turning people into sexual immoralists. He says the transference to the analyst and its persistent fixation are mere monogamy symbols and as such symptomatic of repression. The truly healthy state for the neurotic is sexual immorality. Hence he associates you with Nietzsche. It seems to me, however, that sexual repression is a very important and indispensable civilizing factor, even if pathogenic for many inferior people. Still, there must always be a few flies in the world's ointment. What else is civilization but the fruit of adversity? I feel Gross is going along too far with the vogue for the sexual short circuit, which is neither intelligent, nor in good taste, but merely convenient, and therefore anything but a civilizing factor.

With best regards,

Most sincerely yours, JUNG

48J

Dear Professor Freud,   Burghölzli-Zürich, 10 October 1907

Heartiest thanks for the excellent photograph and the splendid medallion. I am delighted with them. I'll send you my picture at once, although such an exchange seems almost absurd.

Yesterday and again today I felt furious with Weygandt,[30] who has published an exceedingly stupid article in Ziehen's *Monatsschrift*. It is one of the worst bits of drivel I have ever read. And mean, too! I know Weygandt personally, he is a super-hysteric, stuffed with complexes from top to bottom, so that he can't get a sensible word out of his gullet; he is even dumber than Aschaffenburg. I would never have believed the German academics could produce so much beastliness . . .

I would like to ask your sage advice about something else. A lady, cured of obsessional neurosis, is making me the object of her sexual fantasies, which she admits are excessive and a torment to her. She realizes that the role I play in her fantasies is morbid, and therefore wants to cut loose from me and repress them. What's to be done? Should I continue the treatment, which on her own admission gives her voluptuous pleasure, or should I discharge her? All this must be sickeningly familiar to you; what do you do in such cases?

A fortnight ago we had the first meeting of our 'Freudian' society, with twelve participants; lecture by Riklin on 'The Confessions of a Beautiful Soul' and by Dr Maier on a case of catatonia. Second meeting tomorrow. Director Dr Bertschinger of Schaffhausen will report on his negative experiences with Bezzola's tricks, Dr Abraham on purposivity in sexual dreams. The whole thing is going very well, great interest all round, lively discussion. I have the joyful feeling of participating in endlessly fruitful work. I have also converted the first theologian to your cause (our chaplain at the clinic!). That is something of an event . . .

With best regards and very many thanks,

Most sincerely yours, JUNG

[30] Wilhelm Weygandt, professor of psychiatry at Würzburg.

49J

Dear Professor Freud, Burghölzli-Zürich, 28 October 1907
... Your last two letters contain references to my laziness in writing.
I certainly owe you an explanation. One reason is my work load,
which hardly gives me a breather even in the evenings; the other is to
be found in the realm of affect, in what you have termed my 'self-
preservation complex' – marvellous expression! And indeed you
know that this complex has played many a trick on me, not least in
my Dem. praec. book. I honestly do try, but the evil spirit that (as
you see) bedevils my pen often prevents me from writing. Actually –
and I confess this to you with a struggle – I have a boundless admiration for you both as a man and a researcher, and I bear you no
conscious grudge. So the self-preservation complex does not come
from there; it is rather that my veneration for you has something of
the character of a 'religious' crush. Though it does not really bother
me, I still feel it is disgusting and ridiculous because of its undeniable
erotic undertone. This abominable feeling comes from the fact that
as a boy I was the victim of a sexual assault by a man I once
worshipped. Even in Vienna the remarks of the ladies ('enfin seuls',
etc) sickened me, although the reason for it was not clear to me at the
time.

This feeling, which I still have not quite got rid of, hampers me
considerably. Another manifestation of it is that I find psychological
insight makes relations with colleagues who have a strong transference to me downright disgusting. *I therefore fear your confidence.*
I also fear the same reaction from you when I speak of my intimate
affairs. Consequently, I skirt round such things as much as possible,
for, to my feeling at any rate, every intimate relationship turns out
after a while to be sentimental and banal or exhibitionistic, as with
my chief, whose confidences are offensive.

I think I owe you this explanation. I would rather not have said it.
With kindest regards,

Most sincerely yours, JUNG

50J

Dear Professor Freud,   Burghölzli-Zürich, 2 November 1907
I am suffering all the agonies of a patient in analysis, riddling myself
with every conceivable fear about the possible consequences of my
confession. There is one consequence I must tell you right now, as it
might interest you. You will remember my telling you a short dream
I had while I was in Vienna. At the time I was unable to solve it. You
sought the solution in a rivalry complex. (I dreamt that I saw you
walking beside me as a *very, very frail old man.*) Ever since then the
dream has been preying on my mind, but to no purpose. The solution
came (as usual) only after I had confessed my worries to you. *The
dream sets my mind at rest about your + + + dangerousness!* This
idea couldn't have occurred to me at the time, obviously not! I hope
to goodness the subterranean gods will now desist from their chicaneries and leave me in peace.

I don't know whether I am telling you anything new when I say
that the history of Jensen's childhood is now clear to me. A very
beautiful solution is to be found in the stories 'The Red Umbrella'
and 'In the Gothic House'. Both, particularly the first, are wonderful
parallels of *Gradiva*, sometimes down to the finest details. *The problem is one of brother-sister love.* Has Jensen a sister? I refrain from
expatiating on the details, it would only spoil the charm of discovery.

Because of my services as an occultist I have been elected an
'Honorary Fellow of the American Society for Psychical Research'.
In this capacity I have been dabbling in spookery again. Here too
your discoveries are brilliantly confirmed. What do you think about
this whole field of research?

I have the liveliest hopes that you will come to Zürich during the
Christmas holidays. May I count on receiving you as a guest in my
house?

With best regards,

Yours very sincerely, JUNG

51J

Dear Professor Freud,   Burghölzli-Zürich, 8 November 1907

Heartiest thanks for your letter,[31] which worked wonders for me. You are absolutely right to extol humour as the only decent reaction to the inevitable. This was also my principle until the repressed material got the better of me, luckily only at odd moments. My old religiosity had secretly found in you a compensating factor which I had to come to terms with eventually, and I was able to do so only by telling you about it. In this way I hoped to prevent it from interfering with my behaviour in general. In any case I am confident that my humour will not desert me in difficult situations. The goal of our common endeavours provides a salutary and considerably heavier counterweight.

It would be nice if you could pick on Christmas – that is, from the 26th on – for your visit to Zürich. No need at all to think you might inconvenience my chief in any way; he will be 'affairé' as always, and will treat you to a grand display of dedicated, unassuming scientific interest which always bowls the uninitiated over. My chief is the most notable example of a brilliantly successful pseudo-personality, a problem worthy of the sweat of the noble.

Unfortunately Easter is rather far off – my one cogent reason for preferring Christmas.

As to the *Zeitschrift fur Sexualwissenschaft*, a lot depends on the editorship. If the '175-ers'[32] are in charge, that will hardly be a guarantee of its scientific attitude. It is fishy to begin with that you haven't been invited to be a regular contributor. I don't think there is any opening for your ideas there. I believe they will have a smoother passage via psychiatry. The progress of your cause in Switzerland has followed this path, and given the shortness of the time the results have been good. I have now been asked to speak on the significance of your teachings at the cantonal medical society. Right now the

31 (Missing.)
32 Colloquial expression for homosexuals, because section 175 of the German penal code dealt (and still deals) with homosexuality.

second physician of the Préfargier asylum is here to get himself initiated. Dr Jones of London has announced his arrival here on November 25 for the same purpose. So everything is going as well as could be wished. If Germany wants to hang back, others will take the lead. Binswanger jr writes that he will publish from the Jena clinic an analysis with a preface by his uncle – a point that raises several question marks. But in itself it would be all to the good. One thing is certain: the cause will never fall asleep again. The worst thing is being killed by silence, but that stage is over and done with.

With best regards and many thanks,

Most sincerely yours, JUNG

52F

15 November 1907,
Dear friend and colleague,   Vienna, IX, Berggasse 19
I always find that my day has begun well when the post brings me an invitation to a meeting of the society you have named after me; unfortunately it is usually too late for me to take the express and arrive on time. What you say of your inner developments sounds reassuring; a transference on a religious basis would strike me as most disastrous; it could end only in apostasy, thanks to the universal human tendency to keep making new prints of the clichés we bear within us. I shall do my best to show you that I am unfit to be an object of worship. You probably think that I have already begun . . .

I must own to you that I am not working on anything at the moment; but it goes on working inside me without interruption . . .

I hope to hear from you soon.

Yours cordially, DR FREUD

54J

Dear Professor Freud,   Burghölzli-Zürich, 30 November 1907
Last Tuesday I lectured at the medical society for nearly an hour and a half on your researches, to great applause. More than 100 doctors were present. No opposition except from two well known neurologists, who rode the moral hobbyhorse.

Yesterday's meeting of our Freudian society went off very nicely, with much animation. Prof Bleuler opened the proceedings with some priceless doggerel aimed at your critics. Von Monakow[33] was also present and naturally took the verses as referring to himself, which amused all the old hands enormously. One sees what a difference mass suggestion makes – there were twenty-five people present – Monakow shrivelled in his seat. This time the opposition got into hot water. May it be a good omen! ...

Dr Jones of London, an extremely gifted and active young man, was with me for the last five days, chiefly to talk with me about your researches. Because of his 'splendid isolation' in London he has not yet penetrated very deeply into your problems but is convinced of the theoretical necessity of your views. He will be a staunch supporter of our cause, for besides his intellectual gifts he is full of enthusiasm.

Dr Jones, along with my friends in Budapest, has mooted the idea of a congress of Freudian followers. It would be held in Innsbruck or Salzburg next spring, and would be so arranged that the participants would not have to be away from home for more than three days, which should be possible in Salzburg. Dr Jones thinks that at least two people would come from England, and there will certainly be several from Switzerland ...

This week I'm off to Geneva, the second university town where your ideas will never go to sleep again.

With kindest regards,

Most sincerely yours, JUNG

[33] Constantin von Monakow, Swiss neurologist of international repute.

55F

8 December 1907,
Vienna, IX. Berggasse 19
Dear friend and colleague,
In spite of the trouble you seem to be having with your 'complex',
you have delighted me with really interesting news. I can offer you
nothing comparable in return. The congress in Salzburg in spring
1908 would make me very proud; but I suppose I should be in the
way and that you will not invite me. Dr A— has sent (though not to
me) an enthusiastic and, I believe, astute account of your performance at the Zürich society. Your Englishman appeals to me
because of his nationality; I believe that once the English have
become acquainted with our ideas they will never let them go. I have
less confidence in the French, but the Geneva people must be
thought of as Swiss. Claparède's[34] article on the definition of hysteria amounts to a very intelligent judgement on our efforts; the idea
of the building of several storeys comes from Breuer (in the general
section of the *Studies*), the building itself, I believe, ought to be
described rather differently. Claparède would know more about its
plan if he had questioned the patients rather than the good-for-
nothing authors. Still his paper is a step forward; the rejection of
'suggestion' was necessary. I hope he will learn, as a result of your
visit, to take account of a good many things that he still very noticeably neglects.

I was very much pleased to find a reference to a review of Jung,
'The Freudian Theory of Hysteria' in the table of contents of *Folia
Neuro-biologica*, a new journal. I opened to the page given and
indeed found – one line. After this traumatic experience I decided
not to subscribe to this new 'central organ'.

Abraham is coming from Berlin to see me next Sunday.

I spent last week planning and writing a lecture that I delivered on
the sixth in a small hall at Heller's publishing house; about ninety
people were present. It passed off without mishap, which is good
enough for me; it must have been heavy fare for all the writers and

[34] Edouard Claparède, Swiss psychologist and educator.

their wives. *Die Neue Rundschau* acquired the lecture on the foetal stage and will probably publish it. If nothing else, it was an incursion into territory that we have barely touched upon so far, but where I might easily settle down. I see I have forgotten to tell you the title of my lecture! It is: 'Creative Writers and Daydreaming'. In it I speak more of fantasies than of poets, but I hope to make up for it another time.

Let me hear from you soon.

Yours cordially, DR FREUD

56J

Dear Professor Freud,   Burghölzli-Zürich, 16 December 1907

You deceive yourself mightily if you think we are going to let you off coming to Innsbruck or Salzburg! On the contrary, we hope and expect to meet under your chairmanship. It is proposed that the congress be held after the Congress of Psychologists in Frankfurt, ie after April 20. (Unfortunately I cannot remember the exact date at the moment.) I hope this time won't be too inconvenient for you. To make attendance easier, it would be best if the meeting were limited to one evening and one day, so that all participants, even those from the most distant places, would not have to be away from their work for more than three days. As soon as you let me know whether this arrangement suits you, I shall submit definite proposals to the prospective participants.

I am presently negotiating the founding of a journal for which I want to ensure a wide distribution. It is to be international, since we must emancipate ourselves as much as possible from the German market. I'll tell you about it as soon as I have definite results in hand.

Claparède will hold himself in reserve for some time yet as he has no material; he is actually a psychologist. His benevolent neutrality is assured.

Please excuse the brevity of this letter. I am very busy.

Most sincerely yours, JUNG

57F

21 December 1907,
Dear friend and colleague,   Vienna, IX. Berggasse 19

What magnificent plans! You are certainly not lacking in energy. It will be fine for me if the meeting is held after Easter, the sooner the better. If you choose Salzburg rather than Innsbruck – the former is by far the more beautiful and congenial of the two – I can foresee no difficulty on my part, the express from here to Salzburg takes only six hours. But I am still prepared to withdraw if you should decide on second thought that things would go better in my absence – and there is something to be said for that point of view. There is certainly no sense in having me as chairman. That won't do. You or Bleuler must take the lead; nuances, the sharing of roles!

To tell the truth, your plans for the journal please me even more, that is a matter of life or death for our ideas . . .

Abraham was with us from Sunday to Wednesday. More congenial than your account of him, but there is something inhibited about him, no dash. At the crucial moment he can't find the right word. He told me a good deal about Bleuler, in whom he is evidently much interested as a Ψ problem.

I wish you a Merry Christmas,

With kind regards, DR FREUD

59J

Dear Professor Freud,   Burghölzli-Zürich, 2 January 1908

Cordial greetings for the New Year! The past year has brought not a few signs of the rosy dawn, and it is now my heartfelt New Year's wish that the coming year will bring still better things. I needn't repeat how well your crops are coming up; you'll see more of them in Salzburg, I hope . . .

At the moment I am treating another case of severe hysteria with twilight states. It's going well. She is a twenty-six-year-old student. The case is an uncommonly interesting one. I work almost exclusively with dream analyses, the other sources being too scanty. The transference dreams started very early in the most miraculous way, many of them are of somnambulistic clarity. Naturally everything fits in with your theory. The early sexual history is not yet clear, since from the thirteenth year everything is shrouded in retrograde amnesic darkness phosphorescently lit up only by the dreams. The twilight states are similar to those in the case I first published ('Occult Phenomena'). The patient plays to perfection and with positively thrilling dramatic beauty the personality that is her dream ideal. At first I tried to hand over the analysis to our first assistant Dr Maier, but this didn't work out because the patient had already set her cap at me although I purposely never visited her. During her twilight states the doctors and nurses cluster round full of wonderment. On the second day of the analytical treatment, immediately before the emergence of the main complex, there occurred a twilight state that lasted for two days. Then no more, except that once, on the day the transference became clear to her, she went to a woman friend and staged a defensive twilight state lasting two and a half hours, for which she blamed herself the next day and showed every sign of remorse. She possesses in rare degree the capacity for arguing about the existence or non-existence of the symptoms. At present she is expecting a visit from her lover, but is afflicted with a ructus.[35] She is always standing at the window, looking out to see if he is coming. At night she dreams that she is collecting 'protozoa' from the window and giving them to some shadowy figure. The ructus appeared for the first time after her sixteenth year, when she noticed that her mother wanted to marry her off. She refused – disgust – fear of pregnancy – ructus. She now *expects* her beloved *at the window*; she is 'expecting' a child from her lover (ructus), and *from the window* she fetches the protozoa, which she at once recognizes as embryological. There are swarms of such things. Cases like this always console me for the widespread neglect of your teachings. We are on to a really good thing and can be glad of it.

35 Belching, sometimes an accompaniment of pregnancy.

On January 16th I shall be giving a public lecture and hope to interest a wide audience in the new research. This just about exhausts my New Year's news. May I ask you to give my best wishes for the New Year to your wife and your whole family?

Ever sincerely yours, JUNG

62J

1st Congress for Freudian Psychology[36]
Dear Sir,

From many quarters the followers of Freud's teachings have expressed a desire for an annual meeting which would afford them an opportunity to discuss their practical experiences and to exchange ideas. Since Freud's followers, though few in numbers at present, are scattered all over Europe, it has been suggested that our first meeting should take place immediately after this year's 3rd Congress for Experimental Psychology in Frankfurt (22–25 April), so as to facilitate the attendance of colleagues from Western Europe. The proposed place of meeting is *Salzburg*.

The provisional programme is as follows:

26 April, evening Arrival and assembly in Salzburg.
27 April Meeting. Chairman: Prof Dr S. Freud.
28 April Departure.

Lectures, presentation of case material, written questions are *very welcome*. Applications should be sent to the undersigned *before 15 February*.

Should you wish to attend the meeting, you are politely requested to communicate your decision to the undersigned *by 5 February*. The definitive programme will be sent to you later.

Burghölzli–Zürich   Very truly yours, *Dr C. G. Jung*
January 1908   Privatdocent in Psychiatry

[36] Printed circular.

64F

Dear friend and colleague,

25 January 1908,
Vienna, IX. Berggasse 19

I admire your energy and will try to help you with your work. We shall be glad to arrange for accommodation in Salzburg; I am pretty well acquainted with the city and its hotels; we should merely have to know first roughly how many persons are to be provided for, and whether you favour something fashionable or something simple. On Wednesday I shall submit your invitation to my society; then I shall be able to tell you how many of our members wish to attend.

I also accept the chairmanship (!) since you insist, and will say something or other, what I don't know yet; your saying 'nothing special', was a great relief to me . . .

This week influenza has been raging in my house and unless I am very much mistaken I am coming down with it myself. My daughter[37] had at the same time an abdominal irritation connected with a stitch abscess, an after-effect of her appendectomy. She is now recovering nicely.

I shall be able to use a few more invitations.

Heartfelt thanks for your efforts. Do please consider the state of my health in judging the present letter,

Yours cordially, FREUD

I am far from begrudging you your trip to southern France before our congress.

65J

Dear Professor Freud,   Burghölzli–Zürich, 25 January 1908

Yesterday evening (at our little Freud gathering) Dr A— conveyed to me your greetings and your injunction that I should write to you more often. As you see, I'm doing it! Best thanks for the greetings –

[37] Mathilde, born 1887.

but I'm always afraid of boring you with my all too frequent letters. In the end you would be forced to complain of my manic busyness. Perhaps you have already done so in another connection, to wit, the pretentious title of the circular. Dr Jones in London was quite shocked by it. I have therefore sent out a special circular to the few people invited, explicitly stressing the *completely private nature* of the project. Actually this may be superfluous, but I think one can never be careful enough. Dr Abraham has already announced a lecture on the psychosexual differences between Dem. praecox and hysteria.

I hope you will be pleased with the proposed arrangements. I am on tenterhooks for your opinion. You will now have received my primitive lecture and wondered at the *sentiments* that peek through it – *sentiments d'incomplétude* compensated by sentimental posing. If you can't appeal to people's heads then maybe you can get at their hearts. I am an odd mixture of fear and courage, both of them extreme and off balance.

I have just received the galleys of my Amsterdam lecture. Publication won't be long now.

Have you read the Berlin discussion in the *Neurologisches Zentralblatt*? You will see that friend Bezzola has discovered the once falsely so-called 'Breuer–Freud' method. Isn't that something? Liepmann is slyly making himself a little door through which he will suddenly burst upon the scene as the one who knew all about these vulgar things ages ago. He has struck the right note: 'Stale news!' Such will be the inscription over the portal leading to the first circle of the purgatorio of your theory. A pity there are never enough good men around to applaud loudly whenever these weaklings, mixtures of muck and lukewarm water, have to eat humble pie.

I have a sin to confess: I have had your photograph enlarged. It looks marvellous. A few of our circle have acquired copies. So, like it or not, you have stepped into many a quiet study!

With best regards,

Most sincerely yours, JUNG

66F

27 January 1908,
Vienna, IX. Berggasse 19

Dear friend and colleague,

You are joking about your *sentiments*! Your lecture is charming; too bad I haven't got you here to shake your hand; I'd shake it more than once. Spirit of my spirit, I can say with pride, but at the same time something artistic and soft, lofty and serene, something ingratiating that I could never have produced, for I still have the difficulties of the work in my bones. I shall do my best to have it printed soon; the negotiations about the publisher are drawing to an end.

How can you imagine that I would ever complain of your too frequent letters or of your 'manic' busyness. I have really missed your letters during the last few weeks, and as for your busyness, I must have a similar bent even though it has never been fully developed, because I approve exceedingly of what you are doing. Splendid of you to be impudent for my sake; I am not lacking in impudence but only in the kind of relations with people that would enable me to show it.

As a companion piece to Bezzola and Liepmann I offer you Meyer in the issue of *Archiv für Psychiatrie* that appeared today. Remarks on your *Dementia Praecox*. His main objection: everyone has delusions of being injured. Feebleminded arguments of this sort are possible because these gentlemen have learned nothing, they have never developed a psychological insight on the basis of dreams or of everyday life. I believe that if they were analysed it would turn out that they are still waiting for the discovery of the bacillus or protozoon of hysteria as for the messiah who must after all come some day to all true believers. When that happens a differential diagnosis from Dem. pr. ought to be a simple matter, since the hysteria parasite will no doubt have only one stiff whiplike appendage, while that of Dem. pr. will regularly show two and also take a different stain. Then we shall be able to leave psychology to the poets! . . .

I hope your whole family is well. I shall write to you briefly after our Wednesday session. With kind regards,

As ever, FREUD

70F

Dear friend,   17 February 1908, Vienna, IX. Berggasse 19
May I, after adequate preparation, cast off the 'colleague' in expressing my satisfaction that your influenza has been vanquished and that
your silence did not result from any complex. I can sympathize with
your complaints, for I myself have not been feeling very *bright* since
my illness, and have been beset by all kinds of little difficulties that I
would naturally prefer to do without. Especially here in Vienna it is
so easy to get the impression that nothing can be done, that nothing
can be changed, that one is attempting the impossible, helping Sisy-
phus to roll his stone, etc. But these moods pass and I still have a
long wait until the holidays.

You have no doubt received my little paper with the hysteria
formulas. Other trifles are forthcoming; I am determined not to let
any more work be wrung from me, such work always turns out far
inferior to what one does spontaneously. Take my urgent advice,
arm yourself with ill temper against all unreasonable demands. We
definitely need a journal of our own. I am sure you will resume your
efforts as soon as your temperature is down to normal. To start a
German publication would not be at all bad; with your name you
should have no difficulty in finding a decent German publisher. Deuticke would certainly be willing, but to be born in Vienna is no
advantage for a new undertaking. I can't see why your *Diagn. Asso.
Studies* should stand in the way. The papers for the second volume
could continue to be published in their old place, and when you
come to the third volume you could change over, if that is still your
plan.

I shall attend to our accommodations in Salzburg as soon as you
let me know how many people are expected. From here there will be
from twelve to fourteen; though I hope that not all those who have
applied will come, because they are not all fit to exhibit. Here I must
often content myself with very little. If there is still time to do anything about the programme, I must ask you to do what you can to
thwart my talkative Viennese; otherwise we shall all drown in the

torrent of words. You could impose a time limit and politely reject certain communications as inappropriate. I am thinking for instance, of a paper on 'Psychophysical Parallelism' that Dr Schwerdtner, one of my contingent, wants to read; it can only be a piece of dilettantism and is sure to take up an enormous amount of time. We needn't worry too much about the man himself who is new in the circle and rather retiring. I would not like us to make too poor a showing in your eyes, which is a distinct possibility. You may ask why I myself don't do what I can to stop them. I do, but these people are so dreadfully sensitive and naturally they have no *égards* for me; they are much more likely to show consideration for you, the 'distinguished foreigner'. You know what prestige foreigners enjoy in Vienna.

To pass on to something more pleasant, the prospect of Bleuler's presence rather confuses me. I have mixed feelings towards him and I should like to honour him in some way. Don't you think it would be a good idea to offer him the chairmanship? My Viennese will be much better behaved with him, and by providing the battlecry I play enough of a role. Do support me in suggesting this change in the programme ...

At last I come to science. I have been in contact with a few paranoia cases in my practice and can tell you a secret. (I write paranoia and not Dem. pr. because I regard the former as a good clinical type and the latter as a poor nosographical term) ... The paranoid form is probably conditioned by restriction to the homosexual component. My old analysis (1896) also showed that the pathological process began with the patient's estrangement from her husband's *sisters*. My one-time friend Fliess[38] developed a dreadful case of paranoia after throwing off his affection for me, which was undoubtedly considerable. I owe this idea to him, ie to his behaviour. One must try to learn something from every experience. The breaking down of sub-

---

[38] Wilhelm Fliess (1858–1928), Berlin otolaryngologist, Freud's closest friend until 1900; see Jones, I, ch 13, and Freud, *The Origins of Psychoanalysis: Letters to Wilhelm Fliess, Drafts and Notes, 1887–1902* (New York and London, 1954). After the friendship was ended, Freud became critical of Fliess's scientific work because of its highly speculative character.

limations in paranoia belongs to the same context. Altogether I have a good many budding and incomplete ideas to tell you about. Too bad that we shall not be exactly undisturbed in Salzburg!

Yours cordially, FREUD

71F

Dear friend,   18 February 1908, Vienna, IX. Berggasse 19
Don't take fright: after this I promise you a long pause. This is merely a postscript to reiterate my yesterday's suggestion that we offer Bleuler the chairmanship in Salzburg. You will be doing me a great favour if you pass on this wish of mine as a personal request. I consider it quite appropriate and in a way more dignified that he rather than I should take the chair. It would seem odd if I as an outlawed knight were to preside over the diet that has been called to defend my rights against the imperial authorities. On the other hand, it would be quite honourable for me and would also make a better impression abroad, if he, the oldest and most authoritative of my supporters, should take the lead in the movement in my favour.

Also, my Viennese will behave better under his chairmanship, in short everything will be fine if he accepts. I do hope that you will agree with me and use your influence with him.

I decided when I started this note not to write about anything else. So my kind regards and thank you for your efforts.

Yours, FREUD

72J

Dear Professor Freud,   Burghölzli–Zürich, 20 February 1908
I thank you with all my heart for this token of your confidence.[39]
The undeserved gift of your friendship is one of the high points in my life which I cannot celebrate with big words. The reference to
[39] Freud's salutation in 70 F.

Fliess – surely not accidental – and your relationship with him impels me to ask you to let me enjoy your friendship not as one between equals but as that of father and son. This distance appears to me fitting and natural. Moreover it alone, so it seems to me, strikes a note that would prevent misunderstandings and enable two hard-headed people to exist alongside one another in an easy and unstrained relationship.

I have read your hysteria formulas with the greatest pleasure. In my opinion they are very successful and will remove many misunderstandings and false views. I regret very much that these theses did not come into my hands earlier, that is, before the Amsterdam lecture. They would have made my work considerably easier; as you will soon see, it bears traces of laborious formulation and polishing, yet fails to do full justice to your ideas. I hope that while reading it you will bear in mind that it was my most fervent wish to present matters in such a way as to strike the line of least resistance among the opposition. If I may say so, you ought not to bury your theses in this second-rate journal with a dubious prognosis, but should furnish them with examples and publish them in a more conspicuous place. They would do a great deal of good and nip in the bud all the schematisms and syllogisms that will predictably attach themselves to my lecture. Your theses afford an extremely lively and realistic insight into your way of thinking and working; subtly coping with the knots and rough edges of the material, your work is true research in the deepest sense of the word. You have thereby shattered the fable that you lay down axioms and have shown that your science is eternally young and alive, which only a handful of people have believed until now; in my case, for instance, only after I had the good fortune to get to know you personally . . .

Your views on paranoia have not lain fallow. I have been able to confirm them many times over. Only the thing is not yet ripe. I have therefore kept silent about it so far. The detachment of libido, its regression to autoerotic forms, is probably well explained by the self-assertion, the psychological self-preservation of the individual. Hysteria keeps to the plane of 'preservation of the species', paranoia (Dem. pr.) to the plane of self-preservation, ie autoerotism . . . The paranoiac always seeks inner solutions, the hysteric outer ones, probably, and often quite obviously, because in paranoia the complex becomes an absolutely sovereign and incontrovertible fact, whereas in hysteria it is always a bit of a comedy, with one part of the personality playing the role of a mere spectator . . .

I have just received your short letter[40] with its affective perseveration in regard to Bleuler. I shall do as you wish, but must candidly confess that in this and similar matters he is not likely to listen to me. Nevertheless I shall work on him in the hope that he will at least take over the chair when you are lecturing. But as I said, when you get to know Bleuler you will find him a man who is far above all that. There is nothing, but absolutely nothing, of the Geheimrat about him. He has that magnificent Zürich open-mindedness which I count as one of the highest virtues.

I should be very glad to hear something about paranoia in your next letter, and especially what you think of the views I have expressed.

I hope you will soon have recovered, as thoroughly as I, from the influenza.

With best thanks for the offprint and kind regards.

Yours very sincerely, JUNG

74F

Dear friend,   25 February 1908, Vienna, IX. Berggasse 19
What you write about your chief sounds reassuring. I shall admire the phenomenon as it deserves; it is indeed a rare virtue, of which I myself do not feel capable.

Your judgement of the hysteria formulas and even more so your other observations about my work have given me a rarely experienced satisfaction. I know that what you say is true, that my manner of working is indeed honest, which is why my knowledge is so

[40] 71 F.

fragmentary and why I am usually incapable of handling a presentation of any length. I have suppressed my habit of conscious speculation as radically as possible and have absolutely forsworn the temptation to 'fill in the gaps in the universe'. But except for you, who believes me? ...

Your observations on paranoia have struck a chord in me. You really are the only one capable of making an original contribution; except perhaps for O. Gross, but unfortunately his health is poor. I shall write you my fantasies about paranoia soon, they coincide in part with your ideas. Today I am too tired from monotonous hard work and need a Sunday to catch my breath. You are right, the thing is not yet ripe and I can't work with the shadowy memories now at my disposal. Consequently I wish you would take the whole problem over.

Many thanks for your English offprint, I shall read it Sunday. Let me know when you need my inquiries about accommodation in Salzburg.

With kind regards,

Yours ever, FREUD

77F

Dear friend,   5th March 1908, Vienna, IX. Berggasse 19
... I have one more suggestion for you. I want to give the floor to a noble spirit who can be present only in the form of a quotation, to wit, Friedrich Schiller, in whose correspondence with Körner (letter of 1 December 1788) our secretary Otto Rank has found a delightful passage in justification of our psychoanalytic technique.[41] It would

---

[1] The passage which Rank read at the Wednesday meeting of 4 Mar '08 and at Salzburg is as follows: 'It would seem to be unfortunate and detrimental to the creative process for the intellect to examine the ideas that press in upon it too closely while they are still as it were in the gateway. Considered in itself, an idea may seem hazardous and unpromising but perhaps another idea that comes after it will lend it importance; in combination with others that may seem

take Rank only a few minutes to read it and it would close our morning on a suitable note. Rank, who is coming with us, is a pleasant, intelligent youngster. He has qualified in mechanical engineering and is now studying Latin and Greek for admission to university. He is twenty-three; he must have sent you his monograph on 'The Artist'; some of it is not quite clear, but it contains the best explanation of my complicated theories to have reached me thus far. I expect a good deal of him once he has got himself an education . . .

With kind regards and sincere thanks for all the trouble you are taking.

Yours, FREUD

79J

Dear Professor Freud,   Burghölzli–Zürich, 11 March 1908
I am sorry I can't get around to answering letters as promptly and fully as you do. I always have a mass of other things to attend to before I can put myself in the right mood to answer your letters. I can never be rushed; if I am, all thoughts instantly go out of my head.

First I must go into the paranoia question. I have the feeling I ought to talk to you personally about it, as I ought to know your material; then your theory would be more intelligible to me. For instance, the Fl. case helped me greatly in understanding your views, since I always knew what you had in mind. Your line of thought on

---

equally inept, it may prove to be a useful component. This the intellect is unable to judge unless it retains the idea long enough to consider it in combination with these others. In a creative mind, it seems to me, the intellect has withdrawn its guard from the gates; ideas rush in pellmell, and only when many are at hand does it survey and examine them. – You critics, or whatever you may call yourselves, are ashamed or afraid of the passing moments of madness which occur in all creative minds, and whose greater or lesser duration distinguishes the thinking artist from the dreamer.' *Schillers Briefwechsel mit Körner* (1847).

the paranoia question seems to be very different from mine, so I have great difficulty in following you. For you the choice-of-neurosis problem seems to play a crucial role. This is something I daren't touch. At present I am interested only in the way *alleviation of the complex may be obtained*. The following case may serve as an example: A thirty-four-year-old woman declared that the assistant doctor, together with the nurse and an old woman (a patient), had burnt a child (uncertain whether it was the nurse's or the patient's!). Erotic advances to the doctor. The nurse is young and pretty, and the patient likes her very much. Pat. is sexually dissatisfied with her marriage and has to support an old mother. So: transference to the doctor, identification with the nurse, assimilation of the old patient as mother. She represses her marriage, also her children, makes a new, unadmitted transference (to the doctor), simultaneously obtaining wish fulfilment in the role of the pretty nurse. All this in the form of an accusation that could easily pass over into persecution mania. Thus the complex is alleviated by the assertion that it is not in her but is being played out in objective reality by other people. By this means a *very firm dissociation* is achieved. The mechanism is an exaggeration of the normal mechanism of *depotentiating reality*, its purpose being to make the dissociation absolute; that is my view . . .

I marvel at your colossal capacity for work which enables you to produce scientific articles on top of your daily labours. That would be quite beyond me.

I don't rightly know yet what I shall say in Salzburg. In any case no significant novelties will be forthcoming. I feel rather shaky, because here we are still stuck in the rudiments.

No thanks are due to me for the arrangements – the pleasure is mine.

As soon as I have all your data I shall get the programme printed.
With best regards,

Most sincerely yours, JUNG

82F

Dear friend,   14 April 1908, Vienna, IX. Berggasse 19
This letter will be waiting for you when you get home. I am sorry to hear that you have been unwell and that you have been obliged to take a short holiday rather than a long one. With your youthful stamina you ought to make short shrift of any illness.

Three of your papers are lying on my desk. The first, the one you did in collaboration with Bleuler, displeases me with its hesitations and concern over the good opinion of E. Meyer;[42] you have forbidden me to speak of the second, your long-awaited Amsterdam report; the third, which is the third number of my *Papers on Applied Psychology*, is a pure delight with its resoluteness and clarity and, as befits such clear thinking, the language is enchantingly warm and beautiful. How boldly you here proclaim the psychic aetiology of psychic disorders, from which you shrank back in the other papers. In this one, to be sure, you were free to express your own opinion, you were speaking only to laymen and ladies; in the others you were hampered by a spirit of compromise and by concern over the prejudices of physicians and the incomprehension of our colleagues!

Oddly enough, I have been reading in your Amsterdam paper that child hysteria does not enter this context, whereas I myself have been toying with the idea of working up my analysis of a hysterical phobia in a five-year-old boy for the congress. But I doubt if this plan will be carried out.

I am well, but I have worked so hard these last few weeks that I am quite at my wits' end. I shall need half a day of solitude before plunging into the social whirl of our Salzburg gathering. During this period of hard work my insights have become more and more secure, the unanimous opposition of all the psychiatric bureaucrats in this Western world can no longer make the slightest impression on me . . .

I am hoping to find a moment in Salzburg for a private talk with you about paranoia. Be sure to turn up in full vigour.

Yours cordially, FREUD

[42] Ernst Meyer, professor of psychiatry at Königsberg.

83J

Dear Professor Freud,   Burghölzli–Zürich, 18 April 1908
Your last letter upset me. I have read a lot between the lines. I don't
doubt that if only I could *talk* with you we could come to a basic
understanding. Writing is a poor substitute for speech. Nevertheless I
will try to offer some rather incoherent explanations.

1 *Lecture to laymen.* The point was to make the public aware of
the psychological connections that are found in psychosis. Hence the
strong emphasis on the psychogenic factor. There was no reason to
talk about the actual aetiology.

2 *Aetiology of Dem. praec.* The aim here was to set out our conception of the aetiology. From lack of analytical experience Bleuler
stresses the organic side, I the other. I think *very many* cases of Dem.
praec. are due exclusively to purely psychological conflicts. But
besides these there are undoubtedly not a few cases where a physical
weakness of some kind precipitates the psychosis. One would have to
be a spiritualist to believe in an exclusively psychogenic aetiology
here. I never have; for me the 'constitution' has always played a
fairly significant role. That is why I was actually rather relieved when
I saw that you had modified your earlier view of the genesis of hysteria. As you have observed, in discussing the aetiology one gets
entangled in the most hopeless difficulties, all of which seem to me to
have one point of origin: our totally mistaken conception of the
brain's function. Everywhere we are haunted by psyche = *substantia*,
playing on the brain *à la piano*. The monistic standpoint – psyche =
inwardly perceived function – might help to lay this ghost. But I
won't go on philosophizing. You yourself will have thought out the
logical consequences long ago. The whole question of aetiology is
extremely obscure to me. The secret of the constitution will hardly
be unveiled from the psychological side alone.

3 *Amsterdam report.* Here I have done bad work, as I am the first
to admit. In spite of this I shall be grateful for any criticism. It's
nonsense about my forbidding you to speak of it! I can only learn
from your criticism. The chief drawback is its brevity. I had to do a

lot of cutting. A second and more important drawback is the elementary approach that was forced on me by the ignorance of the public.

Child hysteria must fall outside the formula applicable to adults, for whom puberty plays a large role. A specifically modified formula must be established for child hysteria. All the rest I have written as my conscience dictated. I am really no propagandist; I merely detest all forms of suppression and injustice. I am eager to hear of my errors, and hope to learn from them.

Binswanger has now got married so is no longer in Jena. His address is: Kreuzlingen, Canton Thurgau . . .

I too hope very much that we can snatch an hour in Salzburg for a talk on some of the things that are still hanging in mid air.

With best regards,

Most sincerely yours, JUNG

I may be wrong but it seems to me that this letter has an oddly dry tone. It is not meant that way, for a man can also admit his bad mood with a smile. Unfortunately the smile doesn't come through the style – an aesthetic fault that has already driven me to pen a PS.

84F

Dear friend,   19 April 1908, Vienna, IX. Berggasse 19
Happy Easter! Hard feelings must not be nursed. If I was cranky and seemed so, there is much more room – in this case – for a somatic than for a psychogenic aetiology. I am so exhausted by work and lack of recreation that I shall surely make the *same* impression on you in Salzburg. What I mean is I am not at all angry with you. My letter is being written under the impression of my second reading of your *Content of the Psychoses*, for which work I feel great affection. It gives me a picture of you from several different angles. It has in it a great deal of what I esteem in you, not only your insight but also your fine artistic feeling and the seeds of greatness. It stands in marked contrast to a manuscript by your Berlin rival (A.), which is

to occupy my fourth number, staunch in its support but lacking just that spark (here the ucs. of both writer and receiver smile), and also to your collaboration with Bleuler. In my fatigue I failed to bring out the true constellation; my displeasure was so much more evident than my pleasure, which struck no chord in me, feeling as I did. This, I believe, was the situation, from which I did indeed exclude your Amsterdam report; of course I could equally well have expressed my gratitude to you for putting such zeal into so difficult and dangerous a task. Only the sentence about child hysteria struck me as incorrect. The conditions here are the same, probably because every thrust of growth creates the same conditions as the great thrust of puberty (every increase in libido, I mean). After all, it has never been my habit to reproach you with your partial disagreements, but rather to be pleased with your share of agreement. I know it will take you time to catch up with my experience of the past fifteen years. I am rather annoyed with Bleuler for his willingness to accept a psychology without sexuality, which leaves everything hanging in mid air. In the sexual processes we have the indispensable 'organic foundation' without which a medical man can only feel ill at ease in the life of the psyche.

I thoroughly dislike the notion that my opinions are correct, but only in regard to a part of the cases. (Substitute point of view for opinions.) That is not possible. It must be one thing or the other. These characteristics are fundamental, they can't vary from one set of cases to another. Or rather: they are so vital that an entirely different name should be given to the cases to which they do not apply. Thus far, you know, no one has seen this other hysteria, Dem. pr., etc. Either a case is our kind or nothing is known about it. I am sure that basically you agree with me.

There. Now I have avowed the full extent of my fanaticism and venture to hope that the injury to your feelings will not survive the interval that separates us from our meeting in Salzburg.

A chat with you there will do me at least a world of good. However, we shall also have to talk about Otto Gross; he urgently needs your medical help; what a pity, such a gifted, resolute man. He is addicted to cocaine and probably in the early phase of toxic cocaine paranoia. I feel great sympathy for his wife: one of the few Teutonic women I have ever liked . . .

Keep well, I hope to find you unruffled when we meet in Salzburg.

Yours cordially, FREUD

The Salzburg Congress

What was in effect the First International Psychoanalytic Congress took place at Salzburg on Monday 27 April.

86J

Dear Professor Freud,   Burghölzli–Zürich, 30 April 1908
I am in two minds as to whether I should apply a business or an emotional yardstick to the Salzburg congress. On balance the results were very good, and this bodes well for the success of our *Jahrbücher*. . .

As to sentiments, I am still under the reverberating impact of your lecture, which seemed to me perfection itself. All the rest was simply padding, sterile twaddle in the darkness of inanity . . .

. . . I beg you to have patience with me and confidence in what I have done up till now. I always have a little more to do than be just a faithful follower. You have no lack of those anyway. But they do not advance the cause, for by faith alone nothing prospers in the long run.

With kind regards and many thanks,

Most sincerely yours, JUNG

87F

Dear friend,   3 May 1908, Vienna, IX. Berggasse 19
So you too are pleased with our meeting in Salzburg? It refreshed me a good deal and left me with a pleasant aftertaste. I was glad to find you so flourishing and every suspicion of resentment melted

away when I saw you again and understood you. I know you are in a phase of 'negative oscillation' and are now suffering the counter effects of the great influence you have exerted on your chief all this time. It is not possible to push without being pushed. But I am quite certain that after having moved a few steps away from me you will find your way back, and then go far with me. I can't give you any reason for this certainty; it probably springs from a feeling I have when I look at you. But I am satisfied to feel at one with you and no longer fear that we might be torn apart. You will just have to be patient with some of my idiosyncrasies . . .

Jones and Brill have been to see me twice . . . Jones is undoubedly a very interesting and worthy man, but he gives me a feeling of, I was almost going to say racial strangeness. He is a fanatic and doesn't eat enough. 'Let me have men about me that are fat,' says Caesar, etc. He almost reminds me of the lean and hungry Cassius. He denies all heredity; to his mind even I am a reactionary. How, with your moderation, were you able to get on with him?

I have a great favour to ask of you. It has not escaped me that a rift is in the making between you and Abraham. There are so few of us that we must stick together, and a rift for personal motives is less becoming in us psychoanalysts than in anyone else. I regard him as a man of great worth and I should not like to be obliged to give him up, though there can be no question of his replacing you in my eyes. Accordingly, I have this request to make of you: be helpful if he consults you about the publication of his dementia paper, and accept the fact that this time he took the more direct path, whereas you hesitated. Apart from that, you have every advantage over him. In this question the merit will probably lie with the detailed work and not with the pronunciamento. We mustn't quarrel when we are besieging Troy . . .

With kind regards,

As ever, FREUD

90F

Dear friend,   6 May 1908, Vienna, IX. Berggasse 19
Enclosed the certificate for Otto Gross. Once you have him, don't let
him out before October when I shall be able to take charge of him.

Your news of Marhold's offer sounds splendid. For politeness'
sake, wait for Deuticke, but I doubt that he will make a better offer.
Two semi-annual volumes strike me as a much better idea than a
single annual one ...

Well, this is another success for you. I am fifty-two today; supposing I have another ten working years ahead of me, I shall still be
able to make quite a contribution to our work.

Yours with a cordial handshake, FREUD

91J

Dear Professor Freud,   Burghölzli–Zürich, 7 May 1908
Following your wish I will wait until I have heard from Deuticke. Or
should I write to him? Otherwise it might go too slowly. Deuticke
would be more attractive to me than Marhold, as the firm is sounder.
Let's hope D. offers even better conditions.

In the first volume, that is, the first published part of it, there
should unquestionably be a list, ie a compilation of brief abstracts of
all those works that have to do with our cause, by which I mean
chiefly all your books and your numerous articles that are scattered
all over the place, as well as those of your pupils. To ensure complete
coverage, it would be best if one of your people were to draft the
abstracts in chronological order *under your supervision* ...

... Of all your pupils I consider Abraham the most suitable, since
he understands these things. I am sure he would gladly take over at
your request. So let him deal with all the Viennese works – his own
included, of course! You would be doing me a great service if you
sounded him out.

You will see from this suggestion that my objective judgement of A. is not in the least impaired. For that very reason I have an undisguised contempt for some of colleague A.'s idiosyncrasies. In spite of his estimable qualities and sundry virtues he is simply not a *gentleman*. In my eyes just about the worst thing that can happen to anyone. I am always ready to subordinate my judgement to someone who knows better, but in this case I find myself in agreement with a large number of people whose opinions I respect. In Salzburg I was able to prevent a scandal only by imploring a certain gentleman, who wanted to shed light on the sources of A.'s lecture, to abandon his plan. This gentleman wasn't a Swiss, nor was he one of my pupils, who (like me) can only gaze in quiet wonderment at such productions but can't help taking note of the facts. Up till now nothing has ever been done from my side that might have led to the rift; on the contrary it is A. who is pulling in that direction. The latest piece of effrontery (which, be it said, I could not imagine him capable of before) is the news that he will send me his lecture unaltered for publication. Naturally I wouldn't put up with that, for a journal edited by me has to be thoroughly clean and decent and should not publish any plagiarism of your intellectual work or mine.

You can rest assured that so long as A. behaves himself decently everything will remain the same on my side. But if he goes too far, an explosion will be unavoidable. I hope very much that A. will be mindful of how far one may go. A break would be a great pity and not in the interests of our cause. He can avoid this eventuality *very easily* by a *little bit* of decency.

I should be most grateful if you could get A., or some other person who might seem to you even more suitable, to start on the abstracts as soon as possible.

Many thanks in advance! With best regards,

Most sincerely yours, JUNG

92F

Dear friend,   10 May 1908, Vienna, IX. Berggasse 19
Thank you for your birthday wishes; let us as always confront the future with confidence; it looks promising...

We didn't manage to talk enough about A. in Salzburg. An experience of my own gives me a vague idea of how you feel, but this time I think you are much too hard on him. I am sure there was no *animus injuriandi* on his part. I threw out the suggestion, he heard it from you and corresponded with me about it as well. His appropriation of it is perfectly acceptable to me, I only regret that *you* didn't appropriate it. I believe that your reaction to him must be interpreted as a summation of your previous reactions.

As reporter on the Vienna literature I should like to propose little Rank rather than Ab. You know from his 'Artist' how well he can formulate my ideas. I am eagerly awaiting the outcome of your negotiations.

Yours cordially, FREUD

93J

Dear Professor Freud,   14 May 1908
Deuticke offers 50 marks per printed sheet, 60 marks for papers by you, Bleuler, and me – fee for editing: 200 marks. It's even better than Marhold! If you agree, we will go to Deuticke. Please give your approval. For the title we, that is Bleuler and I, suggest: 'Jahrbücher für Psychoanalyse und Psychopathologie'. The first chiefly for you, the second for us, ie for works from our laboratory...

What do you think about the hiatus in Psycho-analysis? May I know your reasons?

Only a short letter for now as I have Gross with me. He is taking up an incredible amount of time. It seems to be a definite obsessional neurosis. The nocturnal light obsession has already gone. We are now down to the infantile identification blockages of a specifically homosexual nature, I am eager to see how it turns out.

Most sincerely yours, JUNG

94F

Dear friend,   19 May 1908, Vienna, IX. Berggasse 19
... Now to Gross! I can imagine how much of your time he must be taking. I originally thought you would only take him on for the withdrawal period and that I would start analytical treatment in the autumn. It is shamefully egotistic of me, but I must admit that it is better for me this way; for I am obliged to sell my time and my supply of energy is not quite what it used to be. But seriously, the difficulty would have been that the dividing line between our respective property rights in creative ideas would inevitably have been effaced; we would never have been able to disentangle them with a clear conscience. Since I treated the philosopher Swoboda[43] I have had a horror of such difficult situations.

I think your diagnosis of Gross is correct. His earliest childhood memory (communicated in Salzburg) is of his father warning a visitor: Watch out, he *bites*! He remembered this in connection with my Rat Man story.

I should prefer to write *Psychoanalyse* without a hyphen ...
But these are trifles.
Kind regards to yourself and Bleuler.

Yours ever, FREUD

---

[43] Hermann Swoboda, Austrian psychiatrist, who had become involved in a
dispute with Fleiss over the priority of a published idea, and Freud was drawn
in.

95J

Dear Professor Freud,   Burghölzli-Zürich, 25 May 1908
... You must be wondering why I am so slack in writing these days. I
have let everything drop and have spent all my available time, day
and night, on Gross, pushing on with his analysis. It is a typical
obsessional neurosis with many interesting problems. Whenever I
got stuck, he analysed me. In this way my own psychic health has
benefited. For the time being Gross is *voluntarily* going through with
the opium withdrawal. Until the day before yesterday, I had been
giving him the full ration so as not to upset the analysis by arousing
feelings of privation. Yesterday he voluntarily, and with no feelings
of privation, reduced the dose from 6.0 to 3.0 [grams] per day. Psychically his condition has improved a lot, so that the future looks less
sombre. He is an extraordinarily decent fellow with whom you can
hit it off at once provided you can get your own complexes out of the
way. Today is my first day of rest; I finished the analysis yesterday.
So far as I can judge, all that remains now will be gleanings from a
very long string of minor obsessions of secondary importance.

The analysis has yielded all sorts of scientifically valuable results
which we shall try to formulate soon ...

With best regards,

Most sincerely yours, JUNG

98J

Dear Professor Freud,   Burghölzli–Zürich, 19 June 1908
At long last I have a quiet moment in which to gather my wits
together for a letter. Until now the Gross affair has consumed me in
the fullest sense of the word. I have sacrificed days and nights to him.
Under analysis he voluntarily gave up *all* medication. The last three
weeks we worked only with very early infantile material. Little by

little I came to the melancholy realization that although the infantile complexes could all be described and understood, and although the patient had momentary insights into them, they were nevertheless overwhelmingly powerful, being permanently fixated and drawing their affects from inexhaustible depths. With a tremendous effort on both sides to achieve insight and empathy we were able to stop the leak for a moment; the next moment it opened up again. All these moments of profound empathy left not a trace behind them; they quickly became insubstantial, shadowy memories. There is no development, no psychological yesterday for him; the events of early childhood remain eternally new and operative, so that notwithstanding all the time and all the analysis he reacts to today's events like a six-year-old boy, for whom the wife is always the mother, every friend, everyone who wishes him well or ill always the father, and whose world is a boyish fantasy filled with heaven knows what monstrous possibilities.

I am afraid you will already have read from my words the diagnosis I long refused to believe and which I now see before me with terrifying clarity: Dem. praec.

The diagnosis has been amply confirmed for me by a very careful anamnesis and partial psychanalysis of his wife. His exit from the stage is in keeping with the diagnosis: the day before yesterday Gross, unguarded for a moment, jumped over the garden wall and will doubtless turn up again in Munich ere long, to go towards the evening of his fate.

In spite of everything he is my friend, for at bottom he is a very good and fine man with an unusual mind. He is now living under the delusion that I have cured him and has already written me a letter overflowing with gratitude, like a bird escaped from its cage. In his ecstasy he has no inkling of the revenge which the reality he has never even glimpsed will wreak upon him. He is one of those whom life is *bound* to reject. He will never be able to live with anybody in the long run. His wife sticks it out only because Gross represents for her the fruits of her own neurosis. I now understand her too, but cannot forgive her on that account.

I don't know with what feelings you will receive this news. For me this experience is one of the harshest in my life, for in Gross I discovered many aspects of my own nature, so that he often seemed like my twin brother – but for the Dementia praecox. This is tragic. You can guess what powers I have summoned up in myself in order to cure him. But in spite of the sorrow of it, I would not have missed this experience for anything; for in the end it has given me, with the help of a unique personality, a unique insight into the nethermost depths of Dementia pr.

What is fixated by the disease is not any kind of complex arising in later life but the earliest infantile sexual complex. The ostensibly later 'outbreak' of the disease is nothing but a secondary conflict, an '*enchevêtrement*'[44] resulting from his infantile attitude, and as such soluble but only up to a point. In hysteria there is both Pompeii and Rome, in D. pr. only Pompeii. The devaluation of reality in D. pr. seems to be due to the fact that the flight into the disease takes place at an early infantile period when the sexual complex is still completely autoerotic; hence the persistent autoerotism.

Meanwhile I still have an unspeakable amount of work to do, as I have to catch up with all the business that has accumulated in the interim . . .

Bleuler, sad to say, is festooned with complexes from top to bottom; only recently he was again disputing the sexual explanation of rhythm. But he can't be pinned down, talks resistance-language, so that communication ceases of itself, and then compensates with fanatical candour and affability. In the end it gets on one's nerves, for one likes human beings around one and not complex-masks.

Should Gross turn to you later, please don't mention my diagnosis; I hadn't the heart to tell him. His wife knows everything.

With kindest regards,

Most sincerely yours, JUNG

[44] = entanglement.

99F

My dear friend,　　　　　21 June 1908, Vienna, IX. Berggasse 19
I have a feeling that I should thank you most vigorously – and so I do – for your treatment of Otto Gross. The task should have fallen to me but my egoism – or perhaps I should say my self-defence mechanism – rebelled against it ...

... Deeply as I sympathize with Otto Gr., I cannot underestimate the importance of your having been obliged to analyse him. You could never have learned so much from another case; and a further good result, I see, is that your views have once again come much closer to mine. I wasn't worried though. At one time, yes, before our last meeting. But just seeing you in Salzburg, though there was hardly a chance of talking to you, I knew that our views would soon be reconciled, that you had not, as I had feared, been alienated from me by some inner development deriving from the relationship with your father and the beliefs of the Church but merely by the influence of your chief. I must own, I was not entirely pleased with Bleuler, he sometimes made me feel rather creepy, but after a while I felt sure that I would not lose you to *him*. 'Complex-mask', incidentally, is a magnificent term; the fact that you have hit upon it indicates that inwardly you have fully prevailed over him ...

In conclusion a little personal item: I recently came across your birthdate in a medical directory: 26 July, a day we have been celebrating for many years; it's my wife's birthday!

With kind regards,

As ever, FREUD

We'll exchange notes about Stekel another time.

100J

Dear Professor Freud,   Burghölzli–Zürich, 26 June 1908
I thank you with all my heart for your last letter.
There have been further developments in the Gross affair. According
to the latest report from Frau Dr Gross to my chief, Gross is acting
really paranoid. He declared for instance that he couldn't remain in
his hotel in Zürich because he had noticed that some men on the
upper floor were spying on his mental state (!); in his flat in Munich
he heard a voice in the street calling 'Is the doctor at home?' Then he
heard knockings in the walls and on the upper floor. He torments his
wife just as before. The wretched woman is probably heading for a
breakdown. Despite her admirable points she is one of those people
who won't listen to reason but prefer to be hurt. Apparently she
wants to tie her whole fate to this symptomatic action.

   If I can possibly manage it during the coming year I shall visit you
again for a few days. I see no other way of discussing the concept of
D. pr. *sive* schizophrenia *sive* paranoia that is weighing on my mind.
In my opinion the negative father transference explains nothing,
firstly because it is not absolute in Gross's case and secondly because
in most other cases of D. pr. we have the exact opposite, as also in
hysteria. The only differences, I find, are the infantile fixation, the
infantile associations and the absolute but long drawn out incura-
bility – the permanent exclusion of sizeable chunks of reality. I am
now treating a large number of highly educated hysterics and can see
the absolute difference between D. pr. and hysteria in these cases, and
can only marvel at the profundity of your views. I wish Gross could
go back to you, this time as a patient, not that I want to inflict a
Gross episode on you too, but simply for the sake of comparison.
That would be a gain for science, because with the D. pr. problem
nine-tenths of the psychiatric problems would be solved . . . Probably
because I am angry that you see my efforts to solve the D. pr. problem in a different light.

   I am delighted with the July 26 parallel! Best regards,

   Yours sincerely, JUNG

101F

Dear friend,   30 June 1908, Vienna, IX. Berggasse 19
Why, of course! We're not living in different centuries, not even on different continents. Why shouldn't we get together to discuss a matter of such importance to both of us? The only question is when would be the best time and whether I should go to see you or you come to see me . . .

I am still expecting editorial answers to the questions I asked you in my last letter. I have had news of Gross from Jones, who is with you now, I presume. Unfortunately there is nothing to be said of him. He is addicted and can only do great harm to our cause.

I am overjoyed at the prospect you open up for the coming months and send you my kindest regards.

Yours, FREUD

103F

Dear friend,   Berchtesgaden, Dietfeldhof, 18 July 1908
I have been here for a few days and am recovering very quickly from all my ailments.

I am delighted at the prospect of seeing you and talking with you for a few days. Of course I accept the dates you suggest and will be with you in Zürich in the latter half of September. I hope to find you rested, for I know how heavy a burden you have taken on and am also well aware that Otto Gross has been a dreadful weight on your shoulders. Were it not for my confidence in your strength and endurance, I should fear to tax you further with whole days of discussion. These thoughts are inspired not by my feeling of friendship for you but by the consideration that I need you, that the cause cannot do without you – less than ever since the founding of the *Jahrbuch* . . .

I thought you knew more than I about Jones. I saw him as a

fanatic who smiles at my faint-heartedness and is affectionately indulgent with you over your vacillations. How true this picture is, I don't know. But I tend to think that he lies to the others, not to us. I find the racial mixture in our group most intersting; he is a Celt and consequently not quite accessible to us, the Teuton and the Mediterranean man ...

With kind regards,

Sincerely, FREUD

106F

Dear friend,   Berchtesgaden, Dietfeldhof, 13 August 1908
... I am very much looking forward to my visit to Zürich-Burghölzli. I gladly accept your invitation to stay with you; in the absence of your little family I trust I won't be in the way. I have various plans in mind, first of all to demolish the resentment that is bound to accumulate in the course of a year between two persons who demand a good deal of each other, to obtain a few personal concessions from you, and to discuss a few points with you very thoroughly – for this I am not making any preparation. My selfish purpose, which I frankly confess, is to persuade you to continue and complete my work by applying to psychoses what I have begun with neuroses. With your strong and independent character, with your Germanic blood which enables you to command the sympathies of the public more readily than I, you seem better fitted than anyone else I know to carry out this mission. Besides, I'm fond of you; but I have learned to subordinate that factor.

Let me recapitulate your programme. From September 1 to 15 you will be on holiday, which must be respected. From the 15th to 26th you will be in Burghölzli, exposed to my visit. I was planning to arrive towards the end of this period, because I shall be in England beginning September 1st and should like to make full use of my time there. If I have had enough in three weeks, I shall be with you on September 23 or 24; after all I can't burden you for more than

two or three days. If I come sooner, I shall also leave sooner and
treat myself during the last week of September to a bit of southern
air, which I should hate to forgo this year. I say nothing about Bleuler, I have abandoned the thought of winning him over because
membership in our group is so clearly contrary to his practical
interests. You would not have invited me if you did not know that
Bleuler has no objection and will not interfere with us . . .

I am gradually recovering from the ravages of this last year's toil,
but my night life is still unpleasantly active. One thing and another
have turned my thoughts to mythology and I am beginning to suspect that myth and neurosis have a common core . . .

I have received proof of the second edition of *The Interpretation
of Dreams* and of the *Studies*. We shall be making considerable
demands on the market this autumn.

I hope to hear from you before our meeting. With kind regards,

As ever, FREUD

107J

Dear Professor Freud,   Burghölzli–Zürich, 21 August 1908
I am eagerly looking forward to your visit, which you are going to
extend by several days. We shall have plenty to talk about – you may
be sure of that. I shall be at home again from September 8th to the
28th. Come any time you like during those twenty days. I shall
banish all intrusions that might encroach upon our sessions, so we
can count on being undisturbed. Prof Bleuler has nothing against
your visit, how much he has for it no one knows, least of all himself.
So there is no need for further worry. He is extremely well behaved
and obliging at all times and will put himself out to provide benevolent background. (The unmistakably venomous tone of these sentences refers to certain happenings of an internal nature which justify
my feelings.) . . .

Recently I had a visit from Prof Adolf Meyer of the State Pathological Institute in New York. He is *very* intelligent and clear headed

and entirely on our side in spite of the toxin problem in Dementia praecox. In addition he's an anatomist. A while ago I received some offprints from Sir Victor Horsley[45] and from a third party the news that he is interested in our work.

My holiday starts tomorrow evening, thank God. I intend to make the best of it by fleeing into the inaccessible solitude of a little Alpine cabin on Mount Säntis.

I am very glad you are coming as there are all sorts of things to clear up.

Please give Ferenczi[46] my very cordial regards. He is highly deserving of your goodwill.

If you should write again in the near future, please send the letter to the usual address; everything will be forwarded.

With best regards,

Most sincerely yours, JUNG

108J

Dear Professor Freud,   Burghölzli–Zürich, 9 September 1908
I got back from my holiday yesterday, much too early for my subjective feelings. Still, the holiday brought me a little recuperation so that I am in a somewhat fresher mood for work. The impetus, however, is slight.

I hope my last letter, written about eighteen days ago, reached you safely. I am sending this to Vienna as I don't know your English address. Please let me know fairly soon when you are thinking of coming. I'd like to arrange things in such a way that I have as little as possible to do with the donkey work in the clinic during your visit. I am looking forward so much to talking with you again in peace, for since I saw you in Vienna very, very many things have changed, much is new and further progress has been made. In this respect

[45] British brain surgeon.
[46] Sandor Ferenczi (1873–1933), Hungarian ventriloquist; introduced by Jung, he became Freud's close friend and psychoanalytic collaborator.

Gross as a contrast, no matter how hard to digest, did me a world of good. In spite of his prickliness, talk with him is wonderfully stimulating. I have missed that no end. Only once since then have I had the luck to talk with a really intelligent man, and that was with Prof Meyer of New York. I think I have already told you about his radical views in my last letter. Bleuler is difficult to bear with in the long run; his infantilisms are intolerable and he ruthlessly acts out his complexes by dint of displacements (naturally!). It's still very hard to talk to him as I am highly suspicious of his goodwill, etc etc.

I hope you are having good weather in England and *omnium rerum satietatem.*

With best regards,

Most sincerely yours, JUNG

Freud in England and Zürich

While Jung had been vacationing alone in an Alpine retreat south of Appenzell, some forty miles east of Zürich, Freud left Berchtesgaden on 1 September for England, travelling via the Netherlands. (His only previous visit to England had been in 1875, during the summer when Jung was born; he did not go again until 1938.) Freud spent a week visiting his half-brothers Emanuel and Philipp in Manchester, Blackpool, and elsewhere, and another week alone in London; on 15 September he left with Emanuel for Berlin, where he visited his sister Marie, or Mitzi (married to Moritz Freud). He was in Zürich 18–21 September, staying in Jung's flat at the Burghölzli.

110F

15 October 1908
My dear friend and heir,   Vienna, IX. Berggasse 19
The days we spent so auspiciously together in Zürich have left me in high good humour. Please tell your dear wife that one passage in her letter gave me particular pleasure . . .

Your chief and his wife called on us last Friday evening. He is definitely the more bearable of the two. He was as amiable as his stiffness permitted. He came out in defence of infantile sexuality, for which only two years ago he was 'without comprehension'. Then both of them pounced on me, insisting that I should replace the word 'sexuality' with another (on the model of autism); this, they claimed, would put an end to all resistance and misunderstanding. I said I had no faith in such a happy outcome; anyway, they were at a loss to provide this better term.

With kind regards to you and your wife.

Yours, FREUD

112F

Dear friend,   8 November 1908, Vienna, IX. Berggasse 19
I have been paralysed as a correspondent by a mass of work that keeps me gasping, and by a domestic event. My daughter[47] has become engaged to a man of her choice, she is to be married in a few months and the young people are creating quite a commotion. I hope that your work is in full swing again; we must make great progress in this working year, both in our thinking and in our activity.

I have started work on a paper. The title – 'A General Exposition of the Psychoanalytic Method' – tells all. It is getting ahead very slowly; at present I can write only on Sundays, and then only a few pages. In any event it is to round out the second volume of the *Collected Papers* which Deuticke is prepared to publish and in which 'Dora' is to reappear. A Mr Parker[48] of Columbia University absolutely insists on having a paper from me; maybe I shall offer him this one, but since, as our translator Brill writes, he is opposed on principle to any mention of sexuality, it seems probable that nothing will come of it. Brill also tells me that you are to contribute an article. He

[47] Mathilde; married on 7 Feb '09 to Robert Hollitscher.
[48] William B. Parker, lecturer at the university; an editor of the journal *World's Work*.

writes that Morton Prince[49] keeps sending out warnings against our 'trend'.

I won't say much about the most recent wave of abuse. Forel's attacks are chiefly on you, probably out of ignorance. Professor Mehringer in Graz (slips of the tongue) is outdoing himself in vicious polemics. Moll's book is dishonest and incompetent; a discussion of it is scheduled for our next Wednesday. On the credit side I can now announce that the second edition of *The Interpretation of Dreams*, a copy of which is here on my desk, will reach you in a few days.

Frau C— did actually come to me a fortnight ago; a very serious case of obsessional neurosis, improvement is bound to be very slow. The reason for her preference for me was that Thomsen had advised her against me, saying that treatment by me would only make her condition much worse. But that fell in with her need for punishment.

I am very eager to hear from you and Burghölzli, and most of all to learn that your dear wife, who has felt obliged to write a second letter of thanks, is well.

With kindest regards,

Yours, FREUD

113J

Dear Professor Freud,　　　Burghölzli–Zürich, 11 November 1908
Magna est vis veritatis tuae et praevalebit![50] What one might call the dismal news in your last letter – Meringer, Morton Prince, Dr Parker – has bucked me up no end. Nothing is more detestable than to blow the horn of instant public acclaim and settle down on densely populated ground. Hence I am delighted by the vigorous opposition we provoke. Obviously there are plenty more waiting to make fools of themselves. Even Forel[51] still has a chance to do so at the eleventh

49 Psychiatrist of Boston, editor of the *Journal of Abnormal Psychology*.
50 'Great is the power of your truth and it shall prevail.'
51 Auguste Henri Forel (1848–1931), Swiss neurologist and entomologist; director of the Burghölzli before Bleuler.

hour. For some time now I have noticed the gentle zephyrs of prudery blowing across from America, for which Morton Prince seems to have a quite special organ. Everyone is terribly afraid for his practice, everyone is waiting to play a dirty trick on someone else. That is why we hear so little of the people who have worked with me and visited you. In America they are simply pushed to the wall . . .

My wife and I congratulate you heartily on your daughter's engagement!

Best regards, JUNG

114F

Dear friend,   12 November 1908, Vienna, IX. Berggasse 19
I agree with you completely. It is an honour to have plenty of enemies! Now that we can live, work, publish and enjoy a certain companionship, life is not at all bad and I should not want it to change too soon. When the day of 'recognition' comes, it will be to the present what the gruesome magic of the Inferno is to the holy boredom of the Paradiso. (That is, of course, the other way around.) . . .

Moll's[52] book on the sex life of the child is both meagre and – dishonest. What a mean, malicious soul, and what a narrow mind he must have. Even your chief has now accepted infantile sexuality. True, he wants to call it something different, for fear of offending the squeamish, perhaps sexity, on the model of autism.

I am delighted with your good humour. You will be able to cope with both pupils and enemies, I have no doubt whatever.

The Interpretation of Dreams is already out, but I have no copies yet. In a few days it should bring you greetings from

Yours cordially, FREUD

PS. We hope your dear wife is very well.

[52] Albert Moll, Berlin sexologist.

118F

Dear friend,   11 December 1908, Vienna, IX. Berggasse 19

By the same post you will receive an offprint of the 'Sexual Theories of Children'. I can account for my delayed reaction – not a usual failing of mine – by overwork and indisposition. No need to look for an explanation on your side. The note of freedom in your letters since it is settled that you are to be your own master comes as an answer to my heartfelt wishes. You will see what a blessing it is to have no master over you. The conjunction – social liberation, birth of a son,[53] paper on the father complex – suggests to me that you are at a crossroads in your life and have taken the right direction. My own fatherhood will not be a burden to you, there is little I can do for you, and I am accustomed to giving what I have.

I must say, your regret at being unable to play the ideal hero-father ('My father begot me and died') struck me as very premature. The child will find you indispensable as a father for many many years, first in a positive, then in a negative sense! We are very glad that mother and child are doing so well. Is your wife nursing the baby herself? (Feminine curiosity.) . . .

I am so obsessed by the idea of a nuclear complex[54] in neuroses such as is at the heart of the case of Little Herbert that I cannot make any headway. A recent observation tempted me to trace the poisoning complex, when it is present, back to the infant's interpretation of its mother's morning sickness. I also have some dim notions on the theory of projection in paranoia; I must have them worked out in time for your anticipated visit next spring.

The other day I received a paper from Frank in which he carries his tail several inches lower and even gives it a friendly wag now and then. But it is obvious that anyone who makes use of hypnotism will

53 Franz Karl Jung.
54 Holograph: *Kerncomplex*. The first occurrence (in this correspondence) of this term, in place of which Freud began using 'Oedipus complex' in 1910.

not discover sexuality. It is used up, so to speak, in the hypnotic process.

With kind regards,

Yours ever, FREUD

119J

Dear Professor Freud,   Burghölzli–Zürich, 15 December 1908
I enclose two drafts for the title page of the *Jahrbuch*. Please let me know which version seems to you more suitable. In support of his suggestion Bleuler argues that he can make only quite modest contributions and can therefore not put his name on the same line as yours. My objection to this is that I am *most unwilling* to let myself be pushed so conspicuously to the forefront, for I know it would be to our detriment. I am too young, and success is the hardest to forgive. Hence I fear that certain contributors who are happy to be published under *your* aegis would not appreciate my appearing to head the project. So I hope you will opt for the version that bears some semblance to my suggestion. Naturally it went against the grain to put Bleuler's name before yours; I did so only because Bleuler has the advantage of being Professor publicus ordinarius. There's not much to choose between his third version and his second, though the third is a little better.

Many thanks for the offprint. It is very good to have all the theories together at last. Yesterday I came across a new theory (in a case of hysteria) – the incubation theory: one must warm the body in order to get it with child. I think this is done occasionally.

I thank you very much for your last letter, which I hope to be able to answer in detail soon.

In haste with best regards!

Most sincerely yours, JUNG

120F

Dear friend,   17 December 1908, Vienna, IX. Berggasse 19
I approve your arguments and support your suggestion. I object to Bleuler's attitude on the ground that his modesty defeats its purpose, ie it can only hurt us both. It is easy to see that if his name comes first this reflects not an order of rank but an alphabetical order, as is customary in such publications. For the same reason it would be an order of rank and highly objectionable if my name were to come first.

I should also like to suggest a slight change in your draft. It has to do with titles and is designed to conceal my nakedness.

Directed by

Prof Dr E. Bleuler	and Prof Dr Sigm. Freud
Director of the Psychiatric Clinic	of Vienna
in Zürich	

My 'professor'[55] is only a title and cannot be put in anywhere else. I hope I have convinced you of the importance of this change.

Well, however the two of you work it out, my heartfelt wishes for the birth of Jung's *Jahrbuch*, as everyone will call it.

Very cordially yours, in haste, FREUD

[55] Freud was granted the right to use the title of professor in 1902, but this did not confer academic standing in the university. (See Jones, I, pp 372ff/339ff.) Bleuler, on the other hand, was a full professor holding a chair in psychiatry.

123F

Dear friend,   30 December 1908, Vienna, IX. Berggasse 19
First a resounding prosit for the year 1909, which looks so promising
for you and for our cause. Special good wishes to your little son, who
is now embarking on psychic labours that we still have no conception of. Many thanks for your thoughtful Christmas present,
which by association has recalled to my mind the splendid days in
Burghölzli. I have it all to myself – an unusual occurrence – the rest
of the family has rejected it with indignation. I like it much better
than the sample I tasted at your house.[56] I am amazed to hear that
you knew nothing about Abraham. I gather, then, that he has not
written to you that he is withdrawing the 'other' abstracts and reiter-
ating his request for the publication of his review of my work in the
first number? His letter to me sounded as if he had *already written* to
you. But I can only rejoice that he has thought better of it; since he is
so completely wrong, you will find it easier to forgive him now than
last time. Just pretend to know nothing. Take my word for it that I
gave him a good dressing down. Too bad, too bad.

Now finally I come to the news that I have been invited by Clark
University, Worcester, Mass, Pres Stanley Hall,[57] to deliver four to
six lectures in the first week of July. They expect my lectures to give
a mighty impetus to the development of psychotherapy over there.
The occasion: the twentieth (!) anniversary of the founding of the
university. I have declined without even consulting you or anyone
else, the crucial reason being that I should have had to stop work two
weeks sooner than usual, which would mean a loss of several thousand kronen. Naturally the Americans pay only $400 for travel ex-
penses. I am not wealthy enough to spend five times that much to
give the Americans an impetus. (That's boasting; two-and-a-half to
three times as much!) Janet, whose example they invoke, is probably

56 Miss Anna Freud has recollected that the present was a cheese.
57 G. Stanley Hall (1844–1924), professor of psychology and pedagogics at
   Clark University as well as president. At first sympathetic to psychoanalysis,
   and a charter member (1911) of the American Psychoanalytic Association, he
   later drew closer to Adler's school.

richer or more ambitious or has no practice to lose. But I am sorry to
have it fall through on this account, because it would have been fun.
I don't really believe that Clark University, a small but serious institution, can postpone its festivities for three weeks ...

Sincerely yours, FREUD

May we remain close together in 1909!

125F

Dear friend,   17 January 1909, Vienna, IX. Berggasse 19
At last a Sunday when I am able to chat with you. During the week
there is too much work ...

Your courageous friend Pfister[58] has sent me a paper for which I
shall thank him at length. It's really too nice of him – a Protestant
clergyman – though rather upsetting to me to see Ψ A enlisted in the
fight against 'sin'.

I was nauseated by Peterson's paper on the seat of consciousness.
There is a good deal to be said about America. Jones and Brill write
often, Jones's observations are shrewd and pessimistic, Brill sees
everything through rose-coloured spectacles. I am inclined to agree
with Jones. I also think that once they discover the sexual core of our
psychological theories they will drop us. Their prudery and their
material dependence on the public are too great. That is why I have
no desire to risk the trip there in July. I can't expect anything of
consultations. Kraepelin had an easier time of it. Anyway I have
heard nothing more from Clark University. But I have had a very
nice letter from Campbell,[59] who asks for contributions, etc.

I am glad to say there is better news from Abraham. He absolutely
denies that he took my reprimand amiss; he has been ill, which ac-

---

58 Oskar Pfister (1873–1956), Protestant pastor of Zürich, founding member of
   the Swiss Psychoanalytic Society (1910); remained with Freud after 1914.
   Co-founder (with Emil Oberholzer) of the new Swiss Society for
   Psychoanalysis.
59 Charles Macfie Campbell, Scottish psychiatrist, in New York since 1908.

counts for his long silence. True, he does not explain why he told me he had made his complaint when in reality he hadn't, but at least this enables you to treat the whole incident as *non arrivé*. It was very kind of you, I should say, to give his paper first place in the *Jahrbuch* after Little Hans ...

We are certainly getting ahead; if I am Moses, then you are Joshua and will take possession of the promised land of psychiatry, which I shall only be able to glimpse from afar ...

Franz Karl is thriving, I trust. You will receive an announcement of my daughter's marriage, which is to take place on February 7.

Don't keep me waiting as long for an answer as I once kept you.

Cordially yours, FREUD

126J

Dear Professor Freud,   Burghölzli–Zürich, 19 January 1909
As you wished, I am hastening to answer your letter at once. I am delighted with your good news. All goes well with us too, except for the last two days which were taken up with enforced inactivity and influenza. Today my head is more endurable.

I am glad you appreciate my efforts to be as indulgent as I can with Abraham. I should be extremely grateful if you could cure him in time. Since getting to know more about the practice of a nerve specialist this year, I understand Abraham's touchiness very well. What a bitter brew it is! Whenever I find myself stuck with some hopeless resistance, I have to think not so much of you (for I know how quick you are to find a way out) as of my other analytical fellow sufferers, who are obliged to make a living out of their patients' resistances and have as little wisdom to fall back on as I have.

Pfister is a splendid fellow, a neurotic himself of course, though not a severe one. Nothing scares him, a redoubtable champion of our cause with a powerful intelligence. He will make something of it. What? I don't know yet. Oddly enough, I find this mixture of medicine and theology to my liking. His present aim is naturally sublimation, permissible enough in a man of his intelligence. You will shortly receive another longish paper from him. He is feverishly busy. Another very good man, recruited by the young Binswanger, is Dr Häberlin, formerly director of a teachers' college, now privatdocent of philosophy in Basel. He has founded a school for problem children there, where he teaches 'analytically'. He divides psychology into 'pre-Freudian' and 'post-Freudian'! Which tells a lot.

Our little circle is thriving. Last time there were twenty-six participants. Monakow again made *acte de présence* but is as dumb as ever. There's a revolution going on among our pedagogues. I have been asked to give a special course of lectures introducing your psychology. Meanwhile Bleuler, with an air of innocence, has quietly handed the teaching post for mental hygiene over to Riklin without even consulting me. This is the second time a teaching post has slipped through my fingers, not without Bleuler's passive connivance. Teaching posts, you see, are important things with us because we have no honorary professorships. My academic prospects are therefore very bad, though at present this doesn't worry me too much. Other successes are a consolation.

The Americans are a horse of a different colour. First I must point out with diabolical glee your slip of the pen: you wrote 'your prudishness' instead of 'their prudishness'. We have noticed this prudishness, which used to be worse than it is now; now I can stomach it. I don't water down the sexuality any more.

You are probably right about the trip to America . . .

Now for a few observations:

First the so-called 'baby pains', the little syncopes with a slight eclampsia during and after feeding. The convulsion is usually very mild, a rolling of the eyes upwards and twitchings of the facial muscles around the mouth, occasionally also a jerking of the arm or leg. It gives the impression of a 'sucking orgasm' (rhythmic action – orgasm), perhaps also 'satiation orgasm' (?). The convulsion of the facial muscles often produce a kind of laughing, even at a time when babies can't laugh yet. The first active mimetic attempts are: staring at a shiny object, opening the mouth, clicking the tongue, mimetic convulsion = laughing or crying. In the course of normal development this much of the infantile reflex-convulsion is retained. Children who later get eclamptic attacks when teething, or with intestinal worms, have retained rather more of this mechanism, most of all *epileptics* (abdominal aura). I think these things deserve closer investigation.

Contributions by my four-year-old Agathli: the evening before Fränzli's birth I asked her what she would say if the stork brought her a little brother? 'Then I shall kill it,' she said quick as lightning with an embarrassed, sly expression, and would not let herself be pinned down to this theme. The baby was born during the night. Early next morning I carried her to my wife's bedside; she was tense and gazed in alarm at the rather wan looking mother, without showing any joy; found nothing to say about the situation. The same morning, when Mama was alone, the little one suddenly ran to her, flung her arms round her neck and asked anxiously: 'But, Mama, you don't have to die, do you?' This was the first adequate affect. Her pleasure over the baby was rather 'put on'. Up till now the problems had always been: why is Granny so old? What happens to old people anyway? 'They must die and will go to heaven.' – 'Then they become children again,' added the little one. So somebody has to die in order to make a child. After the birth A. went to stay for several weeks with her grandmother, where she was fed exclusively on the stork theory ... Finally, on my advice, my wife enlighted A., who showed not the least surprise on hearing the solution. (Children grow in the mother like flowers on plants.) Next day I was in bed with influenza. A. came in with a shy, rather startled look on her face, wouldn't approach the bed but asked: 'Have you a plant in your tummy too?' Ran off merry and carefree when this possibility was ruled out ... The three-year-old Grethli ridicules the stork theory, saying that the stork brought not only her little brother but the nurse as well.

What an enchantment such a child is! ...

With best regards,

Most sincerely yours, JUNG

129F

Dear friend,   25 January 1909, Vienna, IX. Berggasse 19

I know, once a psychoanalyst has his first successes behind him, he is in for a hard, bitter time during which he will curse Ψ A and its originator. But then things arrange themselves and he arrives at a *modus vivendi*. Such are the realities! *C'est la guerre*. Perhaps my article on Methodology (which I am having trouble finishing) will help you all to cope with the most obvious problems, but probably not very much. However, it is only in struggling with difficulties that we learn, and I am not too displeased that Bleuler has deprived you of a teaching post. You will be a teacher in any event, sooner or later you are sure to have all the teaching you want, but one must be driven into Ψ A-tical experience. It's good to have no alternative. 'Only those who have no alternative do their best,' as (more or less) C.F. Meyer[60] has the man on Ufenau say. I often appease my conscious mind by saying to myself: just give up wanting to cure; learn and make money, those are the most plausible conscious aims.

I have had another letter from Pfister, very intelligent and full of substance. Think of it, me and the *Protestantische Monatshefte!* But it's all right with me. In some respects a psychoanalyst who is also a clergyman works under better conditions, and besides, I presume, he will not be concerned with money. Actually all teachers ought to be familiar with our subject, if only for the sake of the healthy children. For this reason I give a joyful prosit to your course for teachers! ...

Your Agathli is really charming. But surely you recognize the main features of Little Hans's story. Mightn't everything in it be typical? I am setting high hopes in a neurotic nuclear complex which gives rise to two chief resistances: fear of the father and disbelief towards grown-ups, both fully transferable to the analyst. I am convinced that we shall discover still more and that our technique will benefit by it.

Recently I glimpsed an explanation for the case of fetishism. So far it concerns only clothing and shoes. But it is probably universal,

[60] Zürich poet of the nineteenth century.

Here again repression, or rather idealization of the substitute for the repressed material. If I see any more cases, I shall tell you about them.

With kind regards to you and your now complete family,

Yours, FREUD

Jung's editorial preface in the Jahrbuch. *I:1:*

'*In the spring of 1908 a private meeting was held in Salzburg of all those who are interested in the development of the psychology created by Sigmund Freud and in its application to nervous and mental diseases. At this meeting it was recognized that the working out of the problems in question was already beginning to go beyond the bounds of purely medical interest, and the need was expressed for a periodical which would gather together studies in this field that hitherto have been scattered at random. Such was the impetus that gave rise to our* Jahrbuch. *Its task is to be the progressive publication of all scientific papers that are concerned in a positive way with the deeper understanding and solution of our problems. The* Jahrbuch *will thus provide not only an insight into the steady progress of work in this domain with a great future, but also an orientation on the current state and scope of questions of the utmost importance for all the humane sciences.*

'*Dr C. G. Jung*
'*Zürich, January 1909*'

132F

Dear friend,　　　　　24 February 1909, Vienna, IX. Berggasse 19
Middle or end of March is all the same to me. Suit your own convenience. Splendid that you are bringing your wife. Or am I wrong in extending the 'we' from the one trip to the other? During your visit I shall not be able to abandon my practice entirely, but I shall keep it within limits. I shall not be as busy as I was at this time two years ago, provided there is no change between now and then.

I am looking forward in high good spirits to your second visit: since the last one things have changed for the better. My people (I am referring mainly to my family) are also very eager to see you and are busily discussing whether you like this or that to eat. You have also built up an excellent reputation as a guest.

My children[61] are expected here on Sunday and ought to pass through Zürich on Saturday. Whether they can stop, I do not know, but if they do, you can be sure of their visit. Possibly they will arrive soon after this letter; or perhaps homesickness will spur them to haste or perhaps they have stayed too long in Lyons.

I read your remarks on hysterical-epileptic convulsions with interest. I didn't react because I know nothing about this side of it. Maeder's[62] idea of starting to attack epilepsy on the basis of hysteria rather than the other way round strikes me as very promising. He is altogether an excellent man.

What leisure I have been able to spare from my correspondence with you in the last few weeks I have used for correspondence with Pfister and the Americans. The former seems a splendid fellow. From Jones and about him I have received very strange news and I am in very much the same situation as you when he was with Kraepelin. Brill, our translator, is certainly a thoroughly honest soul. We shall have plenty to talk about.

Ferenczi's presence will make us all very happy. He will probably come over on Sunday; on the other days we shall be able to talk alone, which is a good thing too.

Your answers to my family inquiries were very indirect. I hope all is well. With kind regards,

Yours, FREUD

133J

Dear Professor Freud,   Burghölzli–Zürich, 7 March 1909

Your telegram today has thrown me into a fluster. I hope you haven't put a bad construction on my longish silence. I have been

61 Mathilde and Robert Hollitscher.
62 Alphonse Maeder, Swiss psychotherapist; supported Jung after the break.

waiting a fortnight for this Sunday in order to write to you in peace. All this time I have been under a terrific strain day and night. I had a mass of correspondence to cope with every evening I happened to be free. All the other evenings were taken up with invitations, concerts, three lectures, etc. Also my house building is giving me a great deal to do. I didn't want to write to you until I could defintely say when I am coming. The fixing of this date is particularly difficult for me, *still* chained by the neck, as I have also to consider the wishes of my colleagues. The last and worst straw is that a complex is playing Old Harry with me: a woman patient,[62a] whom years ago I pulled out of a very sticky neurosis with greatest devotion, has violated my confidence and my friendship in the most mortifying way imaginable. She has kicked up a vile scandal solely because I denied myself the pleasure of giving her a child. I have always acted the gentleman towards her, but before the bar of my rather too sensitive conscience I nevertheless don't feel clean, and that is what hurts the most because my intentions were always honourable. But you know how it is – the devil can use even the best of things for the fabrication of filth. Meanwhile I have learnt an unspeakable amount of marital wisdom, for until now I had a totally inadequate idea of my polygamous components despite all self-analysis. Now I know where and how the devil can be laid by the heels. These painful yet extremely salutary insights have churned me up hellishly inside, but for that very reason, I hope, have secured me moral qualities which will be of the greatest advantage to me in later life. The relationship with my wife has gained enormously in assurance and depth ... I think I have now entered the stage of convalescence, thanks to the buffetings fate has given me.

Your joy over the *Jahrbuch* is my joy too. Now the bed is dug for the stream ...

I am looking forward eagerly to the Vienna trip and not least to recuperating from all my batterings.

With kindest regards,

Most sincerely yours, JUNG

[62a] Sabina Spielrein. See p. 150, n. 67.

134F

Dear friend,   9 March 1909, Vienna, IX. Berggasse 19
Many thanks for your telegram and letter, which (the telegram in itself did the trick) put an end to my anxiety. I evidently still have a traumatic hyperaesthesia towards dwindling correspondence. I remember its genesis well (Fliess) and should not like to repeat such an experience unawares. In the end – though I could imagine that certain obstacles must have accumulated in your overcrowded existence and though I had rejected the idea of illness as too neurotic – in the end I just had to hear from you so as to be able to inform you of a matter which now occupies my thoughts and about which I have written to others.

This I shall dispose of first, then I shall have a free mind with which to answer your very interesting letter. You recall that last December I received an invitation from Clark University in Worcester, Mass, which I had to decline because the festivities during which my lectures were to be delivered were scheduled for the second week in July and I would have lost too much money by the transaction. At the time you yourself regretted that I was unable to manage it. Well, a week ago a second invitation came from Stanley Hall, the president of Clark University, who at the same time informed me that the festivities had been postponed to the week of September 6. Also the travel allowance has been increased not inconsiderably from $400 to $750. This time I have accepted, for at the end of August I shall be free and rested. On October 1 I hope to be back in Vienna. I must admit that this has thrilled me more than anything else that has happened in the last few years – except perhaps for the appearance of the *Jahrbuch* – and that I have been thinking of nothing else. Practical considerations have joined forces with imagination and youthful enthusiasm to upset the composure on which you have complimented me. In 1886, when I started my practice, I was thinking only of a two-month trial period in Vienna; if it did not prove satisfactory, I was planning to go to America and found an existence that I would subsequently have asked my fiancée in Hamburg to share. You see, we both of us had nothing, or more precisely, I had a large and impoverished family and she a small inheritance of roughly 3000fl from her Uncle Jacob, who had been a professor of classical philology in Bonn. But unfortunately things went so well in Vienna that I decided to stay on, and we were married in the autumn of the same year. And now, twenty-three years later, I am to go to America after all, not, to be sure, to make money, but in response to an honourable call! We shall have a good deal to say about this trip and its various consequences for our cause.

I too have had news of the woman patient through whom you became acquainted with the neurotic gratitude of the spurned. When Muthmann[63] came to see me, he spoke of a lady who had introduced herself to him as your mistress, thinking he would be duly impressed by your having retained so much freedom. But we both presumed that the situation was quite different and that the only possible explanation was a neurosis in his informant. To be slandered and scorched by the love with which we operate – such are the perils of our trade, which we are certainly not going to abandon on their account ...

Good. I shall expect you and your dear wife for dinner on Friday the 19th. Amuse yourself as you see fit during the day, in the evenings and on Sunday we shall exchange our experiences of these last months. I have no need to tell you how much such meetings with you mean to me both professionally and personally. Unfortunately I can return only a small part of your hospitality, but I hope you have no other social commitments here.

Very cordially yours, FREUD

135J

Dear Professor Freud,   Burghölzli–Zürich, 11 March 1909
I must answer you at once. Your kind words have relieved and comforted me. You may rest assured, not only now but for the future, that nothing Fliess-like is going to happen. I have experienced so much of that sort of thing; it has taught me to do the

[63] Arthur Muthmann, Basel neurologist.

contrary at all times. Except for moments of infatuation my affection is lasting and reliable. It's just that for the past fortnight the devil has been tormenting me in the shape of neurotic ingratitude. But I shall not be unfaithful to Ψ A on that account. On the contrary, I am learning from it how to do better in the future. You mustn't take on about my 'theological' style, I just felt that way. Now and then, I admit, the devil does strike a chill into my – on the whole – blameless heart. The story hawked round by Muthmann is Chinese to me. I've never really had a mistress and am the most innocent of spouses. Hence my terrific moral reaction! I simply cannot imagine who it might have been. I don't think it is the same lady. Such stories give me the horrors.

I must congratulate you heartily on your American triumphs. I believe you will get an American practice in the end. My American has been behaving quite well so far. I am all agog for more news . . .

If you are going to America in September, I earnestly hope that you will put in a week with us here as a way-station. You will have all the holiday peace and quiet that could be wished for, and we'll then be living *procul negotiis* in the country. We are boldly taking it for granted that you will come. After all, the road to America runs through Zürich too. (This piece of impudence was only half intentional, otherwise I would have deleted the sentence.)

With kindest regards, also from my wife.

Most sincerely yours, JUNG

The Jungs again in Vienna

Carl and Emma Jung were in Vienna from Thursday 25 March to Tuesday 30 March (Jones, II, p 57/51). Beyond what the next two letters tell us, nothing more is known of this visit.

According to family records (as communicated by Mr Franz Jung), Jung terminated his work at the Burghölzli at the end of March. The visit to Vienna, therefore, and Jung's bicycle tour in Italy in mid April, must have been celebratory holidays. After resigning from the Burghölzli, Jung continued to lecture as privatdocent in the university until April 1914.

138J

Dear Professor Freud,   Burghölzli–Zürich, 2 April 1909

Worry and patients and all the other chores of daily life have beset me again and quite got me down for the first two days. Now I am slowly coming to the surface and beginning to bask in the memory of the days in Vienna . . .

12 April.

When I left Vienna I was afflicted with some *sentiments d'incomplétude* because of the last evening I spent with you. It seemed to me that my spookery[64] struck you as altogether too stupid and perhaps unpleasant because of the Fliess analogy. (Insanity!) Just recently, however, the impression I had of the last named patient smote me with renewed force. What I told my wife about it also made the deepest impression on her. I had the feeling that under it all there must be some quite special complex, a universal one having to do with the prospective tendencies in man. If there is a 'psychanalysis' there must also be a 'psychosynthesis' which creates future events according to the same laws . . .

That last evening with you has, most happily, freed me inwardly from the oppressive sense of your paternal authority. My unconscious celebrated this impression with a great dream which has preoccupied me for some days and which I have just finished analysing. I hope I am now rid of all unnecessary encumbrances. Your cause must and will prosper, so my pregnancy fantasies tell me, which luckily you caught in the end. As soon as I get back from Italy I shall begin some positive work, first of all for the *Jahrbuch.*

I hope you had a good Easter holiday and feel the better for it . . .

With kindest regards,

Yours gratefully, JUNG

[64] While Freud and Jung were discussing precognition and parapsychology in the former's study, and after Freud had rejected the subject as 'nonsensical' there was a loud report in the bookcase. Jung predicted that another would follow in a moment, and that indeed happened. Jung gave this account in *Memories* . . . According to Jung, Freud told him that they must make an unshakable bulwark of the sexual theory, 'against the black tide of mud of occultism' (*Memories*).

139F

Dear friend,   16 April 1909, Vienna, IX. Berggasse 19
I hope this letter doesn't reach you for a while. I'm sure you see what
I mean. I simply prefer to write now while the feelings aroused by
your last letter are still fresh.

I wrote your wife a card from Venice, where I went on an Easter
trip in the vain hope of getting a foretaste of spring and a little rest. I
thought you were already bicycling in northern Italy.

It is strange that on the very same evening when I formally
adopted you as eldest son and anointed you – *in partibus infidelium*[65]
– as my successor and crown prince, you should have divested me of
my paternal dignity, which divesting seems to have given you as
much pleasure as I, on the contrary, derived from the investiture of
your person. Now I am afraid of falling back into the father role
with you if I tell you how I feel about the poltergeist business. But I
must, because my attitude is not what you might otherwise think.
I don't deny that your stories and your experiment made a deep impression on me. I decided to continue my observations after you left,
and here are the results. In my first room there is constant creaking
where the two heavy Egyptian steles rest on the oaken boards of the
bookshelves. That is too easy to explain. In the second, where we
heard it, there is seldom any creaking. At first I was inclined to
accept this as proof, if the sound that was so frequent while you were
here were not heard again after your departure – but since then I have
heard it repeatedly, not, however, in connection with my thoughts
and never when I am thinking about you or this particular problem
of yours. (And not at the present moment, I add by way of a challenge.) But this observation was soon discredited by another consideration. My credulity, or at least my willingness to believe,
vanished with the magic of your personal presence, once again, for
some inward reasons that I can't put my finger on, it strikes me as
quite unlikely that such phenomena should exist; I confront the de-
spiritualized furniture as the poet confronted undeified Nature after

[65] 'in the lands of the unbelievers'.

144

the gods of Greece had passed away. Accordingly, I put my fatherly hornrimmed spectacles on again and warn my dear son to keep a cool head, for it is better not to understand something than make such great sacrifices to understanding. I also shake my wise head over psychosynthesis and think: yes, that's how the young people are, the only places they really enjoy visiting are those they can visit without us, to which we with our short breath and weary legs cannot follow them.

Then, invoking the privilege of my years, I become garrulous and speak of one more thing between heaven and earth that we cannot understand. Some years ago I discovered within me the conviction that I would die between the ages of 61 and 62, which then struck me as a long time away. (Today it is only eight years off.) Then I went to Greece with my brother and it was really uncanny how often the number 61 or 60 in connection with 1 or 2 kept cropping up in all sorts of numbered objects, especially those connected with transportation. This I conscientiously noted. It depressed me, but I had hopes of breathing easy when we got to the hotel in Athens and were assigned rooms on the first floor. Here, I was sure, there could be no number 61. I was right, but I was given 31 (which with fatalistic licence could be regarded as half of 61 or 62), and this younger, more agile number proved to be an even more persistent persecutor than the first. From the time of our trip home until very recently, 31, often with a 2 in its vicinity, clung to me faithfully. Since my mind also includes areas that are merely eager for knowledge and not at all superstitious, I have since attempted an analysis of this belief, and here it is. It made its appearance in 1899. At that time two events occurred. First I wrote *The Interpretation of Dreams* (which appeared postdated 1900), second, I received a new telephone number, which I still have today: 14362. It is easy to find a factor common to these two events. In 1899 when I wrote *The Interpretation of Dreams* I was 43 years old. Thus it was plausible to suppose that the other figures signified the end of my life, hence 61 or 62. Suddenly method entered into my madness. The superstitious notion that I would die between the ages of 61 and 62 proves to coincide with the conviction that with *The Interpretation of Dreams* I had completed my life work, that there was nothing more for me to do and that I might just as well lie down and die. You will admit that after this substitution it no longer sounds so absurd. Moreover, the hidden influence of W. Fliess was at work; the superstition erupted in the year of his attack on me.

You will see in this another confirmation of the specifically Jewish nature of my mysticism. Otherwise I incline to explain such obsessions as this with the number 61 by two factors; first heightened, unconsciously motivated attention of the sort that sees Helen in every woman, and second by the undeniable 'compliance of chance', which plays the same part in the formation of delusions as somatic compliance in that of hysterical symptoms, and linguistic compliance in the generation of puns.

Consequently, I shall receive further news of your investigations of the spook complex with the interest one accords to a charming delusion in which one does not oneself participate.

With kind regards to you, your wife and children,

Yours, FREUD

140J

Dear Professor Freud,   Burghölzli–Zürich, 12 May 1909

I must again make amends for a sin of omission. Once more you haven't heard from me for a long time. Well, I got back safe and sound from Italy and found your letter awaiting me. I am entirely of your opinion that one must be careful not to be carried away by impressions or indulge in expectations and plans that go too far. The trouble is that one is so eager to discover something. However, I have not gone over to any system yet and shall also guard against putting my trust in those spooks.

Pfister was here the day before yesterday and relayed your greetings. He says your daughter has recently been operated on. I hope there won't be anything serious, ie complications. P. of course was full of you and of his warm reception in your family. I hope you got a good impression of him. He is, all told, a very acceptable theologian with admirable traits of character. He also told me that Moll was with you at the same time. What was *that* black spirit doing in your house? Amazing that the fellow was not ashamed after all his pestering. Quite spineless, obviously. I am dying to hear of the warm reception you gave *him*.

The 'psychoanalytic questionnaire' is a horrid fact which I have now seen with my own eyes. A perfectly idiotic concoction that does Hirschfeld no credit. I find the desecration of the word 'psychoanalytic' unforgiveable. It is most regrettable, to say the least, that Abraham and Stein have subscribed to this sorry rigmarole. I feel like protesting at this infamous bamboozlement of the public. In Zürich everyone is sedately shocked.

I am still at Burghölzli as my house has naturally not been finished on time. We move on May 25th. From then on my address is Küsnacht bei Zürich . . .

All well here. With kindest regards,

Most sincerely yours, JUNG

141F

Dear friend,   16 May 1909, Vienna, IX. Berggasse 19
Once more I am writing to Burghölzli. You know how much pleasure your letters give me, but I am far from wishing to burden you with the obligation of a formal correspondence at times when you have other things to do and nothing to say to me. Still, I hope you will not be surprised to hear from me as often as my own need prompts me to write.

We have all grown very fond of Pfister. He is really an acceptable priest, and he has even helped me by exerting a moderating influence on my father complex. We were like old friends in no time; he is a little fulsome in his enthusiasm, but there is nothing false or exaggerated in his warmth. Whether he will be able to preserve his residue of faith for long strikes me as doubtful; he is only at the beginning of a far reaching development, and the bad company he keeps is bound to have its effect. Moll's visit provided a contrast staged by fate. To put it bluntly, he is a brute; he is not really a physician but has the intellectual and moral constitution of a pettifogging lawyer. I was amazed to discover that he regards himself as a kind of patron of our movement. I let him have it; I attacked the passage in his notorious book where he says that we compose our case histories to support our theories rather than the other way round, and had the pleasure of listening to his oily excuses: his statement was not meant as an insult, every observer is influenced by his preconceived ideas, etc. Then he complained that I was too sensitive, that I must learn to accept justified criticism; when I asked him if he had read 'Little Hans', he wound himself up into several spirals, because more and more venomous, and finally, to my great joy, jumped up and prepared to take flight. At the door he grinned and made an unsuccessful attempt to retrieve himself by asking me when I was coming to Berlin. I could imagine how eager he must be to return my hospitality, but all the same I wasn't fully satisfied as I saw him go. He had stunk up the room like the devil himself, and partly for lack of practice and partly because he was my guest I hadn't lambasted him enough. Now of course we can expect all sorts of dirty tricks from him. And then I called Pfister into the room.

My daughter's abscess has finally cleared up and she is feeling better than before the incident. She is coming to see us today for the first time. I am glad the trouble has been taken care of now, rather than later, on some serious occasion like childbirth.

Foerster has delivered a lecture here but made no mention of me in it. Kurt Redlich, who[66]

66 The rest of the letter is missing.

143F

Dear Friend,   3 June 1909, Vienna, IX. Berggasse 19
Hurrah for your new house! I would say it louder and longer if I
didn't know how you Swiss disliked emotional effusions. This year
my trip to America deprives me of the pleasure, but I hope before
too long to admire your house and enjoy the company of its inhabitants.

Of course I understood your silence and even now I would leave
you more time if another letter – which I enclose – had not reached
me at the same time as yours. Weird! What is she? A busybody, a
chatterbox, or a paranoiac? If you know anything about the writer
or have some opinion in the matter, would you kindly send me a
short wire, but otherwise you must *not* go to any trouble. If I don't
hear from you, I shall assume that you know nothing . . .

I should like very much to talk with you about America and have
your suggestions. Jones threatens me, not entirely without ulterior
motive, with the absence of all leading psychiatrists. I expect nothing
of the moguls. But I wonder if it might not be a good idea to con-
centrate on psychology since Stanley Hall is a psychologist, and
perhaps to devote my three to four lectures entirely to dreams, from
which excursions in various directions would be possible. Of course
these questions have little practical interest in view of my inability to
lecture in English.

With very special regards to you, your wife and children in your
new house.

Yours, FREUD

144J

Im Feld, Küsnacht bei Zürich,
4 June 1909

Dear Professor Freud,

In accordance with your wish I sent you a telegram this morning, framing it as clearly as I could. At the moment I didn't know what more to say. Spielrein[67] is the person I wrote you about. She was published in abbreviated form in my Amsterdam lecture of blessed memory. She was, so to speak, my test case, for which reason I remembered her with special gratitude and affection. Since I knew from experience that she would immediately relapse if I withdrew my support, I prolonged the relationship over the years and in the end found myself morally obliged, as it were, to devote a large measure of friendship to her, until I saw that an unintended wheel had started turning, whereupon I finally broke with her. She was, of course, systematically planning my seduction, which I considered inopportune. Now she is seeking revenge. Lately she has been spreading a rumour that I shall soon get a divorce from my wife and marry a certain girl student, which has thrown not a few of my colleagues into a flutter. What she is now planning is unknown to me. Nothing good, I suspect, unless perhaps you are imposed upon to act as a go-between. I need hardly say that I have made a clean break. Like Gross, she is a case of fight-the-father, which in the name of all that's wonderful I was trying to cure *gratissime* (!) with untold tons of patience, even abusing our friendship for that purpose. On top of that, naturally, an amiable complex had to throw an outsize monkey wrench into the works. As I have indicated before, my first visit to

[67] Sabina (or Sabine) Spielrein (1885–1941), of Russian origin. 1905–11 studied medicine at the University of Zürich; MD 1911. Later in 1911 she became a member of the Vienna society. From 1912, in Berlin. In 1921–3, Dr Spielrein (then called Spielrein-Scheftel) practised in Geneva; Jean Piaget underwent his didactic analysis with her. In 1923, she returned to the Soviet Union and taught at the North Caucasus University, Rostov on the Don, and was listed in the *International Journal* as a member of the Russian society until 1933, after which year the psychoanalytic movement was officially abolished in the Soviet Union. Spielrein was murdered by German troops that occupied Rostov in 1941.

Vienna had a *very* long unconscious aftermath, first the compulsive infatuation in Abbazia, then the Jewess popped up in another form, in the shape of my patient. Now of course the whole bag of tricks lies there quite clearly before my eyes. During the whole business Gross's notions flitted about a bit too much in my head. Incidentally, Gross hasn't sent me his book. I shall try to buy it. Could you give me the name of the publisher? Gross and Spielrein are bitter experiences. To none of my patients have I extended so much friendship and from none have I reaped so much sorrow.

Heartiest thanks for your blessings on my house! I take them as the best omen . . .

. . . I have inscribed your classic apophthegm 'Just give up wanting to cure' in block letters on my heart, for the above reasons. I have learnt my lesson for keeps . . .

With kindest regards, JUNG

145F

Dear friend,   7 June 1909, Vienna, IX. Berggasse 19
Since I know you take a personal interest in the Sp. matter I am informing you of developments. Of course there is no need for you to answer this.

I understood your telegram correctly, your explanation confirmed my guess. Well, after receiving your wire I wrote Fräulein Sp. a letter in which I affected ignorance, pretending to think her sugges- tion was that of an over-zealous enthusiast. I said that since the matter on which she wished to see me was of interest chiefly to myself, I could not take the responsibility of encouraging her to take such a trip and failed to see why she should put herself out in this way. It therefore seemed preferable that she should first acquaint me with the nature of her business. I have not yet received an answer.

Such experiences, though painful, are necessary and hard to avoid. Without them we cannot really know life and what we are dealing with. I myself have never been taken in quite so badly, but I have

come very close to it a number of times and had *a narrow escape*. I
believe that only grim necessities weighing on my work, and the fact
that I was ten years older than yourself when I came to ΨA, have
saved me from similar experiences. But no lasting harm is done.
They help us to develop the thick skin we need and to dominate
'counter-transference', which is after all a permanent problem for us;
they teach us to displace our own affects to best advantage. They are
a *'blessing in disguise'*.

The way these women manage to charm us with every conceivable
psychic perfection until they have attained their purpose is one of
nature's greatest spectacles. Once that has been done or the contrary
has become a certainty, the constellation changes amazingly . . .

With a confident handshake and kind regards,

Sincerely yours, FREUD

146J

	Im Feld, Küsnacht bei Zürich
Dear Professor Freud,	12 June 1909

Many thanks for your letter. I had to tell myself that if a friend or
colleague of mine had been in the same difficult situation I would
have written in the same vein. I had to tell myself this because my
father-complex kept on insinuating that you would not take it as you
did but would give me a dressing down more or less disguised in the
mantle of brotherly love. For actually it is too stupid that I of all
people, your 'son and heir', should squander your heritage so heed-
lessly, as though I had known nothing of all these things. What you
say about intellectual overvaluation is right on every point, and to
cap it I still have the absurd idea of some kind of moral obligation.
All that is too stupid, but useful [last word in bold type and letter-
spaced] . . .

Today my children have moved into the new house. Everything is
going well, including my practice, which makes me very happy. Frl

E— is a gorgeous case. Did she tell you about her experiences with doctors? She seems to be dangerous. (Here I tweak myself severely by the ear.)

With many kind regards,

Yours, JUNG

147F

Dear friend,   18 June 1909, Vienna, IX. Berggasse 19
Your being invited to America is the best thing that has happened to us since Salzburg; it gives me enormous pleasure for the most selfish reasons, though also, to be sure, because it shows what prestige you have already gained at your age. Such a beginning will take you far, and a certain amount of favour on the part of men and fate is a very good thing for one who aspires to perform great deeds.

Of course your joy is now beginning to be clouded by the same concerns as mine, culminating in the question: What am I to say to those people? On this score I have a saving idea, which I shall not keep secret from you. Here it is: we can think about it on shipboard, on our long walks round the deck. Otherwise I can only refer you to the astute observation with which you yourself recently allayed *my* misgivings: that the invitation is the main thing, that the audience is now at our mercy, under obligation to applaud whatever we bring them.

A most gratifying detail is that you too are sailing on the *G. Washington*. We shall both be very nice to Ferenczi . . .

Fraülein Spielrein has admitted in her second letter that her business has to do with you; apart from that, she has not disclosed her intentions. My reply was ever so wise and penetrating; I made it appear as though the most tenuous of clues had enabled me Sherlock Holmes-like to guess the situation (which of course was none too difficult after your communication) and suggested a more appropriate procedure, something endopsychic, as it were. Whether it will be effective, I don't know. But now I must entreat you, don't go too far in the direction of contrition and reaction. Remember Lassalle's fine sentence about the chemist whose test tube had cracked: 'With a slight frown over the resistance of matter, he gets on with his work.' In view of the kind of matter we work with, it will never be possible to avoid little laboratory explosions. Maybe we didn't slant the test tube enough, or we heated it too quickly. In this way we learn what part of the danger lies in the matter and what part in our way of handling it ...

With kind regards to you and the lady of the new house.

Cordially yours, FREUD

148J

Im Feld, Küsnacht bei Zürich
Dear Professor Freud,   21 June 1909
I have good news to report of my Spielrein affair. I took too black a view of things. After breaking with her I was almost certain of her revenge and was deeply disappointed only by the banality of the form it took. The day before yesterday she turned up at my house and had a *very decent* talk with me, during which it transpired that the rumour buzzing about me does not emanate from her at all. My ideas of reference, understandable enough in the circumstances, attributed the rumour to her, but I wish to retract this forthwith. Furthermore, she has freed herself from the transference in the best and nicest way and has suffered no relapse (apart from a paroxysm of weeping after the separation). Her intention to come to you was not aimed at any intrigue but only at paving the way for a talk with me. Now, after your second letter, she has come to me in person. Although not succumbing to helpless remorse, I nevertheless deplore the sins I have committed, for I am largely to blame for the high-flying hopes of my former patient. So, in accordance with my original principle of taking everyone seriously to the uttermost limit, I discussed with her the problem of the child, imagining that I was talking theoretically, but naturally Eros was lurking in the back-

ground. Thus I imputed all the other wishes and hopes entirely to my patient without seeing the same thing in myself. When the situation had become so tense that the continued perseveration of the relationship could be rounded out only by sexual acts, I defended myself in a manner that cannot be justified morally. Caught in my delusion that I was the victim of the sexual wiles of my patient, I wrote to her mother that I was not the gratifier of her daughter's sexual desires but merely her doctor, and that she should free me from her. In view of the fact that the patient had shortly before been my friend and enjoyed my full confidence, my action was a piece of knavery which I very reluctantly confess to you as my father. I would now like to ask you a great favour: would you please write a note to Frl Spielrein, telling her that I have fully informed you of the matter, and especially of the letter to her parents, which is what I regret most. I would like to give my patient at least this satisfaction: that you and she know of my 'perfect honesty'. I ask your pardon many times, for it was my stupidity that drew you into this imbroglio. But now I am extremely glad that I was not mistaken, after all, about the character of my patient, otherwise I should have been left with a gnawing doubt as to the soundness of my judgement, and this would have been a considerable hindrance to me in my work.

I am looking forward very much to America. I have booked a passage on the *G. Washington*, a very expensive cabin, however. You have set my mind at rest about Marcinowski, I need no further documents.

You will have received a letter from the *studiosus* Honegger[68] which will surely amuse you. The young man is very intelligent and subtle minded; wants to take up psychiatry, once consulted me because of loss of reality-sense lasting a few days. (Psychasthenia = libido introversion = Dem. praec.) Indirectly, I am nudging him towards analysis so that he can analyse himself *consciously*; in that way he may perhaps forestall the automatic self-disintegration of Dem. pr.

---

[68] Johann Jakob Honegger, Jr (1885–1911), psychiatrist of Zürich, worked at Burghölzli and at Territet. His father, also a psychiatrist, was Adolf Meyer's teacher. The present correspondence is a principal source of information about Honegger.

Your letter has just arrived – many thanks! Reality has already consoled me. All the same I am grateful for your sympathetic interest ...

Best regards,

Gratefully yours, JUNG

149F

Dear friend,   30 June 1909, Vienna, IX. Berggasse 19
It is high time I wrote you again. Yours would have reconciled me to greater misdeeds on your part; perhaps I am already too biased in your favour. Immediately after receiving your letter I wrote Fräulein Sp. a few amiable lines, giving her satisfaction, and today received an answer from her. Amazingly awkward – is she a foreigner by any chance? – or very inhibited, hard to read and hard to understand. All I can gather from it is that the matter means a great deal to her and that she is very much in earnest. Don't find fault with yourself for drawing me into it; it was not your doing but hers. And the matter has ended in a manner satisfactory to all. You have been oscillating, as I see, between the extremes of Bleuler and Gross. When I think that I owe your ultimate conversion and profound conviction to the same experience with Gross, I cannot possibly be angry and can only marvel at the profound coherence of all things in this world.

Now to myself. My energy is pretty well exhausted, except for one undertaking. In a fortnight I shall be going to Munich and from there to Ammerwald (address follows). This one undertaking is my paper about the Rat Man. I am finding it very difficult; it is almost beyond my powers of presentation; the paper will probably be intelligible to no one outside our immediate circle. How bungled our reproductions are, how wretchedly we dissect the great art works of psychic nature! Unfortunately this paper in turn is becoming too bulky. It just pours out of me, and even so it's inadequte, incomplete and therefore untrue. A wretched business. I am determined to finish it before leaving and to do nothing more before setting sail for our America. I'm too tired this year . . .

 With kind regards to you and yours,

 Sincerely yours, FREUD

The Clark Conference

Freud met Jung and Ferenczi on 20 August at Bremen (see below, 329 F) and the following day the three sailed on the North German Lloyd ship George Washington. *During the voyage, they analysed one another's dreams, and Jung has recounted one of his own dreams* (Memories, *pp 158ff), which foreshadowed his concept of the collective unconscious.*

 They arrived in New York on Sunday evening 29 August, and were joined by Brill and later by Jones. The week was given to sightseeing and entertainment, and on Saturday evening 4 September, the party departed by steamer for an overnight voyage to Fall River, Massachusetts, then by train via Boston to Worcester, the site of Clark University.

 Freud and Jung were guests in Stanley Hall's home. Freud gave five lectures, at eleven o'clock each morning, Tuesday to Saturday; Jung gave three during the week; both spoke in German. The participants in the conference included William Stern, of Munich, and Leo Burgerstein, of Vienna; from the United States, William James, Adolf Meyer, Franz Boas, E. B. Titchener, and in particular James Jackson Putnam. At the closing ceremony, on Saturday 11 September, honorary doctorates of law were conferred on Freud (in psychology) and on Jung (in education and social hygiene).

 During the following two days, Freud, Jung, and Ferenczi travelled extensively; west to Niagara Falls and back east to Keene, New York, in the Adirondack mountains near Lake Placid, where they spent four days at the Putnam family camp. During the weekend, they returned to New York, whence they embarked on Tuesday morning the 21st, aboard the Kaiser Wilhelm der Grosse. *They arrived in Bremen on 29 September . . .*

155J

Dear Professor Freud,   Küsnacht bei Zürich, 1 October 1909
Here I stand on your doorstep with a letter of welcome to greet you
in Vienna on resumption of work. For my part I have got down to it
in real earnest. I feel in top form and have become much more
reasonable than you might suppose. My wife is bearing up splendidly
under the psychoanalysis and everything is going *à merveille*. On
the journey back to Switzerland I never stopped analysing dreams
and discovered some priceless jokes. A pity there's no time for this
now. How are you? and the stomach? Well, I hope . . .

It is amazing how our work is spreading among the primary
school teachers here. A young teacher was with me today, asking for
advice; for months he has been treating his severely hysterical wife
with good results and extraordinary understanding; he is also treating one of his pupils who suffers from a phobia. The scalpel is being
cold-bloodedly wrested out of the doctors' hand. What do you say
to this? The young man also tells me that in Zürich people have
started calling me names, particularly colleagues. Understandable,
because now their reputation is at stake. One must let the forest fire
rage, there's no stopping it now. In Zürich a Dr *Bircher* (please note
the name!) has set up as a psychoanalyst. Formerly he believed in
uric acid and apple sauce and porridge. Naturally he hasn't a clue.
He is very much to be warned against, especially as he is much in
vogue and assiduously avoids personal relations with me.

All's well with my family, and I hope with yours too. Most cordial
regards,

Yours, JUNG

157J

Dear Professor Freud,   Küsnacht bei Zürich, 14 October 1909

Occasionally a spasm of homesickness for you comes over me, but only occasionally; otherwise I am back into my stride. The analysis on the voyage home has done me a lot of good. I have much zest and little opportunity for scientific work, by which I do not mean instructing students. In this respect I am doing far too much at present. What would you think if I planned to organize things in such a way as to exploit the situation financially a bit? I find it quite as necessary to guard myself against so-called normal people as against neurotics (the differences between them are remarkably small). I hold myself justified in this depravity, for these people will draw a fat profit later on while I merely lose time and energy for work.

How goes it with your daughter, or rather, your two daughters? You say you found both your elder daughters ill.

Have you seen the new article by Friedländer?[69] And Siemerling's,[70] I think in the *Archiv*, on the *Jahrbuch*? Imagine, Friedländer was with me yesterday, sweet as sugar and wagging his tail. He would like to be answered *à tout prix*, you were absolutely right. Unless the fellow has taken it into his head to convert me, I simply don't know what his real purpose was in coming. He told me he would be delighted to have more contacts with us so as to learn something from our work. (A damned sight too many patients seem to be demanding psychoanalytic treatment, don't you think?) He must have a mighty big bee in his bonnet that leaves him no peace. From all this I gather that our opponents are inconsolable because of our inviolate silence. He tried to work up my enthusiasm for a public appearance, so naturally I put on an unenthusiastic air. I distrust the fellow, especially as I cannot believe that he has any real scientific interests. He must be pursuing a quite different purpose which is still opaque to me. He wants to come again tomorrow, to sit in at a

[69] Adolf Albrecht Friedländer (1870–1949), psychiatrist then at the Hohe Mark Sanatorium, near Frankfurt a. M.; an aggressive critic of psychoanalysis.

[70] Ernst Siemerling, German psychiatrist, critic of psychoanalysis.

conference with my students. I almost hope these people will remain our opponents for a long time to come . . .

I am obsessed by the thought of one day writing a comprehensive account of this whole field [mythology], after years of fact finding and preparation, of course. The net should be cast wide. Archaeology or rather mythology has got me in its grip, it's a mine of marvellous material. Won't you cast a beam of light in that direction, at least a kind of spectrum analysis *par distance*? . . .

In my family all is well, thanks to lots of dream analysis and humour. The devil seems to have been beaten at his own game.

With many kind regards,

Yours sincerely, JUNG

158F

Dear friend,   17 October 1909, Vienna, IX. Berggasse 19
I am glad to find a number of things in your letter that call for an immediate answer. This is Sunday and I am entitled to rest from a hard week's work. Actually I have a great deal to tell you and discuss with you. Let's start with the business matters.

I hope and trust Friedländer hasn't got anything out of you. He is an unsavoury individual, even in his private affairs; he left his country because of some crooked business, he owes his clinic to his marriage to a woman he has since then divorced, and is now operating it for his former father-in-law, etc. All he wanted of us, it seems to me, was a kind of rehabilitation through our hostility. Now he is inconsolable because we have shown by our silence that we regarded him as unfit to duel with, so to speak. Either he has some specially beastly plan in visiting you, or he is stupid as well; can he think that we don't notice the contrast between the sweets he is dispensing and his public statements? In private the fellow deserves to be treated with all possible rudeness, in our literature we must simply ignore him; he is plain riffraff . . .

. . . Your idea of getting some profit out of your students strikes

me as quite justified. Couldn't you announce a course of lectures –
call it 'An Introduction to the Technique of ΨA' – and let your
'guests' enroll at a reasonable fee?[71] It can do no harm to clarify
your relations ...

I am glad you share my belief that we must conquer the whole field
of mythology. Thus far we have only two pioneers: Abraham and
Rank. We need men for more far reaching campaigns. Such men are
so rare. We must also take hold of biography. I have had an inspiration since my return. The riddle of Leonardo da Vinci's character has suddenly become clear to me. That would be a first step in the
realm of biography. But the material concerning L. is so sparse that I
despair of demonstrating my conviction intelligibly to others. I have
ordered an Italian work on his youth and am now waiting eagerly for
it. In the meantime I will reveal the secret to you. Do you remember
my remarks in the 'Sexual Theories of Children' (second *Short
Papers*) to the effect that children's first primitive researches in this
sphere were bound to fail and that this first failure could have a
paralysing effect on them? Read the passage over: at the time I
did not take it as seriously as I do now. Well, the great Leonardo
was such a man; at an early age he converted his sexuality into an
urge for knowledge and from then on the inability to finish anything
he undertook became a pattern to which he had to conform in all his
ventures: he was sexually inactive or homosexual. Not so long ago I
came across his image and likeness (without his genius) in a
neurotic ...

Many thanks for your 'family news', in the extended sense as well.
My daughter, who was twenty-three yesterday, is having trouble
again with postoperative inflammation; but at least she is cheerful
and generally in good health. The developments are uncertain. As
for the second, her stay in Karlsbad has not helped her. Both grand-
mothers are shaky. All in all nothing very serious.

My week's work leaves me numb. I would invent the seventh day
if the Lord hadn't done so long ago. Forgive this long letter; writing
it has enabled me to take stock of myself. Except on Sunday

[71] In an unpublished letter to Ferenczi, 4 Nov '09, Jung wrote: 'I am now asking
100 frs for a three-week course.'

afternoon I cannot possibly work for Worcester. Once this unpleasant task is over I want to start working methodically for the
Jahrbuch again. Nothing much can be expected of me on weekday
evenings. Quite against my will I must live like an American: no
time for the libido.

Your good news of your family has given me great pleasure.

With kind regards,

Sincerely yours, FREUD

159J

Dear Professor Freud,   Küsnacht bei Zürich, 8 November 1909
You will, no doubt, have arrived at a fair explanation of my long
silence. It's just that one has so much to do, and I expect this is the
case on your side as well. Many thanks for the long letter. Meanwhile, some more news has cropped up. But back to the past first.

Friedländer: I treated him in the 'grand' or haughty manner and
received him in the circle of my four foreigners. They started talking
in English, and it turned out afterwards that he doesn't understand a
word. Yet he acted so sagely that I never noticed it. Otherwise I was
polite, keeping my distance. Pfister also suffered a visitation from
him, likewise Foerster . . .

One of the reasons why I didn't write for so long is that I was
immersed every evening in the history of symbols, ie in mythology
and archaeology. I have been reading Herodotus and have made
some wonderful finds (eg Book 2, cult at Papremis). Now I am reading the four volumes of old Creuzer, where there is a huge mass of
material. All my delight in archaeology (buried for years) has sprung
into life again. Rich lodes open up for the phylogenetic basis of the
theory of neurosis. Later I want to use some of it for the *Jahrbuch*.
It's a crying shame that already with Herodotus prudery puts forth
its quaint blossoms; on his own admission he covers up a lot of
things 'for reasons of decency'. Where did the Greeks learn that from

so early? I have discovered a capital book in Knight's *Two Essays on the Worship of Priapus*, much better than Inman, who is rather unreliable. If I come to Vienna in the spring, I hope to bring you various ancient novelties.

As a basis for the analysis of the American way of life I am now treating a young American (doctor). Here again the mother-complex looms large (cf the *Mother-Mary cult*). In America the mother is decidedly the dominant member of the family. American culture really is a bottomless abyss; the men have become a flock of sheep and the women play the ravening wolves – within the family circle, of course. I ask myself whether such conditions have ever existed in the world before. I really don't think they have.

With kind regards,

Yours, JUNG

160F

Dear friend,   11 November 1909, Vienna, IX. Berggasse 19
It probably isn't nice of you to keep me waiting 25 days (from October 14 to November 8; I checked because I suspected one of Fliess's 23-day periods, but wrong again) for an answer – as though the promptness and length of my last letter had frightened you away. I don't wish to importune you in the event that you yourself don't feel the need of corresponding at shorter intervals. But I can't help responding to my own rhythm, and the only compromise action I am capable of is not to post the letter I am now writing until Sunday. For I am obliged to reserve Sunday for my American lectures, the first of which is already on the high seas.

As for Forel, I too think we should join. Please tell him so for both of us. Then he may let us know what the purpose of his society is.

Your idea about Bleuler is excellent. We must persuade him to contribute his discussion of principles[72] to the *Jahrbuch* (third half-volume); if you think it advisable, I shall ask him myself, just let me

[72] This article by Bleuler is sometimes called his 'apologia' in this correspondence.

know when. That will oblige him to show special moderation, and besides, it is the only solution compatible with his position as director. There can be no objection to discussion in our own camp; still, it must be constructive. You are quite right, a discussion with Stekel will also be inevitable. He is a slovenly, uncritical fellow who undermines all discipline; I feel the same as you do about him. Unfortunately, he has the best nose of any of us for the secrets of the unconscious. Because he is a perfect swine, whereas we are really decent people who submit only reluctantly to the evidence. I have often contradicted his interpretations and later realized that he was right. Therefore we must keep him and distrust him and learn from him ...

I was delighted to learn that you are going into mythology. A little less loneliness. I can't wait to hear of your discoveries. I ordered Knight in July but haven't received it yet. I hope you will soon come to agree with me that in all likelihood mythology centres on the same nuclear complex as the neuroses. But we are only wretched dilettantes. We are in urgent need of able helpers ...

... Eitingon is the only one I can talk to here; we take walks in the evening and I analyse him just in passing. He is leaving tomorrow.

With kind regards to you and your family,

Yours, FREUD

162J

Küsnacht bei Zürich, 15 November 1909

Pater, peccavi – it is indeed a scandal to have kept you waiting twenty-five days for an answer. From the last paragraph of your letter it is clear why the intervals need to be shorter: you seem to be very isolated in Vienna. Eitingon's company cannot be counted among the highest joys. His vapid intellectualism has something exasperating about it. If I appear to be such a sterile and lazy correspondent it is because I am positively wallowing in people and social life here. I spend much of my time with young Honegger – he is so intelligent and subtle minded. Hardly a day goes by without an exchange of ideas. Thus I fill up my gaps and do not sense the passing of twenty-five days. Well, it is scandalous and shall not happen again. I will arrange matters with Forel at once, and for you too. Bleuler, I hear, has already joined. He is chewing the cud of countless resistances. His main grudge against us is that he is incapable of doing ΨA. He also seems to think that we back up Stekel in every particular. (I am very glad that we are in agreement on St. A dictionary of dream symbols! Good Lord, that's all we needed! Too bad he's usually right.)

Now to better things – mythology. For me there is no longer any doubt what the oldest and most natural myths are trying to say. They speak quite 'naturally' of the nuclear complex of neurosis. A particularly fine example is to be found in Herodotus: at Papremis, during the festival in honour of the mother of Ares (Typhon), there was a great mock battle between two opposing crowds armed with wooden clubs. Many wounded. This was a repetition of a legendary event: Ares, brought up abroad, returns home to his mother in order to *sleep* with her. Her attendants, not recognizing him, refuse him admission. He goes into the town, fetches help, overpowers the attendants and sleeps with his mother. These flagellation scenes are repeated in the Isis cult, in the cult of Cybele, where there is also self-castration, of Atargatis (in Hierapolis), and of Hecate: whipping of youths in Sparta. The dying and resurgent god (Orphic mysteries, Thammuz, Osiris [Dionysus], Adonis, etc) is everywhere phallic. At the Dionysus festival in Egypt the women pulled the phallus up and down on a string: 'the dying and resurgent god'. I am painfully aware of my utter dilettantism and continually fear I am dishing you out banalities. Otherwise I might be able to say more of these things. It was a great comfort to me to learn that the Greeks themselves had long since ceased to understand their own myths and interpreted the life out of them just as our philologists do ...

I was most interested in your news about Oedipus. Of the *dactyls* I know nothing, but have heard of St Cosmas that people kiss his great *toe* and offer up wax phalli *ex voto*. Can you give me sources for the Oedipus myth and the Dactyls? A counterpart of the nunlike Vestal Virgins would be the self-castrated priests of Cybele. What is the origin of the New Testament saying: 'There be eunuchs which have made themselves eunuchs for the kingdom of heaven's sake'? Wasn't self-castration practically unheard of among the Jews? But in neighbouring Edessa self-castration of the Atargatis priests was the rule. In that same place, incidentally, there were 180-foot high 'spires' or minarets in phallic form. Why is the phallus usually represented as winged? (Joke: 'The mere thought lifts it.') Do you know those early mediaeval lead medallions in Paris, on one side the Christian cross, on the other a penis or vulva? And the penis-cross of Sant' Agata de' Goti? (Inaccurate illustration in Inman.) There seem to be indications of early mediaeval phallus worship . . .

With many kind regards,

Yours, JUNG

163F

Dear friend,   21 November 1909, Vienna, IX. Berggasse 19
At last you have realized how Vienna fare must taste to me now that I have been spoiled by my six weeks' absence. Then I need say no more about it . . .

I am delighted with your mythological studies. Much of what you write is quite new to me, eg the mother-lust, the idea that priests emasculated themselves to punish themselves for it. These things cry out for understanding, and as long as the specialists won't help us, we shall have to do it ourselves.

. . . Oedipus, I believe I have told you, means swollen foot, ie erected penis. Quite by accident I recently hit on what I hope is the ultimate secret of foot fetishism. In the foot it has become permissible to worship the long lost and ardently longed-for woman's penis of the primordial age of infancy. Evidently some people search as passionately for this precious object as the pious English do for the ten lost tribes of Israel . . .

Something to remember: the evil eye is an excellent proof of the contention that envy and hostility always lurk behind love. The apotropaea are entirely in our possession, they are always consolations through sexuality; as onanism is in childhood. It has also been explained to me why a chimney sweep is regarded as a good omen: *chimney sweeping* is an action symbolic of coitus, something Breuer certainly never dreamed of. All watch charms – pig, ladder, shoe, chimney sweep, etc – are sexual consolations.

With kind regards to yourself and family,

FREUD

164J

Dear Professor Freud,   Küsnacht bei Zürich, 22 November 1909
You have no doubt received the postcard with the various names. It is from the meeting of Swiss psychiatrists in Zürich. It was a *historic moment*! The meeting was absolutely packed. Three lectures on ΨA were on the programme – Bleuler: Freudian Symptoms in Dem. praec.; Frank: Psychoanalytical Treatment of Depressive States; Maeder: On Paranoids. The whole interest centred on these. The Tübingen, Strassburg, and Heidelberg clinics were officially represented by assistants. Dr Seif of Munich was present, as well as an assistant of Pick's in Prague, two directors of sanatoria from Würtemberg, one from the Bergstrasse, etc. The opposition was headed by a medical friend of Foerster's, who only emitted a miserable squeak. Forel was on our side, although he fought against infantile sexuality, but mildly. Your (that is, our) cause is *winning all along the line*, so that we had the last word, in fact we're on top of the world. I was even invited by German colleagues to give a holiday course on ΨA. This is something I shall have to think about.

So – that was the first prank. Monakow and company lay on the floor, totally isolated. Now for once they can savour the joys of being in the minority. One circumstance came to my aid, and I exploited it. Forel first attacked Monakow because of the rival founding of the neurologists' society. I resolutely took Forel's part, thereby winning him over so that his subsequent opposition was very mild. This political coup made a deep impression, so deep that the opposition no longer dared to show its face. The whole discussion, which was very lively, centred exclusively on ΨA.

The psychiatrists' society is ours. The rival neurologists' society is a defensive and offensive alliance between Monakow and Dubois. The (unwritten) programme of the two societies will be: Freud and Antifreud.

Now it's Germany's turn.

With many kind regards,

Yours, JUNG

166F

Dear friend,   2 December 1909, Vienna, IX. Berggasse 19
That revenge has anything to do with my failure to answer your victory letter before now is something which I should naturally deny and you affirm – in accordance with the customary ΨA sharing of roles. But you will admit that work, fatigue and America add up to an excellent rationalization. The truth is that I am rather low in health and spirits, but I am hoping for an improvement, for I was able at the end of the month to reduce my work schedule by two hours and the fourth of the Worcester lectures was sent off the day before yesterday. Since you have already promised to treat me better, my complaints can no longer be construed as blackmail . . .

. . . It will interest you to know that we have become worthy of the Dürerbund. In their Christmas catalogue my books, especially those in the *Applied Psychology Papers*, are reviewed at length and warmly recommended, though to be sure in so turgid and unintelligible a style that my little Sophie exclaimed: it's good you know what you want, you'd never find out from reading that. All the same, Heller says recognition from Dürerbund betokens significant progress in the good opinion of the German people.

So Germany is coming along! Aren't we (justifiably) childish to get so much pleasure out of every least bit of recognition, when in reality it matters so little and our ultimate conquest of the world still lies so far ahead?

With kind regards to you and your wife,

Sincerely yours, FREUD

170J

Dear Professor Freud,   Küsnacht bei Zürich, 25 December 1909
My attempt at criticism, though it looked like an attack, was actually a defence, which is why I apparently had to tilt at the '*omnipotence* of thoughts'. Of course the term is dead right as well as elegantly concise and trenchant, for that's how it is, especially in D. pr. where new fundamentals are constantly being uncovered by it. All this has shaken me very much, in particular my faith in my own capacities. But most of all I was struck by your remark that you longed for archaeologists, philologists, etc. By this, I told myself, you probably meant that I was unfit for such work. However, it is in precisely these fields that I now have a passionate interest, as before only in Dem. pr. And I have the most marvellous visions, glimpses of far ranging interconnections which I am at present incapable of grasping, for the subject really is too big and I hate impotent bungling. Who then is to do this work? Surely it must be someone who knows the psyche and has the passion for it. D. pr. will not be the loser. Honegger, who has already introduced himself to you, is now working with me with *great* understanding, and I shall entrust to him everything I know so that something good may come of it. It has become quite clear to me that we shall not solve the ultimate secrets of neurosis and psychosis without mythology and the history of civilization, for *embryology* goes hand in hand with *comparative anatomy*, and without the latter the former is but a freak of nature whose depths remain uncomprehended. It is a hard lot to have to work alongside the father creator. Hence my attacks on 'clinical terminology'.

31 Dec. The Christmas holidays have eaten up all my time, so I am only now in a position to continue my letter. I am turning over and over in my mind the problem of antiquity. It's a hard nut! Without doubt there's a lot of infantile sexuality in it, but that is not all. Rather it seems to me that antiquity was ravaged by the struggle with *incest*, with which sexual *repression* begins (or is it the other way round?). We must look up the history of family law . . .

With many kind regards and wishes,

As ever, JUNG

171F

Dear friend,   2 January 1910, Vienna, IX. Berggasse 19
My New Year's greetings have been postponed by my waiting for your letter. I didn't want our correspondence to get out of kilter again. Today it has come belatedly and I give you my greetings loudly and officially. They are also addressed to the beautiful house which I hope to see this year. Because this summer we are planning to go somewhere with woods and a lake and a certain altitude in French Switzerland, where some of the mountain resorts are warmer than Austria, and of course we shall make a long stopover in Zürich on the way. That is our plan at least. May the powers of fate not frustrate it!

Your letter gave me special pleasure in these lovely quiet holidays. It is gratifying in every way. You feel the need of discussing certain fundamental problems with me; that is wonderful. And you promise me your visit for next spring. Will the congress interfere with that? No, of course not. My wife thought you would come to Vienna first and then take me with you to Nuremberg, or come back to Vienna with me from there. I don't know what you have in mind, but I think it could be combined with the congress; my minimum expectation is that after the congress we should spend a day strictly alone in Nuremberg or somewhere else, and share our problems and budding projects. I should very much like you to accept the Easter date, but I have the following objection to Tuesday: it would mean travelling on Easter Monday, which would not suit some of us. One must really knock off for three days in order to be rested for one day's work, and also to have some time for personal relationships . . .

Your displeasure at my longing for an army of philosophical collaborators is music to my ears. I am delighted that you yourself take this interest so seriously, that you yourself wish to be this army; I could have dreamed of nothing better but simply did not suspect that mythology and archaeology had taken such a powerful hold on you. But I must have hoped as much, for since October something has diverted me from working in those fields, though I have never for a moment doubted their importance for our purposes. I have an excellent opinion of Honegger, who probably offers the best prospects. But may I confide a source of misgiving? I don't think it would be a good idea to plunge directly into the general problem of ancient mythology; it strikes me as preferable to approach it in a series of detailed studies. Perhaps you have had the same idea. What I have valued in the specialists was simply the sheer knowledge that is so hard for us to acquire. But that after all is not an impossible task. I have reread your detailed remarks with close attention; I know the other fellow has an easier time of it if one does not interfere with him . . .

Of my own flashes of inspiration – I am quite well again and correspondingly unproductive – I can confide only one. It has occurred to me that the ultimate basis of man's need for religion is *infantile helplessness*, which is so much greater in man than in animals. After infancy he cannot conceive of a world without parents and makes for himself a just God and a kindly nature, the two worst anthropomorphic falsifications he could have imagined. But all that is very banal . . .

This is my prelude to the chat which I am so looking forward to, but which is evidently not to take place for quite some time. I assure you that I shall be briefer in later phases of this new year. Kind regards to you and your wife. On this occasion I cannot repress the hope that the year 1910 holds something as pleasant as our American trip in store for our relationship.

Yours cordially, FREUD

173J

Dear Professor Freud,   Küsnacht bei Zürich, 10 January 1910
Many thanks for your heartening letter. Mythology certainly has me
in its grip. I bring to it a good deal of archaeological interest from my
early days. I don't want to say too much now but would rather wait
for it to ripen. I have no idea what will come out. But I quite agree
with you that this whole field must first be divided up for monograph
treatment, which shouldn't be too difficult as there is any amount of
typical material that crops up now here, now there in variant form.
So that's no problem. The main *impedimentum* is lack of knowledge,
which I am trying to remedy by diligent reading...

It is with the greatest joy that I hear you will be coming to Switzerland in the summer. *When* will it be? My wife is looking forward to
the company as eagerly as I. Your suggestion that I come to Vienna
before or after Nuremberg has fallen upon equally fertile ground.
Whether it will be before or after I don't yet know, because my
military service is giving me a lot of bother this year – I must count
on seven weeks or more. I shall know my sentence in a few days and
will then give you a definite date...

Many kind greetings,

Most sincerely yours, JUNG

174F

Dear friend,   13 January 1910, Vienna, IX. Berggasse 19
I am answering you without delay in the interest of the congress...

And now I have a suggestion: a good subject for your talk would
be our trip to America and the situation of psychoanalysis over
there. That will impress and encourage our people. I have been con-
templating a paper on the prospects for ΨAtical therapy; I could
weave in a discussion of technique. If you insist on case material, I
shall probably have to fall back on my little piece on the love life of

men, which may be too specialized and besides our people here are familiar with it. At the moment I have nothing else. All the same, I do think our ΨAtical flag ought to be raised over the territory of normal love life, which is after all very close to us; maybe I'll contribute the few pages to the *Jahrbuch* . . .

I should like to bring up an idea of mine that has not yet fully ripened: couldn't our supporters affiliate with a larger group working for a practical ideal? An International Fraternity for Ethics and Culture is being organized in pursuit of such ideals. The guiding spirit is a Bern apothecary by the name of Knapp, who has been to see me. Mightn't it be a good idea for us to join as a group? I want no dealings with the anti-alcohol organization. I have asked Knapp to get in touch with you. Forel is a leading light in the fraternity.

I feel confident that the three months between now and the congress will bring us many gratifying developments.

Kindest regards, FREUD

175J

Dear Professor Freud,　　　Küsnacht bei Zürich, 30 January 1910
At last I can settle down to write to you at leisure . . . During the time when I didn't write to you I was plagued by complexes, and I detest wailing letters. This time it was not I who was duped by the devil but my wife, who lent an ear to the evil spirit and staged a number of jealous scenes, groundlessly. At first my objectivity got out of joint (rule one of psychoanalysis: principles of Freudian psychology apply to everyone except the analyser) but afterwards snapped back again, whereupon my wife also straightened herself out brilliantly. Analysis of one's spouse is one of the more difficult things unless mutual freedom is assured. The prerequisite for a good marriage, it seems to me, is the licence to be unfaithful. I in my turn have learnt a great deal. The main point always comes last: my wife is pregnant again, by design and after mature reflection. In spite of tempestuous complexes my enthusiasm for work is riding high. The new *Jahrbuch*

is practically finished and should go to the printer early in February. It is solid and many sided . . .

I'm afraid I still haven't heard from the army authorities when I have to go on my military exercises, so I can't yet say whether I shall be free before or after Nuremberg.

Your suggestion that I should talk about America at Nuremberg is beginning to simmer. I think I shall do so in the form of a report on the development of the movement in general.

Many kind greetings,

Yours, JUNG

177F

Dear friend,   2 February 1910, Vienna, IX. Berggasse 19
Although experience has taught me to harden myself against the anticipation of your letters, the one that came yesterday gave me great pleasure and even consoled me with its varied contents. Living so far apart, we are bound to have experiences of all sorts that we cannot share. You are living on the high seas, while I often can't help thinking of our little Dalmatian islands where a ship puts in every second Monday . . .

I should have thought it quite impossible to analyse one's own wife. Little Hans's father has proved to me that it can be done. In such analysis, however, it seems just too difficult to observe the technical rule whose importance I have lately begun to suspect: 'Surmount counter-transference.'

I trust you will bring Honegger to Nuremburg with you, he has made a splendid impression on me too by an attempt to analyse me. Perhaps he will bring us Stekel's sensitivity in the interpretation of the unconscious without Stekel's brutality and uncritical approach . . .

I shall gladly go over the list. Here they will certainly be asking me whether and on what conditions 'guests' are desirable.

Kind regards to you and your growing family,

Sincerely yours, FREUD

178J

Dear Professor Freud,   Küsnacht–Zürich, 11 February 1910

I am a lazy correspondent. But this time I have (as always) excellent excuses. Preparing the *Jahrbuch* has taken me an incredible amount of time, as I had to work mightily with the blue pencil. The bulk of the manuscripts goes off today. It will be an impressive affair . . .

Meanwhile, I too have received an invitation from the apothecary Knapp in Bern to join the I.F. I have asked for time to think about it and have promised to submit the invitation to the Nuremberg congress. Knapp wanted to have me also for lectures. The prospect appals me. I am so thoroughly convinced that I would have to read myself the longest ethical lectures that I cannot muster a grain of courage to promote ethics in public, let alone from the psychoanalytical standpoint! At present I am sitting so precariously on the fence between the Dionysian and the Apollinian that I wonder whether it might not be worthwhile to reintroduce a few of the older cultural stupidities such as the monasteries. That is, I really don't know which is the lesser evil. Do you think this fraternity could have any practical use? Isn't it one of Forel's coalitions against stupidity and evil, and must we not love evil if we are to break away from the obsession with virtue that makes us sick and forbids us the joys of life? If a coalition is to have any ethical significance it should never be an artificial one but must be nourished by the deep instincts of the race. Somewhat like Christian Science, Islam, Buddhism. Religion can be replaced only by religion. Is there perchance a new saviour in the I.F.? What sort of new myth does it hand out for us to live by? Only the wise are ethical from sheer intellectual presumption, the rest of us need the eternal truth of myth.

You will see from this string of associations that the problem does not leave me simply apathetic and cold. The ethical problem of sexual freedom really is enormous and worth the sweat of all noble souls. But two thousand years of Christianity can only be replaced by something equivalent. An ethical fraternity, with its mythical Nothing, not infused by any archaic-infantile driving force, is a pure vacuum and can never evoke in man the slightest trace of that age-old animal power which drives the migrating bird across the sea and without which no irresistible mass movement can come into being. I imagine a far finer and more comprehensive task for ΨA than alliance with an ethical fraternity. I think we must give it time to infiltrate into people from many centres to revivify among intellectuals a feeling for symbol and myth, ever so gently to transform Christ back into the soothsaying god of the vine, which he was, and in this way absorb those ecstatic instinctual forces of Christianity for the *one* purpose of making the cult and the sacred myth what they once were – a drunken feast of joy where man regained the ethos and holiness of an animal. That was the beauty and purpose of classical religion, which from God knows what temporary biological need has turned into a Misery Institute. Yet what infinite rapture and wantonness lie dormant in our religion, waiting to be led back to their true destination! A genuine and proper ethical development cannot abandon Christianity but must grow up within it, must bring to fruition its hymn of love, the agony and ecstasy over the dying and resurgent god, the mystic power of the wine, the awesome anthropophagy of the Last Supper – only *this* ethical development can serve the vital forces of religion. But a syndicate of interests dies out after ten years.

ΨA makes me 'proud and discontent', I don't want to attach it to Forel, that hair-shirted John of the Locusts, but would like to affiliate it with everything that was ever dynamic and alive. One can only let this kind of thing grow. To be practical: I shall submit this crucial question for ΨA to the Nuremberg congress. I have abreacted enough for today – my heart was bursting with it. Please don't mind all this storming.

With many kind regards,

Most sincerely yours, JUNG

179F

Dear friend,   13 February 1910, Vienna, IX. Berggasse 19
Yes, in you the tempest rages; it comes to me as distant thunder. And though I ought to treat you diplomatically and humour your obvious distaste for writing with an artificial delay in answering, I am unable to restrain my own precipitate reactions. I can only offer the excuse of practical necessity.

Please tell Knapp that we do not wish to submit the question of the fraternity to our congress just yet, that there are too few of us, that we ourselves are not yet organized, which is true. But you mustn't regard me as the founder of a religion. My intentions are not so far reaching. Considerations of a purely practical, or if you will diplomatic nature led me to make this attempt (which at heart I have already abandoned). I suspect that Knapp is a good man, that ΨA would bring him liberation, and I thought: if we join the fraternity while it is *in statu nascendi*, we shall be able to draw the moralists to ΨA rather than let the Ψ-analysts be turned into moralists. Perhaps the idea was too diplomatic. Glad to abandon it. I was attracted by the practical, aggressive and protective aspect of the programme, the undertaking to combat the authority of State and Church directly where they commit palpable injustice, and so to arm ourselves against the great future adversaries of ΨA with the help of larger numbers and methods other than those of scientific work. I am not thinking of a substitute for religion; this need must be sublimated. I did not expect the fraternity to become a religious organization any more than I would expect a volunteer fire department to do so! ...

I send you my kind regards. I am looking forward to the best of news of you and your family.

Sincerely yours, FREUD

181J

Dear Professor Freud,   Küsnacht/Zürich, 2 March 1910

I was very perturbed by your letter[73] – all sorts of misunderstandings seem to be in the air. How could you have been so mistaken in me? I don't follow. I can't say any more about it now, because writing is a bad business and all too often one misses the right note . . .

Recently I received a letter from Isserlin in Munich asking whether he might attend our meeting. He disagreed with us, but, etc . . . As you know, the man is a member of the blackest Munich clique and slanders us for all he is worth. I beg you to let me know *by return* whether we should allow such vermin to come to N. Myself, I'd rather not have the bastard around, he might spoil one's appetite. But our *splendid isolation* must come to an end one day . . .

Much looking forward to seeing you again. Many kind regards,

Your not in the least vacillating, JUNG

182F

Dear friend,   6 March 1910, Vienna, IX. Berggasse 19

Believe me, there are no further misunderstandings between us, nor do I regard you as 'vacillating'. I am neither so forgetful nor so touchy, and I know how closely we are united by personal sympathy and by pulling on the same cart. I am merely irritated now and then – I may say that much, I trust – that you have not yet disposed of the resistances arising from your father complex, and consequently limit our correspondence so much more than you would otherwise. Just rest easy, dear son Alexander, I will leave you more to conquer than I myself have managed, all psychiatry and the approval of the civilized world, which regards me as a savage! That ought to lighten your heart . . .

. . . I am worried about the immediate future of my daughter who

73 (This letter is missing.)

must undergo another operation. I am eagerly awaiting news of your timetable, so as to know whether we shall have any time together in addition to the few hours at the congress.

Kindest regards, FREUD

183J

Grand Hotel Terminus, Rue St Lazare
Dear Professor Freud,   Paris, le 9 Mars 1910
Now don't get cross with me for my pranks! You will already have heard from my wife that I am on my way to America. *I have arranged everything so as to be back in time for Nuremberg.* Everything else is so arranged that it will function automatically, ie with the help of my wife and the assistance of Honegger, to whom I have entrusted my patients.

I had a severe conflict of duties to overcome before I could make up my mind to travel. But the journey *had* to be made, and it can be because I shall be back in Cherbourg on the afternoon of March 28th, having spent six to seven days in America, enough for a trip to Chicago and a few other things besides. It will also be good for my mental health ...

I send you a hearty farewell and please forgive me all my misdemeanours.

Most sincerely yours, JUNG

From Emma Jung
Dear Professor Freud,   Küsnacht, 16 March 1910
Here at last you have the programme for Nuremberg, from which you will see that your lecture comes first after all. My husband had never said anything about his speaking on the 1st day, and as the title is only 'Report on America' it will not upset the plan. I also think he will be glad not to have to speak first, as he may be arriving in Nuremberg at five in the morning and will probably be rather tired.

Many thanks for your kind letter and offer of help which I shall gladly accept if anything more difficult happens. I can set your mind at rest by telling you that a young friend and pupil of my husband's, Dr Honegger, is deputizing with the patients and looking after the Nuremberg business with me, otherwise I would be rather nervous about everything turning out all right.

Today I am expecting news of my husband's safe arrival in New York; I do hope it comes soon. Incidentally, America no longer has the same attraction for him as before, and this has taken a stone from my heart. It is just enough to satisfy the desire for travel and adventure, but no more than that.

I was very sorry to hear that Frau Hollitscher has had to undergo another operation; I hope she will soon recover and that it will be a lasting success this time. Please give her my warmest greetings and wishes.

I send greetings to you and all your dear ones.

EMMA JUNG

Dr Honegger sends best regards.

The Nuremberg Congress

The Second International Psychoanalytic Congress was held at Nuremberg on 30–31 March 1910. Freud's anxiety over Jung's prior absence in America is evident in what he wrote Pfister 17 Mar 1910: 'I still have not got over your not coming to Nuremberg. Bleuler is not coming either, and Jung is in America, so that I am trembling about his return. What will happen if my Zurichers desert me?' After the congress, however, Freud wrote Ferenczi (3 Apr): 'There is no doubt that it was a great success.'

The chief accomplishment of the meeting was the founding of the International Psychoanalytic Association (Internationale Psychoanalytische Vereinigung), of which Jung was elected president and Riklin secretary; its headquarters were at the place of residence of its president ie then Zürich.

184J

Dear Professor Freud,　　　　　　Küsnacht–Zürich, 6 April 1910
This time I'm settling down quickly to a letter so as not to give the
devil a chance to conduct his well known time-extending experiments. I have reluctantly let Honegger go to his sanatorium in Territet; now my libido is thrashing around for a suitable object. Riklin
will in some measure replace the temporary loss. Nuremberg did him
a lot of good and he is coming much closer to me than before. All the
same I won't let go of Honegger, and will do everything in my power
to carry out this plan . . .

As a perseveration from America I am still reading the interesting
book by Maurice Low, *The American People, A Study in National
Psychology.* He holds the climate largely responsible for the frequency of neurosis in America. There must be something in it, for it
is really too weird that the Indians were unable to populate that
fertile country more densely. Low thinks the colossal differences of
temperature between summer and winter are to blame. Perhaps a
harshly continental climate really is ill suited to a race sprung from
the sea. 'Something is wrong,' as Low says.

When I have fulfilled this duty (the reading of this book) I shall
return to the overflowing delights of mythology, which I always reserve as dessert for the evening.

I found wife, children, and house in good shape, and work
aplenty.

I forget to ask whether Deuticke has inquired about the separate
publication of my child analysis. What do you think? I'd welcome it
myself, but shall take account of business interests and your advice.

Kind regards, JUNG

185F

Dear friend,   12 April 1910, Vienna, IX. Berggasse 19
... I was sorry to hear that you have let Honegger go off. I hope it
will not be for long and that your self-confidence will soon catch up
with your new position; that will obviate a number of delicate situations. In less than a year, I believe, the world will show you who you
are, and a wise man prepares for all eventualities. At last Wednesday's meeting of our society I ceded the presidency to Adler.
They all behaved very affectionately, so I promised to stay on as
chairman of the scientific sessions. They are very much shaken, and
for the present I am satisfied with the outcome of my statesmanship.
Fair competition between Vienna and Zürich can only benefit the
cause. The Viennese have no manners, but they know a good deal
and can still do good work for the movement.

... I have returned rather depressed from our lovely Diet of Nuremberg. Analysis [of my depression] leads far afield to the distress
which the state of my daughter's health causes me – I have been
trying in vain to replace her. You will discern the note of resignation
in *Leonardo*.

Jones writes excellent letters. Couldn't you prod him into setting
up groups in Boston and New York? Isserlin seems almost to be
having lucid moments, if he speaks and thinks as he writes. I send
you kind regards. I shall always be glad to hear from you.

Sincerely yours, FREUD

186J

Dear Professor Freud,   Küsnacht/Zürich, 17 April 1910
I too have now read Isserlin's article and can only see that the fellow
has stooped even lower than before. At the back of it all is still the
same twisted mind, but he has now done a bit of reading and is
worried by the criticism of his associates and by our success. As late

as last autumn, in the holiday course in Munich, he compared the Freudian school with Titania's obsessed lover who woke up one day with an ass's head on him – something his own demon has obviously whispered in his ear. We won't have to wait long for his conversion. His unconscious at last knows this much, that Puck has already 'miracled' the ass's head on to Biehen and Oppenheim. And then all the equivocations! *Your* discovery of repression is nothing, but *his* conception of it suddenly amounts to something. The psychoanalytic method is not worth a button, yet he uses it to clear up the complexes of his patients. When all's said and done, the whole of Herr Isserlin lives and breathes only because of what you and I have discovered, yet he reviles us, not as impudently and loudly as before, but in private and therefore all the more dirtily, and still he can't help trying to cadge an invitation to Nuremberg. What's more he has put into my mouth a piece of nonsense I never said . . .

. . . At present I am pursuing my mythological dreams with almost auto-erotic pleasure, dropping only meagre hints to my friends. I also notice that my whole desire for publication is concentrated on the *Jahrbuch*, which seems to soak up all my libido. Probably it must be so. I often feel I am wandering alone through a strange country, seeing wonderful things that no one has seen before and no one needs to see. It was like that when the psychology of Dementia praecox dawned upon me. Only, I don't yet know what will come of it. I must just let myself be carried along, trusting to God that in the end I shall make a landfall somewhere.

Still no improvement in your daughter's health? Such a confounded twist of fortune – I too would find it hard to bear.

With kind regards and wishes,

Yours sincerely, JUNG

Apropos of Deuticke: I stand firmly by
the bi-annual publication of the *Jahrbuch*.

189J

Dear Professor Freud,

At last I can report to you after the uproar last week. In a private talk beforehand, Bleuler, very huffy and irritable, gave me a flat refusal and expressly declared that he would not join the society – he would dissociate himself from it altogether. Reasons: its aim was too biased, it took too narrow a view of the problems, it was too exclusive, you had slighted Frank in Nuremberg and thereby ostracized him, one didn't want to sit down with everybody (a dig at Stekel). He simply would not join, that was the long and short of it. I told him what the consequences would be, but it was no good. Yesterday we had our constituent assembly, which Frank also attended. The same opposition was shown with the same hollow resistances; another 'reason' they gave was that they didn't want to commit themselves to a confession of faith, etc. In the course of the discussion it became clear that Frank is the grey eminence who has been working on Bleuler. I let the discussion go on until both Bleuler and Frank were properly cornered and were forced to admit that they just didn't want to join. I had so arranged matters that the local group had already constituted itself with twelve members before the meeting took place, which faced them with a *fait accompli*. The overwhelming majority are on our side. Taking your Nuremberg tactics as a model, I postponed the final decision until the next meeting in the hope that Bleuler's resistances will have melted by then. As the evening wore on he became noticeably milder and I almost venture to hope he will come along with us ...

As a matter of fact his whole opposition is a revenge for my resignation from the abstinence societies. (Hence his charge of exclusiveness, narrowness, and bias.) ...

Otherwise all's well. Nuremberg has produced happy results for us all.

Kind regards, JUNG

190F

Dear friend,   2 May 1910, Vienna, IX. Berggasse 19
Your idea of tracing Bleuler's objections back to the abstinence societies is both clever and plausible. Towards them such an attitude is perfectly reasonable, towards our International it is an absurdity. We can't very well inscribe such things as providing freezing schoolchildren with warm clothing on our banners side by side with the furtherance of ΨA. One would be reminded of certain hotel signs: Hotel England and Red Cock. But it's amusing how such an incident brings out the latent resistances in our so-called supporters. In this we are at a great advantage though; when a man stands firm as a rock, all the tottering, wavering souls end by clinging to him for support. Which is just what will happen now, and undoubtedly Bleuler, after setting too high a price on himself, will find out how unpleasant it is to fall between two stools . . .

. . . From Löwenfeld two of our nasty mongrel's accomplishments, also very funny. Of course I shouldn't be letting them out of my hands, but I am counting on you to send them right back, so I can promptly cheer the rightful owner's heart with them.

On the scientific side, just an oddity. I have two patients with nuclear complexes involving their witnessing acts of infidelity on the part of their mothers (the one historical, the other perhaps a mere fantasy). They both tell me about it the same day and preface their story with dreams about *wood*. In one a building supported by wooden posts collapses, in the other the woman is represented *directly* by old wood, ie antique furniture. Now I am aware that boards mean a woman, also cupboards, but I never heard of any close connections between wood and the mother complex. It occurs to me though that wood in Spanish is *madera* = matter (hence the Portuguese name of the island of Madeira) and undoubtedly *mater* lies at the root of *materia* (matter). Force and matter would then be father and mother. One more of our dear parents' disguises.

Things are quite lively in Vienna: I am being treated very tenderly. The two editors have agreed to discuss each number of the

Zentralblatt with me in advance, and I am to have full veto power. The matter of a publisher is not yet settled. Deuticke is reluctant, he wants to wait for the outcome of our negotiations with Bergmann. If nothing comes of them, I'm pretty sure he will be willing. ΨA has been selling well and that mellows him. The *Jahrbuch* is disgracefully late, he puts the blame on the printers. Too bad. A new volume always encourages our friends and annoys our enemies; one would come in very handy right now ...

My daughter's health is definitely a little better; I don't dare expect any more. One becomes so anxious and resigned in old age!

A sign of the times: I have received a letter to the effect that Geheimrat Ostwald[74] would be pleased to have an article from my pen for the *Annalen der Naturphilosophie*. If I were more ambitious, I would already have consented and would know what to write. But I am far from having made up my mind.

I hope you are safely back in your own house, to whose inhabitants I send my kind regards.

Yours ever, FREUD

191J

Dear Professor Freud,   Küsnacht–Zürich, 5 May 1910

Enclosed are the choice documents of modern times: Germany and America! The contortions of the latter are priceless. The so-called freedom of research in the land of the free has indeed been well guarded – the very word 'sexual' is taboo. There's nothing more to be said about that liar and clown Friedländer except that it was a thousand pities Löwenfeld mentioned him at all. He won't do him the same honour a second time, I hope.

This evening I shall have a talk about the society with Dr Maier, my successor with Bleuler. The latest proposition is: out of gratitude for their friendliness and helpfulness towards us, we should hold our

[74] Wilhelm Ostwald, German philosopher and scientist; Nobel Prize for chemistry 1909.

meetings jointly with them, ie present them everything on a silver salver, at no risk to themselves and with no demands upon their backbone. Their naïveté is so staggering that I was dumbfounded. These good people are imitating the neurotic evasions of alcoholics which they themselves pillory so relentlessly. The general wail about coercion is thoroughly understandable if one has ever been present while Bleuler was interrogating an alcoholic. The decision is to be next week. After that no quarter will be given. Let Bleuler and Frank go ahead and found a society together. It will doubtless produce marvellous results for ΨA...

Best regards, JUNG

193J

Dear Professor Freud,   Küsnacht–Zürich, 24 May 1910
Now I have had to get in arrears myself to keep the parallelism going. When you failed to answer me for so long it occurred to me to ask you what was wrong. But I consoled myself with the thought that you must have had good reasons for not writing. I hope your influenza is better and is no longer impeding your strenuous work. I also hope you have good news of your daughter. Here all is well internally, but war rages on the frontier – war with Bleuler, who has refused to join our society. That is why everything has been held up so idiotically ...

On Whitmonday I spoke on 'symbolism' at the Meeting of Swiss Psychiatrists in Herisau, mythological stuff that aroused great applause. Our adversaries have given up the fight, except in the hick papers; officially not one of them has anything to say. Only Bleuler has taken it into his head to carp at the notion of verbal and non-verbal thinking, without advancing anything positive. I shall have the lecture copied, just as it is, and send it to you for an opinion with all its present imperfections ...

I have a great desire to attend the congress in Baden-Baden next Sunday, where Hoche is speaking on 'An Epidemic of Insanity among Doctors'. I am eager to hear this historic outpouring for myself. How delightful to be publicly sneered at as insane! I scarcely think the epidemic is raging anywhere except among us ...

I have got into a tight corner again and am no longer master of my own time. I need help badly, no doubt of that. Honegger's fiancée is doing valuable work as my secretary. I judged her much too unfavourably, she is an excellent worker. Honegger wins all hearts. I think he won't lack for success.

Many kind regards,

Yours very sincerely, JUNG

194F

Dear friend,   26 May 1910, Vienna, IX. Berggasse 19

I was delighted to hear that I shall soon have an opportunity to read another fine piece by you. I won't be quite so busy in June and reading it will be pure joy, especially as I am counting on your formulation to clarify certain vague ideas of my own.

The difficulties in Zürich are of course a product of all-too-human jealousy, hence indirect confirmation of your merit, which had hitherto been hidden from view ... Our main tactic must be not to let Bleuler and his following notice that their secession troubles us in any way. Then they will come to us one by one. For tactical reasons we must therefore found the international association and issue a bulletin as soon as possible. Zürich will not be able to cut much of a figure at first, but don't let that trouble you; don't make concessions with a view to concealing your internal conflicts from our adversaries. ΨAtic candour! There will be an opportunity for revenge, which tastes very good cold. For the present you will be paying the price for the help you once received from Bleuler; it could not have been had for nothing any more than the help I received from Breuer ...

Your idea of attending Hoche's lecture is delightful – I envy you your sense of humour. But are you sure that he has us in mind? If so, it will be splendid publicity. If not, you will be dreadfully bored.

Still another sign of the times. Geheimrat Ostwald and the *Wiener Neue Presse* have asked me for articles. I put the former off, the latter I turned down because I must be especially careful in Vienna.

My daughter is much better. I count fifty days until the holidays. From 14 July to 1 August we shall very probably be in Bistrai near Bielitz, staying with our colleague Jekels.[75]

I am glad things are looking up with Honegger.

With many thanks for your news and an avowal of ardent desire for more.

With kind regards,

Yours FREUD

195F

Dear friend,   30 May 1910, Vienna, IX. Berggasse 19
On the 28th something amusing happened. I must tell you about it. I was in a good humour because Deuticke had told me he was planning to bring out a *third* edition of *The Interpretation of Dreams* next autumn (after one year!) and that the first volume of the *Papers on the Theory of the Neuroses* was soon to be reprinted. At that point a Hofrat Schottländer of Frankfurt phoned to ask me when he might see me for a talk. I asked him to come at nine for coffee. At nine o'clock a card was brought in. On it I read: Hofrat *Fried*länder, Hohe Mark bei Frankfurt am Main. I stood there dumbfounded and had the little man shown in. He denied having misstated his name and pointed out that it is very easy to misunderstand over the phone, but he showed rather too little emotion, he didn't seem surprised or indignant enough. I was certain that he had said Schott, but what could I do? So there was our great enemy. I quickly pulled myself together and hit on an excellent tactic. I'll come to that. But first about the man. He had hardly sat down when he began denouncing. First Ferenczi for having said in his paper on introjection that all our

75 Ludwig Jekels, Vienna-educated Polish psychiatrist, at a sanatorium in Silesia, now Poland.

methods of therapy – electricity, massage, water, etc – owed their effect purely to suggestion, ie transference, when in reality their success in rheumatism etc was unquestionable. I picked up the *Jahrbuch* and showed the demon that F. had spoken exclusively of the treatment of psychoneuroses. Beelzebub pulled in his horns, emitted his well known stench, and went on denouncing. First someone not unknown to you whom he had called on in Zürich; he even remarked (how right he was!) on this person's restraint in not throwing him out ...

The conversation began to amuse me more and more. As I've told you, I developed an excellent technique. Slipping into the father role he was determined to force on me (Pfister was perfectly right), I affected hearty good humour and took advantage of the atmosphere and situation to make the most insulting remarks, which produced exactly the desired effect. He whined and whimpered, but he was helpless against my Ψ-analytic frankness. I told him that he knew nothing of the analytic technique, which accounted for his negative results, that his methods were those of 1895 and that he hadn't learned a thing since that date because he was too well off to bother, what a shame it was that there was no one in his vicinity who might teach him something, that his conversion would make an enormous impression in Germany, that he was essentially a brute, a retarded guttersnipe (this in more polite language, to be sure), that his friendliness and obsequiousness were pure pretence, that I myself had passed the word around not to answer him, because obviously he was itching for attention, etc.

I was having a fiendishly good time, I couldn't get enough. I kept him there until one in the morning. I've forgotten the choicest details, anyway they would take too long to tell ...

To think we have to trouble our heads over such riffraff!

It gives me great satisfaction to reflect that we after all are different.

With kind regards,

Yours, FREUD

Hoche seems indeed to have us in mind if Karlchen Schottländer hasn't been lying again.

196J

1003 Seestrasse, Küsnacht–Zürich,
2 June 1910

Dear Professor Freud,

I was amazed by your news. The adventure with 'Schottländer' is marvellous; of course the slimy bastard was lying. I hope you roasted, flayed, and impaled the fellow with such genial ferocity that he got a lasting taste for once of the effectiveness of ΨA. I subscribe to your final judgement with all my heart. Such is the nature of these beasts. Since I could read the filth in him from his face I would have loved to take him by the scruff of the neck. I hope to God you told him all the truths so plainly that even his hen's brain could absorb them. Now we shall see what his next coup will be. Had I been in your shoes I would have softened up his guttersnipe complex with a sound Swiss thrashing.

Hoche did indeed declare us ripe for the madhouse. Stockmayer was there and has told me about it. The lecture fell into the well known pattern: charges of mysticism, sectarianism, arcane jargon, epidemic of hysteria, *dangerousness*, etc. Isolated clapping. Nobody protested. Stockmayer was quite alone and hadn't the gumption . . .

My mythology swirls about inside me, and now and then various significant bits and pieces are thrown up. At the moment the unconscious 'interest-draughts' centre entirely on the inexhaustible depths of Christian symbolism, whose counterpart seems to have been found in the Mithraic mysteries. (Julian the Apostate, for instance, reintroduced them as being the equivalent of Christianity.) . . . Finally he succeeds with the help of Ahura-Mazda. You will soon get the material where all this is described.

Many kind regards,

Most sincerely yours, JUNG

198J

Dear Professor Freud, 17 June 1910

... Please forgive me for the delay in answering. The break with
Bleuler has not left me unscathed. Once again I underestimated my
father complex. Besides that I am working like mad. I just keep alive
in a breathless rush. It's high time I got some help. Unfortunately
Honegger is coming only at the end of next week. Till then I'll have
to let the correspondence pile up unanswered ...

The founding of our group was a painful affair. We have about
fifteen members, several of them foreigners. As yet we haven't got
down to debating the statutes because of the difficulties at the
Burghölzli. But we have elected Binswanger president and my cousin
Dr Ewald Jung secretary – he is coming along very nicely. Now
the hair in the soup: I proposed holding *occasional* public meetings
and then inviting Burghölzli, etc. Binswanger declared he would
accept the vote for president only if all meetings were held in
common with non-members. I put it to the vote and my proposal fell
through. So now we have a society with a few regular members and
an audience of non-members who do nothing but have all the privileges. I don't like it a bit. But what can I do? I suggested asking your
fatherly advice beforehand but this was turned down. So we in
Zürich limp along making a poor show. You won't be happy about
it. Neither shall I.

Leonardo is wonderful. Pfister tells me he has seen the vulture in
the picture. I saw one too, but in a different place: the beak precisely
in the pubic region. One would like to say with Kant: play of chance,
which equals the subtlest lucubrations of reason. I have read *Leonardo* straight through and shall soon come back to it again. The
transition to mythology grows out of this essay from inner necessity,
actually it is the first essay of yours with whose inner development I
felt perfectly in tune from the start. I would like to dwell longer on
these impressions and brood quietly on the thoughts which want to

unroll in long succession. But the present rush that has already gone on for several weeks leaves me no peace.

... Be patient with me – when Honegger is here I shall be able to breathe more freely and cope with my outer obligations a bit more decently.

I think I have already told you that I received the manuscripts safely, with best thanks.

Many kind regards and again a plea for forgiveness,

Most sincerely, JUNG

199F

Dear friend,   19 June 1910, Vienna, IX. Berggasse 19
I am really sorry to hear of all your overwork and irritation and thank you very much for your friendly explanations. You mustn't suppose that I ever 'lose patience' with you; I don't believe these words can apply to our relationship in any way. In all the difficulties that confront us in our work we must stand firmly together, and now and then you must listen to me, your older friend, even when you are disinclined to ...

Naturally I was very much dismayed not to see you take a firm stand in your first official functions. You know how jealous they all are – here and elsewhere – over your privileged position with me (it is the same with Ferenczi; I mean, his closeness to me is equally begrudged), and I think I am justified in feeling that what people say against you as a result is being said against me ...

The goings-on in Zürich strike me as stupid. I am amazed that you could not summon up the authority to forestall a decision which is quite untenable. Two things are involved: to pay ten francs in dues and put one's name on the list. Why on earth should certain people enjoy all the privileges without meeting these obligations? It will discourage the others from meeting them ...

In your place I should never have given in ...

Now to something more agreeable. I was overjoyed at your

interest in *Leonardo* and at your saying that you were coming closer to my way of thinking. I read your essay with pleasure the day it arrived: I have been thinking about it and will write you more soon. I couldn't reread it today because Ferenczi and Brill have been with me all day – a happy occasion. Friends are after all the most precarious acquisitions . . .

I am suffering from a recurrence of the intestinal trouble I picked up in America and am undergoing treatment. They tell me it is plain colitis and that there is nothing wrong with my appendix. But it is not improving very much; I am on a strict diet that is not compatible with travelling and threatens to interfere with my plans for September. I still count twenty-five days until my well earned holidays. I have a great deal to do in the meantime but I feel cheerful and energetic.

With kindest regards to you and your family, whom you haven't mentioned for quite some time.

Yours ever, FREUD

203J

                                        1003 Seestrasse, Küsnacht–Zürich,
Dear Professor Freud,   24 July 1910
This last week I have been working like mad again. But now thank heavens the holidays have come for me too. This evening I am going sailing on Lake Constance. I have had my boat sent on ahead. Meanwhile Honegger will deputize for me in Zürich. My military service is scheduled for August 14–19. I hope to write to you from Lake Constance once I have got my wits together. The *Jahrbuch* should be out soon. What a torment it has been!

I hope you are enjoying your holidays *procul negotiis*. Kindest regards,

Most sincerely yours, JUNG

205F

Noordwijk, 10 August 1910

Dear friend,   Pension Noordzee

Thus far I have respected your holiday, but yesterday you broke the peace, so now I feel free to write. I am sitting here by the most beautiful beach, watching a fabulous sunset, but I miss various things, and I can't think of anything much to do on a flat beach. Besides, I have no little corner to be alone in and collect my thoughts. On the 29th of the month I am supposed – nothing has been settled yet – to board ship at Antwerp for Genoa with Ferenczi; we are planning to spend September in Sicily. Tomorrow the geographically most distant of our friends is expected here in Noordwijk, where a relative of his owns a villa: Jones from Toronto. He has risen a good deal in my affections this past year.

From the outside world I have received all sorts of news, which combine with what you tell me to give me the impression that we are going through a critical period, a negative fluctuation, in the history of ΨA. My suspicion is confirmed by the behaviour of men with instinct and flair like Marcinowski and Strohmayer (who, Stekel writes, does not wish to be named on the title page of the *Zentralblatt*). Maybe I am to blame, but it is easy to find explanations after the event, and the outcome could not have been foreseen. All the same, when I look at the situation objectively, I believe I went ahead too fast. I overestimated the public's understanding of the significance of ΨA, I shouldn't have been in such a hurry about founding the I. A. My impatience to see you in the right place and my chafing under the pressure of my own responsibility also had something to do with it. To tell the truth, we should have done nothing at all. As it is, the first months of your reign, my dear son and successor, have not turned out brilliantly. Sometimes I have the impression that you yourself have not taken your functions seriously enough and have not yet begun to act in a manner appropriate to your new dignity. Probably all this comes from the impatience of old age. Now we must merely keep still for a while, let the unpleasant events take their course, and meanwhile go on with our work. I have high hopes for the new organ; I hope you will show no hostility towards it, but commit yourself and your closest associates to its support. One who wishes to rule must carefully cultivate the art of winning people; I thought you had great talents in that direction ...

My mood and the atmosphere have prevented me from doing any work here. And I am not capable of enjoying the rest. A number of things, eg the paper on the two principles of Ψ functioning, are already tormenting me like a blocked bowel movement. (There is good reason for the metaphor too.) ... I must answer a silly letter of Löwenfeld's – he thinks I am offended by it. Quite mistakenly, I esteem him personally and don't expect him to understand anything. He wrote to me at length about the horror which my *Leonardo* aroused even in persons 'favourably disposed'. But on this score I feel quite easy in my mind, for I myself am very pleased with *Leonardo*, and I know that it has made an excellent impression on the few who are capable of judging it: you, Ferenczi, Abraham, and Pfister ...

As you see, nothing but petty worries and concerns ...

With cordial wishes for a restful end to your vacation.

Yours ever, FREUD

206J

1003 Seestrasse, Küsnacht–Zürich,
Dear Professor Freud,   11 August 1910
I realize now that my debut as regent has turned out less than brilliantly because of the resistances I contracted in Nuremberg to Adler and Stekel. I shall try to do better next time. So far as the Vienna organ is concerned, I have encouraged everyone in my vicinity to collaborate and shall myself contribute to the first number – nothing much as my hands are pretty empty. It was only to be expected that *Leonardo* would meet with opposition since the intellectual freedom of this work far exceeds that of its predecessors. In the

meantime, I have been reading about Leonardo so as to deepen my impression of your work and get down to the bed-rock – you are right on every point. If we can rely on the facts, it can only have been as you say. What the rabble say about it is neither here nor there; the thing is beautifully done and leads to exalted spheres of knowledge. Only simpletons will stumble over the difficulties of detail. It is a grim pleasure to be God knows how many decades ahead of these duffers.

I try to be as amiable with people as I can. But to get any results I would have to be on duty day and night. Hardly is my back turned than they start getting paranoid. This is not my fault, it's the fault of the progress of your ΨA. It is inevitable that a ray of light should break forth from occasional remarks, revealing the rapid advances in knowledge which till now we have enjoyed in silence. Each of these sparks is a threat and an insult in itself. I am well aware of that and am doing my best to keep quiet, but 'Out of the abundance of the heart the mouth speaketh,' though rarely. I heartily agree that we went ahead too fast. Even among the 'favourably disposed' there are far too many who haven't the faintest idea of what ΨA is really about and especially of its historical significance. My ear is now cocked at our adversaries; they are saying some very remarkable things which ought to open our eyes in several ways. All these mutterings about sectarianism, mysticism, arcane jargon, initiation, etc mean something. Even the deep-rooted outrage, the moral indignation can only be aimed at something gripping, that has all the trappings of a religion. Our ideal should also be: 'Let no one enter here who is ignorant of mathematics.' Might this become a phrase, however unexpected, in the development of ΨA? The keen interest of our theologians is suspicious. And finally, ΨA thrives only in a very tight enclave of like minds. Seclusion is like a warm rain. One should therefore barricade this territory against the ambitions of the public for a long time to come. So I am not in the least worried by this period of depression; it is a guarantee of unsullied enjoyment, like a beautiful valley high in the mountains not yet discovered by Thos Cook & Co. Moreover ΨA is too great a truth to be publicly acknowledged as yet. Generously adulterated extracts and thin dilutions of it should first be handed around. Also the necessary proof has not yet been furnished that it wasn't you who discovered ΨA but Plato, Thomas Aquinas and Kant, with Kuno Fischer and Wundt thrown in. Then Hoche will be called to a chair of ΨA in Berlin and Aschaffenburg to one in Munich. Thereupon the Golden Age will dawn. After the first thousand years ΨA will be discovered anew in Paris, whereupon England will take up the opposition for another five hundred years and in the end will have understood nothing.

After this apocalyptic vision I turn back to the present. I have now been home for three days. On the 14th I go on military service until the end of the month. In September my wife will be confined. At the beginning of October (1–14) I am bicycling to Italy (Verona?). If only you were nearer in September I would visit you for a couple of days. But Sicily is too far . . .

I wish you likewise a good and productive holiday,

Most sincerely yours, JUNG

212F

Dear friend,   Rome, 24 September 1910

I am writing to you on a dark, cold, dismally rainy morning that reminds me of our November. This evening we are planning to leave the Eternal City for home. In the meantime you have no doubt become a father; I hope to find the best news of you waiting for me at home.

The trip has been very rich and has supplied several wish-fulfilments that my inner economy has long been in need of. Sicily is the most beautiful part of Italy and has preserved unique fragments of the Greek past, infantile reminiscences that make it possible to infer the nuclear complex. The first week on the island was delightful, the second, because of the continuous scirocco, a hard trial for poor Konrad.[76] Now at last we feel that we have come through it

[76] Freud's name for his body.

all: the scirocco and the threat of cholera and malaria. September is not the right time of year to enjoy the beauty here. My travelling companion is a dear fellow, but dreamy in a disturbing kind of way, and his attitude towards me is infantile. He never stops admiring me, which I don't like, and is probably sharply critical of me in his unconscious when I am taking it easy. He has been too passive and receptive, letting everything be done for him like a woman, and I really haven't got enough homosexuality in me to accept him as one. These trips arouse a great longing for a real woman . . .

Monday, 26 Sept.

Now I am at home and rather tired from the trip and the change of scene. Still, I want to answer your letter and not delay my congratulations on the birth of your third daughter and my kind regards to your wife.

. . . Some hack has devoted a tender article to *Leonardo* in the Berlin *Sturm*, entitled 'Genius Spat Upon'. Otherwise good, serious things showing that the world is taking an interest in us, an article by Putnam[77] which you too must have, a number of the *Lancet*, in which for variety's sake your 'complexes' are attributed to me, etc . . .

I send you my kind regards and an expression of my certainty that nothing can befall our cause as long as the understanding between you and me remains unclouded.

Yours ever, FREUD

214F

Dear friend,　　　　　1 October 1910, Vienna, IX. Berggasse 19
I am delighted at the cheerful tone of your letters and infer from it that mother and child are doing very well, though you have neglected to say so *aloud*. Pleased with everything you say, only in regard to

[77] James Jackson Putnam (1846–1918), professor of neurology at Harvard; met Freud and Jung at the Clark University lectures. Founder and first president of the American Psychoanalytic Association (1911).

Schottländer you do me an injustice. I kept him that time just to tease and punish him, and I only wish you could have been there to see him squirm. Incidentally, his article had already been sent off to America at the time, he mentioned it if I am not mistaken.

In the meantime I have written a long letter to Uncle Bleuler ... not humble and pleading, more on the severe side, but nevertheless inspired by the consideration that he may feel offended at my not having got in touch with him directly. I tried to explain how unjust it is of him to punish us for rejecting Isserlin's inquisitorial presence and to let our opponents, his honoured colleagues, get away with statements like those of Ziehen and Hoche; I expressed my regret that he should renounce his influence on the development of the movement but assured him that we would survive none the less. I pointed out most emphatically that the gulf between him and his German colleagues is in any event unbridgeable, so sprinkling a little pepper on his anal erogenous zone. I expect no good to come of it, but I believe my step was justified and will not create any trouble for you ...

Today I resumed my practice and saw my first batch of nuts again. I must now transmute the nervous energy gained during my holiday into money to fill my depleted purse. It always takes a week or two before they all turn up, and for a while there is enough resilience and alertness left for scientific work. Later on one is content with sheer survival.

With kind regards and special good wishes to the happy mother.

Yours, FREUD

216F

Dear friend,   23 October 1910, Vienna, IX. Berggasse 19
After my own wallowing in nature and antiquity, I can hardly begrudge you your trip, but I am very glad you are within reach again. I have all sorts of things to tell you.

First you will be interested to hear about Bleuler. The nerve-contact I have made with him led to a copious correspondence and I am just now answering one of his letters. It is difficult with him, his arguments are so vague that I can't pin him down; and if I were to point out his secret motives it would only antagonize him. He does nothing but skirmish with indirect statements. He has expressed a desire for an interview. Since he adds that he cannot get away before Easter when the next congress is presumably to be held, I offered to go to Zürich during the Christmas holidays if he holds out some hope of an understanding. My position is that he is no more indispensable than anyone else, but that his loss would be regrettable and would widen the gulf between us and the others. Consequently it is worth a sacrifice to hold him, of what I don't know yet, certainly not of the association which we have been at so much pains to found and which is destined to do great things. There is an enormous disproportion between his objections to our procedure and the conclusions he draws from them. And he fills in the gap with imponderables and unintelligibles. But he seems to court my good opinion, he believes in the cause and doesn't want to break with us. My awareness that we are indebted to him for your beginnings inclines me in his favour. I can only suggest that we wait and see what comes of our correspondence and possible meeting ...

With kind regards to you and your family.

Yours ever, FREUD

217J

1003 Seestrasse, Küsnacht–Zürich,
Dear Professor Freud,   29 October 1910
Yesterday there was a meeting of our society at which the case of Bleuler was discussed. We decided to 'wait and see'. But nothing was decided about the gaggle of assistants that Bleuler trails behind him and with whom he professes his solidarity ...

Further, in Zürich we have the rule that *only holders of academic degrees* can be accepted as members. Students at most as guests and for limited periods only. I say this because I fear that Ferenczi is starting something with that stage director. But I would like our society to be rigorously restricted to men with academic credentials, otherwise it will be a League of Monists. When I have your approval I will lay the matter before the association . . .

Many thanks for sending me your article in the *Zentralblatt*. But surely the journal brings out offprints as well? I don't quite understand what influence I could exert. To do so, I would have to have personal rapport with the editors, which is totally out of the question in Adler's case. Any such influence can only be exerted through you. The most I can do is criticize – Stekel for his own sweet self and his theoretical superficiality, and Adler for the total absence of psychology. It would be most inopportune to say it aloud. And it's not worth while picking on trivia (such as Schwedenborg instead of Swedenborg). The only way to teach these people is to do it better for oneself.

With kind regards,

Most sincerely yours, JUNG

218F

Dear friend,   31 October 1910, Vienna, IX. Berggasse 19
I hope the niggling tone of my last letter hasn't had a lasting effect and that such features are not present in the final image . . .

And now to politics and the right of self-defence! You speak after my own heart. If I had been alone, my tactics would have been to wait for our adversaries to destroy each other. But now we have become a little band, we have assumed responsibilities towards our supporters, we have a cause to defend before the public. And so we must do violence to our own nature, show that we are capable of adapting ourselves to reality, and do what has to be done as intelligently as possible. For the president of the international association and his mentor (!) the right of self-defence is no longer appropriate; it is time for the witches 'Politics' and 'Diplomacy' and the changeling 'Compromise' to take a hand. But we can make it up to ourselves with humour when we talk about these 'farts' together one day. Of course there must be limits. Cases can easily arise in which the diplomatic approach would be unwise and we must give our nature free rein. Then I am prepared to sally forth arm in arm with you and challenge the century. I have become neither timid nor dishonest, I am merely trying to be impersonal.

You are a master of the art of winning people; I should be glad if in the interest of ΨA you were to make more use of it. I also believe that you have not overcome your dislike of our Viennese colleagues, and that you extend it to the *Zentralblatt*. You are unquestionably right in your characterization of Stekel and Adler; for the latter you have even found the brilliant formula I have always been looking for. I can confide in you, as Montezuma did in his companion in misery, that I am not lying on a bed of roses myself. But it does not befit a superior man like you to bear a grudge against them. Take it with humour as I do except on days when weakness gets the better of me. My guess is that the insides of other great movements would have been no more appetizing if one could have looked into them. There are never more than one or two individuals who find the straight road and don't trip over their own legs . . .

Restriction of membership to holders of academic degrees. Here the statutes leave us free, although their spirit does not tend towards such exclusiveness. Consequently, the Zürich society can accept such a provision without making it obligatory for the other societies. In Vienna it is impossible, if only because we should then have to exclude our secretary of many years (Rank). It would also be a pity to exclude several new and very hopeful student members. Finally, such a 'regressive' measure is not really appropriate in the era of *university extension*. As to any similarities to the League of Monists, that can be avoided by policy and purpose. In Vienna we have only the tacit rule that 'active' patients are not to be admitted. The restriction you plan would never be accepted in Vienna and is also displeasing to me personally . . .

And now at last, after all this rubbish, I can speak to you of science. I am now in a somewhat more productive phase, which is reflected in minor productions. I have contributed a highly educational article on 'Wild Psychoanalysis' to the next number of *Zentralblatt*, another, not much more significant, on the understanding of the concepts neurotic, psychogenic, and hysterical, is intended for a later number. I should feel more secure if you were to read it first ...

With kindest regards,

Yours, FREUD

219J

1003 Seestrasse, Küsnacht–Zürich

Dear Professor Freud,   7 November 1910

All your words shall be treasured in a 'faithful and upright' heart. At present I am frightfully busy. First with patients, secondly with scientific work, thirdly with Honegger, whose worries oppress me. The moment has come, we are in the thick of the mess we spoke of in Nuremberg: the question of his fiancée. The situation has become sickly and unendurable. I have the impression that he hangs on, and thereby hangs himself, but gets stuck in the attempt. It is all very dismal and depressing. As a result I have not had the least help from Honegger. I have to pull the whole cart by myself. My cousin Ewald Jung, on the contrary, is delightful. He has established himself in Winterthur and has a ΨAtic practice.

Your card has just arrived. Bleuler's answer is just what I expected. He is going to hold a big soirée to which Riklin and I are invited. This may well be a bad sign. He stresses our 'personal relationship' only in order to repudiate the official one more easily. Bleuler's virtues are distorted by his vices and nothing comes from the heart. I take a very pessimistic view of things. The younger elements in our society are pressing for separation from Burghölzli but Binswanger is hanging on grimly.

As for my relations with the Vienna people, I admit that not everything is as it should be. The less than cordial reception in Nur-

emberg (I don't mean the election of the pope, but the purely personal aspect) has chilled me somewhat. I have never sought the
presidency and therefore object to being looked at askance or envied
because of it. I think I shall take myself at my own word and come to
Vienna. I shall then pay Adler and Stekel a visit, especially in connection with the *Zentralblatt* . . .

I have been able to finish this boring letter only a paragraph at a
time. There have been too many interruptions. Honegger seems to
have got himself disengaged at last, thus probably saving his skin.
Tomorrow I shall be with Bleuler. Afterwards I will write to you.

Kind regards, JUNG

220J

1003 Seestrasse, Küsnacht–Zürich
Dear Professor Freud,   13 November 1910

The discussion with Bleuler took place last Friday evening. The first
thing he wanted was that I should analyse a dream he had been
keeping for me for five days. Naturally the analysis had to be staged
before the public (to make the exhibition more effective). I hu-
moured him by not mincing any words. He dreamt he was *suckling
his child himself*. Here we have the obvious answer. His wife is still
feeding it. So now he's becoming a woman. He still can't decide
(consciously) to stop producing children. At last he holds *me*, his
child, to his breast again. He is dying to be analysed and torments
himself with delusional ideas: I haven't the time, reject his love, etc.
He does not feel in the least homosexual. Consequently, from love of
me, he is turning himself into a woman and wants to behave exactly
like a woman, to go along with our society only *passively*, to be
scientifically *fecundated* since he cannot express himself *creatively*, is
afraid of being violated. So, for the time being, he won't join chiefly
because of homosexual resistance. He did ask me, though, whether I
would advise him to encourage you to come to Zürich. The whole
apparatus that is being set in motion to win him over gives him

enormous pleasure, so he would be frightfully offended if the negotiations were broken off. You may already have heard from him.
Riklin and I were very sweet with him. Sometime this week I'll invite
him to my place for further softening up. I now have the impression
he will join after all, if we are prepared to pay a very high price.

I hope you have received the proofs of Bleuler's paper for Deuticke by now. Fine how he polishes off our opponents. But unfortunately a good deal of it is vague and tortuous, all from lack of
personal experience. For instance he still has astonishing difficulties
with dream analysis.

All in all, Bleuler has been surprisingly agreeable and obliging. He
has not given one reason for his unwillingness to join. The 'tone' gets
on his nerves, he 'just can't', 'not yet' at least. He has *no conscious
reason*; the dream tells us what the real reason is. It is not, as he says,
that *Stekel* is in the society; *I am the one who is holding him back*.
He throws Isserlin in my face, obviously as a screen for his homosexual resistance. He identifies with Isserlin. Scorned love! In the
light of this analysis I shall have quite a few things to straighten out.

Meanwhile with kindest regards, JUNG

221F

Dear friend,   25 November 1910, Vienna, IX. Berggasse 19
Bleuler's letter enclosed. He starts by confirming the failure of all
attempts at a rational solution, but seems to be assuring us of something else, to wit, that he does not want to forsake us and the cause.
We can only rejoice at the prospect of holding him. But you must
have studied him enough at your last meetings to be able to decide
what is to be done. Would this be possible: purge the Zürich
society, throw the others out mercilessly, create a special place for
him as an elder statesman, and invite him to the scientific sessions,
though not to all of them. But we should have to get along without
him at the congress. Then he would soon feel isolated in Burghölzli
and advise the others to join the society. Would that be feasible? ...

... My spirits are dampened by the irritations with Adler and Stekel, with whom it is very hard to get along. You know Stekel, he is having a manic period, he is destroying all my finer feelings and driving me to despair; I have had just about enough of defending him against everybody. Recently a strong opposition to him has developed in the society. Adler is a very decent and highly intelligent man, but he is paranoid; in the *Zentralblatt* he puts so much stress on his almost unintelligible theories that the readers must be utterly confused. He is always claiming priority, putting new names on everything, complaining that he is disappearing under my shadow, and forcing me into the unwelcome role of the ageing despot who prevents young men from getting ahead. They are also rude to me personally, and I'd gladly get rid of them both. But it won't be possible ...

I hope my tale of woe is a comfort to you in your local difficulties ...

My kind regards to you, your wife and children. Here things are back to normal again after our grandmother's death (in Hamburg),

Yours ever, FREUD

222J

1003 Seestrasse, Küsnacht–Zürich,
Dear Professor Freud,   29 November 1910
I had a faint suspicion that your present attitude to the divergent tendencies of Stekel and Adler is not exactly a simple one. There is in any case a noticeable analogy between Adler and Bleuler: the same mania to make the terminology as different as possible and to squeeze the flexible and fruitful psychological approach into the crude schematism of a physiological and biological straitjacket. Bleuler is another one who fights against shrivelling in your shadow ...

Regretfully I must share your view that, if you came to Zürich, you would have to grit your teeth and lodge with him. Bleuler is extremely touchy, loudly proclaiming that it doesn't matter a hang to him. This would be so miserable for us that I must counsel you to get together with Bleuler in Munich ... The evening Bleuler departs I shall arrive in Munich and hope very much to spend the next day with you. There is no need whatever for you to sacrifice any more time. I now have sufficient contact with Bleuler to hold him to our cause ...

With us everything is going ahead nicely. In Bern the *whole interest* centred on ΨA. In that society it has made a lasting abode for itself.

Have you read Bleuler's apologia?

With many kind regards,

Most sincerely yours, JUNG

We hope you will pay us a fleeting visit in the spring.

223F

Dear friend,   3 December 1910, Vienna, IX. Berggasse 19

If it can be done, splendid. I've written to Bleuler suggesting that we meet in Munich on a Sunday. I hinted *gently* that I was pressed for time and would be quite satisfied if we could get together for a few hours. Now let's hope that he creates no difficulties and suspects nothing. And you will be coming later in the day – a secret, I presume. I find the intrigue delightful. If he insists on coming Monday rather than Sunday, it will cost me a day's work; I shall sacrifice it to him unwillingly, but to you willingly if you can come. If you do, I hope you will be nicer to me than my so-called oldest supporters here, who are finally beginning to get under my skin.

It is getting really bad with Adler. You see a resemblance to Bleuler; in me he awakens the memory of Fliess, but an octave lower. The same paranoia. In the second issue of the *Zentralblatt*, which will also contain your charming bit of school gossip, you will find a review by him of your so-called 'Little Anna'. Read it carefully; otherwise it's hard to see what he is driving at. His presentation suffers from paranoid vagueness. But here one can see clearly how he tries to force the wonderful diversity of psychology into the narrow bed of a single aggressive 'masculine' ego-current – as if the child rejected her femininity and had no other thought than to be 'on top' and play the man. To make his point he is obliged to misinterpret certain elements completely, such as the planing off of the genital organ, and to disregard others, such as her fear that her father will also get a child. The crux of the matter – and that is what really alarms me – is that he minimizes the sexual drive and our opponents will soon be able to speak of an experienced psychoanalyst whose conclusions are radically different from ours. Naturally in my attitude towards him I am torn between my conviction that all this is lopsided and harmful and my fear of being regarded as an intolerant old man who holds the young men down, and this makes me feel most uncomfortable.

Today I received from Putnam the second of his lectures on behalf of our ΨA. An absolutely genuine and straightforward man, a precious acquisition for the cause. He hasn't forgotten to mention you most particularly. Jones has also sent me a transcript of the discussion about it. All the flat, sterile, insipid objections we are accustomed to are to be heard unchanged on the other side of the Great Water; they seem admirably suited to the American prudishness we know so well. In our studies of America, have we ever looked into the source of the energies they develop in practical life? I believe it is the early dissolution of family ties, which prevents all the erotic components from coming to life and banishes the Graces from the land ...

Our movement seems indeed to be spreading vigorously. Not long ago I received a first letter from France (!) from a Dr Morichau-Beauchant, professor of medicine at Poitiers, who reads psychoanalysis, works at it, and is convinced: 'Cette lettre vous montrera que vous avez aussi des disciples en France qui suivent passionnément vos travaux.' *The Interpretation of Dreams* has found readers in Paris and Madrid, as is proved by letters, from persons with German names, I must admit. Of course the negative aspect of my fame is even more pronounced; sometimes it annoys me that no one abuses you – after all you too have some responsibility in the matter. But let's hope the next generation is destined to something better than the role of a 'cultural manure'.

I hope to hear soon that all are well in your house, which is escaping me once again. I am looking forward to our meeting.

With kind regards,

Yours ever, FREUD

228F

Dear friend,   22 December 1910, Vienna, IX. Berggasse 19
Just a few words in haste. I am assuming that you will not leave
Tuesday morning if you arrive Monday evening. I think it would be
more dignified not to conceal from Bleuler that I am expecting you.
He will be leaving Monday noon before your arrival or in the evening after it. In the latter – unlikely – event, the three of us could
spend a few hours together. In any case I have booked rooms at the
Park Hotel.

I am very glad that you see Adler as I do. The only reason the
affair upsets me so much is that it has opened up the wounds of the
Fliess affair. It was the same feeling that disturbed the peace I otherwise enjoyed during my work on paranoia; this time I am not sure to
what extent I have been able to exclude my own complexes, and shall
be able to accept criticism.

Don't be dismayed if you do not find me in the best of health; it
will do me good to see you.

A thousand apologies to the children for taking their papa away at
Christmas time.

Very cordially yours, FREUD

The Munich Meetings

Freud reported on the meetings in Munich in other letters – to Ferenczi, 29 Dec 1910, quoted at length by Jones ('I came to a complete understanding with [Bleuler] and achieved a good personal relationship ... After he left Jung came ... I am more than ever convinced that he is a man of the future'), and to Abraham, 20 Jan 1911, Freud/Abraham Letters, p 98 ('With Bleuler things went well ... We parted as friends').

At the meeting of the Vienna society on 4 January, Freud announced that Bleuler, 'who published in the latest Jahrbuch his magnificent apologia for psychoanalysis, has joined the Psychoanalytic Society in that area and may perhaps soon appear officially as its leader' (Minutes, III).

230J

1003 Seestrasse, Küsnacht–Zürich,
18 January 1911

Dear Professor Freud,

Now that I have partly disposed of the mass of work that always threatens to engulf me after the holidays, I can think of writing to you again. The event that will interest you most is this: Bleuler has now joined the society. I bow to your arts! Binswanger will probably cede the presidency to him. I shall confer with Binswanger on this matter. Last Sunday I invited Bleuler over to my place; he was most amiable, everything went off smoothly, we spent the whole evening talking with a physicist[78] about something far removed from our usual concerns – the electrical theory of light ...

My paper is now in the process of being copied out. It grows and grows. After seeing a performance of *Faust* yesterday, including bits of Part Two, I feel more confident of its value. As the whole thing sprang into life before my eyes, all kinds of thoughts came to me, and

[78] Probably Albert Einstein (1879–1955), then a professor of physics at Zürich University.

I felt sure that my respected great-grandfather[79] would have given my work his placet, the more willingly as he would have noted with a smile that the great-grandchild has continued and even extended the ancestral line of thought. But it is a risky business for an egg to try to be cleverer than the hen. Still, what is in the egg must eventually summon the courage to creep out. So you see what fantasies I must resort to in order to protect myself against your criticism.

They say here that your son Martin has broken his foot skiing. Is that true? . . .

My family is well, and so am I. I am exercising my libido in various ways and testing out the modicum of stupidity that I must allow myself.

I hope Munich has done you good. My beautiful vase arrived safely. After your departure you let me in for some diabolical expenses. Your example was contagious. I bought myself a small oil painting and three marvellous drawings, getting myself in the red for a round 1000 francs. As you see, it cost me a pretty penny to salve my conscience for your beautiful gift. Where objets d'art are concerned I easily go *non compos mentis*. Afterwards I crept home with my tail between my legs. Consequently, I shall have to go hard at it to earn money.

I still owe you a mountain of thanks for Munich!

Most sincerely yours, JUNG

231F

Dear friend,   22 January 1911, Vienna, IX. Berggasse 19

I didn't want to resume our correspondence after the refreshing hours in Munich until I could report that my son was beyond danger of complications and that his temperature was normal, as is now the case. He broke his leg on a skiing trip. He lay motionless in the snow for five hours before help came, and some of his appendages would

79 There was a legend in Jung's family that his grandfather was Goethe's natural son.

certainly have frozen if a friend has not watched over him. This happened at an altitude of some 7800 feet and it was another two and a half days before he could be brought down to a hospital. Well, I suppose such accidents are determined by the same causes as those of non Ψanalysts' sons . . .

Adler is still being consistent with himself and will soon have carried his ideas to their logical conclusion. Recently he expressed the opinion that the motivation even of coitus was not exclusively sexual, but also included the individual's desire to *seem* masculine to himself. It's a nice little case of paranoia. So far it hasn't occurred to him that with such a theory there can be no explanation for the real sufferings of neurotics, their feelings of unhappiness and conflict. On one occasion (since Munich) he defended a part of his system at the society and was attacked from various quarters, not by me. Now that I understand him fully, I have become master of my affects. I shall treat him gently and temporize, though without hope of success – I am enclosing an article by Stekel, which my veto has eliminated from the *Zentralblatt*. Be careful about showing it around; it is too compromising . . .

. . . I don't know why you are so afraid of my criticism in matters of mythology. I shall be very happy when you plant the flag of libido and repression in that field and return as a victorious conqueror to our medical motherland . . .

With kind regards to you and your dear ones,

Yours ever, FREUD

232J

1003 Seestrasse, Küsnacht–Zürich,

31 January 1911

Dear Professor Freud,

Many thanks for all the news in your last letter. As I am laid low with influenza, this will be only a soulless typed letter. Stekel's aphorisms are atrocious. A blessing they were suppressed . . .

I had no idea of the mishap that has befallen your son. In the circumstances it is a miracle that he got off so lightly. These accidents are terribly dangerous. My wife and I send heartfelt wishes for speedy recovery.

Best regards and wishes for your own health,

Most sincerely yours, JUNG

235J

1003 Seestrasse, Küsnacht–Zürich,
Dear Professor Freud,   14 February 1911
First of all I am very glad to hear you are well again. Couldn't anyone smell the gas? From a very discreet source a little of your son's 'complex' story has come to my ears. Is Martin his mother's favourite? I am sure you know the rest as well as I do . . .

Yes, I do have some wishes in regard to the third edition of your *Interpretation of Dreams*: I have criticized Morton Prince's 'Mechanism and Interpretation of Dreams' very sharply and in detail, and have also drilled my seminar students in the most rigorous Freudian usage. Now, I have noticed that my students (and I myself) take exception to the following passages: p 92 (second edition) 'The dreams of young children . . . quite uninteresting compared with the dreams of adults.' This sentence is objectionable in terms of *Freudian* dream interpretation; likewise p 94: 'though we think highly of the happiness of childhood', etc objectionable in terms of the *Freudian* sexual theory. The children's dreams on pp 92 and 93 seem to me insufficiently interpreted; the interpretation uncovers only a superficial layer of the dream, but not the whole, which in both cases is clearly a sexual problem whose instinctual energy alone explains the dynamism of the dreams. But you may have reasons (didactic?) for not revealing the deeper layer of interpretation, just as in the preceding dreams (your own) . . . Naturally one cannot strip oneself naked, but perhaps a model would serve the purpose. I also wish there could be a supplementary bibliography of the literature concerned with your work.

I hope you won't be angry with me for my bold criticism and wishes ...

Many kind regards,

Yours sincerely, JUNG

236F

Dear friend,   17 February 1911, Vienna, IX. Berggasse 19
I see you don't believe me; you seem to think I have my cycles and that suddenly, at certain intervals, I feel the need of looking at the world through rose-coloured spectacles. I see I must give you further details. In the daytime there was no smell of gas because when the cock was closed none escaped. But in the evening from ten to one, when I was working under the desk lamp, the gas escaped from the loose joint between the metal pipe and the rubber tube connected with the lamp. On inspection, a flame shot out of this leak. I smelled nothing because I sat swathed in cigar smoke while the gas gradually mixed with the atmosphere. The result was strange headaches which set in, or increased, in the evening when I was working, and by day annoying lapses of memory, which obliged me to keep asking myself: who said that? when did that happen? etc. I am still very proud of the fact that I did not attribute all this to neurosis, but I admit that I diagnosed it as arteriosclerosis, to which I resigned myself. Well, now the whole thing has cleared up. The headaches gradually stopped within three days after the tube was changed.

As for my son's secret moves, I was aware of the social or, if you prefer, homosexual ones, and definitely expected the accident. He had told me nothing about this projected skiing trip. I knew that a few days before he had been in a fight in the barracks yard and was expecting to be called before a court of honour. As for the erotic or heterosexual motives, I heard of them only later, probably from the same source as yourself. His little adventure will probably set him back a year; I only hope that he comes off with two legs of approximately the same length. But something seems to be wrong with your combinations. He is not his mother's favourite son; on the contrary, she treats him almost unjustly, compensating at his expense for her overindulgence towards her brother, whom he resembles a good deal, whereas, strangely enough, I compensate in my treatment of him for my unfriendliness towards the same person (now in New York) . . .

Many thanks for your remarks about *The Interpretation of Dreams*. In principle I shall take account of them *all*, but everything you say cannot be reflected in changes in the third edition. The supplementary bibliography you wish had already been prepared by Rank. The sentence on p 92 about the dreams of small children will be set right by the addition of 'seem'. It is undeniable that the children's dreams on p 94 are interpreted only superficially, without reference to their sexual motivation, but you yourself provide the explanation when you stress my expository or pedagogic purpose. It is not possible to presuppose a knowledge of the *Theory of Sexuality* in a reader of *The Interpretation of Dreams*, or to inculcate this knowledge while providing an elementary introduction to our conception of dreams. That is why I cannot alter the 1899 text in the light of my findings of 1905. You have very acutely noticed that my incomplete elucidation of my own dreams leaves a gap in the overall explanation of dreams, but here again you have put your finger on the motivation – which was unavoidable. I simply cannot expose any more of my nakedness to the reader . . .

The Society for Psychical Research has asked me to present my candidacy as a corresponding member, which means, I presume, that I have been elected. The first sign of interest in *dear old England*.[80] The *list of members*[81] is most impressive.

With kind regards to you and yours, big and little,

Yours ever, FREUD

[80, 81] In English in the original.

237J

1003 Seestrasse, Küsnacht–Zürich,

Dear Professor Freud,   28 February 1911

Last Sunday, the day I could best have written to you, was clouded by a mighty hangover from the carnival. It was a propitiatory offering to the chthonic gods not to disturb my work.

Many thanks for the information about *The Interpretation of Dreams*. Pp 128/129 (bottom) there is a passage where you make children's dreams an exception to the rule. Just how significant children's dreams can be has been admirably documented by my Gretchen: she dreamt that her 'little friend Hans had pulled his felt hat right down over his head (so that the head was hidden) and she had to swallow it.' Or she dreams of a wolf 'that sits in the tunnel'. She is now five years old. The knowledge of foreskin and glans is remarkable. 'Consequently' she was violently *sick* (at the age of four) when her godfather was here with his fiancée. Grethe was terribly jealous.

I am very busy in my thoughts with the incest problem and have found splendid fantasies among my patients. Something should come of it.

I was very much interested in your announcement of a new dreambook, especially in the parallelism of our points of view. For me dream analysis is still one of the most difficult of our problems, and the most rewarding . . .

One of my young pupils here, Dr Lenz,[82] is a voluntary worker with Geheimrat Kraus[83] at the Second Medical Clinic of the Charité in Berlin. He has been successfully importing ΨA. He writes: 'Kraus is very enthusiastic at present and wants ΨA to be fostered and vigorously promoted at his clinic.' Considering Kraus's standing, he is an acquisition not to be underestimated. He seems to want to make my acquaintance. I am thinking of striking while the iron is hot, and

[82] Emil Lenz, Swiss medical pharmacologist in Berlin.
[83] Friedrich Kraus, professor of medicine, Berlin University.

for this purpose shall betake myself to Berlin (in two to three weeks).
It wouldn't be a bad thing if we made a breach there . . .

I hope all is well with you. Everything fine with us.

Kind regards,

Most sincerely yours, JUNG

238F

Dear friend,   1 March 1911, Vienna, IX. Berggasse 19
. . . I see with at least partial satisfaction that *The Interpretation of Dreams* is becoming obsolete and must be replaced by something better, though for a whole decade I had thought it unassailable. Which means that we have made a good bit of progress . . .

I had already heard that Kraus was interested in ΨA, but I didn't think he would take an active part. Though he was in Vienna before he went to Berlin, I have never seen him here. I only hope that his friendliness to us has a solid basis, eg a wholesome hostility to Ziehen. It would be splendid if you put in an appearance there. It would give you as president an opportunity to inspect one of our local groups for the first time. The Berliners (ie Abraham) are holding up very well.

I congratulate you on the enlargement of your empire, thanks to the founding of the New York group. I trust that from now on no year will pass without some new addition to it . . .

Since the day before yesterday I have been chairman of the Vienna group. It had become impossible to go on with Adler; he was quite aware of it himself and admitted that his chairmanship was incompatible with his new theories. Stekel, who now sees eye to eye with him, followed suit. I have decided, after this unsuccessful attempt, to take the reins back into my own hands and I mean to keep a tight hold on them. Even so, considerable damage may already have been done. The deputy chairman is Hitschmann,[84] who as you know is

---

[84] Eduard Hitschmann, doctor, early (1905) adherent to psychoanalysis; later in USA.

quite orthodox. There was strong opposition to Adler among the older members, whereas the younger and newer men showed considerable sympathy for him. I now feel that I must avenge the offended goddess Libido, and I mean to be more careful from now on that heresy does not occupy too much space in the *Zentralblatt*. I see now that Adler's seeming decisiveness concealed a good deal of confusion. I would never have expected a Ψanalyst to be so taken in by the ego. In reality the ego is like the clown in the circus, who is always putting in his oar to make the audience think that whatever happens is his doing.

In the next few days I am expecting our most exotic supporter, Lt-Colonel Sutherland[85] from Saugor in India, who means to spend two days here on his way to London. England seems definitely to be stirring.

With kind regards to you and your family,

Sincerely, FREUD

247J

Dear Professor Freud,   Central Hotel, Berlin, 31 March 1911

A few words in haste! Just before leaving Zürich I had a telephone call saying that Honegger had committed suicide with morphine. He was to have reported for military duty the next day. The sole motive was to avoid a psychosis, for he did not under any circumstances want to give up living in accordance with the pleasure principle.

I have been well received here and though I haven't seen Kraus I found his whole clinic infected with ΨA. I think things in Berlin are off to a good start. I have had three consultations at the Charité.

Kindest regards,

Most sincerely yours, JUNG

[85] W. D. Sutherland, medical officer; founding member of the London Psycho-Analytical Society, 1913.

248F

Dear friend,　　　　　　2 April 1911, Vienna, IX. Berggasse 19
Fate wills it that I must write to you again before your Easter flight. I
am sorry to hear about Honegger. He was a fine man, intelligent,
gifted, and devoted. I had been counting on him to become an in-
valuable help to you; I know that his loss must be a severe blow to
you. Something in his makeup seems to have rebelled against adapting to the necessities of life. Do you know, I think we wear out quite
a few men. Your impressions of Berlin, on the other hand, are most
gratifying. I have always held that loud abuse has the least lasting
effect ...

I am sorry to hear that Jones is planning to leave Toronto. We
should be at a great loss without him in America. In Zürich we shall
have to make a personal effort with the Americans.

And now for the last time I wish you and your dear wife luck on
your little trip.

Yours cordially, FREUD

252J

　　　　　　　　　　　　　1003 Seestrasse, Küsnacht–Zürich,
Dear Professor Freud,　　　　　　　　　　　　　19 April 1911
I got home yesterday evening in order to leave tomorrow for the
congress in Stuttgart. Since we roared (not rode) through the
countryside, I was unable to write you in a sensible way, for I would
have had to write to you sensibly and that is not possible on picture
postcards. You can easily imagine that the shades of Honegger accompanied me on my journey. This blow struck home. How wasteful
children are, even with their own, precious, irreplaceable lives! Not
to speak of friendship and the distress of other people! When I con-
template his fate I cannot but admit that suicide is a thousand times
better than sacrificing the most brilliant gifts of the mind in all their

abundance to the Moloch of neurosis and psychosis. If only he had left off quarrelling with the order of the world and instead quietly submitted to its necessities! It was his first act of self-sacrifice, and alas it had to be suicide. He did it well, without fuss, no sentimentalities like letters, etc. He prepared a strong injection of morphine without betraying his intentions in any way. There is a touch of grandeur about the manner of his going. I am trying to get hold of any manuscripts he may have left behind (?)[86] so as to save for science anything that can be saved. It is an evil thing that such people, marked by the gods, should be so rare and, when they exist, should be the victims of madness or an early death . . .

Today I have written Bleuler that in your opinion we should print Silberer. Accordingly, I have invited Bleuler to give free rein to his divergent opinion in the *Jahrbuch* in the form of a critique (otherwise his resistance might choke him). Joining the society has done him no good at all. He brushes aside my little civilities with disdain . . .

When I get back from Stuttgart I will write again and tell you what the people are up to there.

Many kind regards,

Most sincerely yours, JUNG

253F

Dear friend,   27 April 1911, Vienna, IX. Berggasse 19
. . . Stekel has moved close to us again, and I should like to treat him more gently. First because all in all he is a good-natured fellow and devoted to me, secondly because I am bound to put up with him as one does with an elderly cook who has been with the family for years, and thirdly and mainly because we have no way of knowing what he may discover and misrepresent if we rebuff him. He is absolutely incorrigible, an offence to all good taste, a true child of the

[86] None survived.

ucs., a 'strange son of chaos', but what he says about the ucs., with which he is on much better terms than we are, is usually right. Yesterday we had a discussion about his book. I read the review in question aloud; he reacted as if he didn't feel spat upon but had only felt a few drops of rain. So it passed off quite well. As an editor he is conscientious and self-sacrificing, which makes him irreplaceable.

With Adler it is different; his behaviour is simply puerile. I should like to throw him out on the next occasion; but Stekel wants to keep him and promises to make him see the light . . .

I don't know if I have told you or anyone else the *core* of the Putnam story, which is really delicious. If I have, you must forgive me, I never know any more whether I have written something or not. My supposed piece of diplomacy was simply an act of vengeance against Putnam. The accent is on the inserted remark 'although he has left his youth far behind him' – because in his article in the *Journal of Abnormal Psychology*, he had written, 'Freud is no longer a young man.' You see, it's my 'old-age complex', whose erotic basis is known to you. It is also the source of a fine example of name-forgetting, which will appear in the *Zentralblatt*[87] . . .

Kind regards to you, your wife and family.

Very cordially yours, FREUD

254J

1003 Seestrasse, Küsnacht–Zürich,

Dear Professor Freud, 8 May 1911

It is bad of me to have kept you waiting again so long. The reason is that I came down last week with an atrocious attack of influenza, caught from my children, so that I could do only the most urgent

[87] Later in *The Psychopathology of Everyday Life*: 'I know I don't much like to think about growing old, and I have strange reactions when I'm reminded of it. For instance, I recently charged a very dear friend of mine in the strangest terms with having "left his youth far behind him", for the reason that once before, in the middle of the most flattering remarks about me, he had added that I was "no longer a young man".'

work with a fearful effort. I hadn't the strength for anything else. Today I am sufficiently recovered to give you at least a sign of life . . .

The New York group has now come into being, and Seif[88] has successfully founded one in Munich. Pleasant news!

My Australian article is finished too. It's about 'The Doctrine of Complexes', a stupid thing you had better not see . . .

As to my intellectual activities, I am at the moment working up some popular small talk on ΨA which a literary magazine, the *Zürcher Jahrbuch*, has wrung out of me. I am trying to be popular again – not to my advantage, as you will see . . .

. . . Occultism is another field we shall have to conquer[89] – with the aid of the libido theory, it seems to me. At the moment I am looking into astrology, which seems indispensable for a proper understanding of mythology. There are strange and wondrous things in these lands of darkness. Please don't worry about my wanderings in these infinitudes. I shall return laden with rich booty for our knowledge of the human psyche. For a while longer I must intoxicate myself on magic perfumes in order to fathom the secrets that lie hidden in the abysses of the unconscious . . .

Kindest regards,

Most sincerely yours, JUNG

[88] Leonard Seif; after 1920, in Adler's school.
[89] After he received this letter, Freud wrote to Ferenczi: 'Jung writes to me that we must conquer the field of occultism and asks for my agreeing to his leading a crusade . . . I can see that you two are not to be held back. At least go forward in collaboration with each other; it is a dangerous expedition and I cannot accompany you.' (Quoted in Jones, vol III.)

255F

Dear friend,   12 May 1911, Vienna, IX. Berggasse 19
This time I have really missed your letters, even more than the news they contain. I am very glad there was nothing worse behind your silence. I haven't been feeling very well myself and I can say without exaggeration that I am intellectually drained. My business prospectus is going off to Australia tomorrow and is evading your inspection for the same reasons of shame and delicacy that have led your article to evade mine. But you will be receiving the preface to *The Interpretation of Dreams* in the next few days. It will have to be changed, Deuticke says it might make an unfavourable impression. And I must admit that the rabble who read these things don't deserve a shred of honesty.

Because of the long interruption I don't know what I have already told you and what I haven't. Not much has been happening. It may be news to you that Stekel has been trying to make up. I have changed my mind and decided to put up with him. But I am becoming steadily more impatient of Adler's paranoia and longing for an occasion to throw him out. Especially since seeing a performance of *Oedipus Rex* here – the tragedy of the 'arranged libido'.

I am aware that you are driven by innermost inclination to the study of the occult and I am sure you will return home richly laden. I cannot argue with that, it is always right to go where your impulses lead. You will be accused of mysticism, but the reputation you won with the *Dementia* will hold up for quite some time against that. Just don't stay in the tropical colonies too long; you must reign at home ...

At home we are worried about Ernst, my third boy, who had a duodenal ulcer or fistula. They say there is no danger. He is being allowed to take his final examinations, but then he will have to spend quite some time in a sanatorium. My wife is in Karlsbad and I shall be going there with my brother on 9 July ...

With la C— I have at last accomplished something through ΨA: her symptoms have grown much worse. Of course this is part of the

1911

process, but there is no certainty that I can get her any farther. I have come very close to her central conflict, as her reaction shows. She is a grave case, perhaps incurable. But we must be consistent with ourselves, these are the very cases from which we have most to learn.

My kind regards. I hope you won't wait quite so long before your next letter.

Yours ever, FREUD

256J

1003 Seestrasse, Küsnacht–Zürich,
Dear Professor Freud, 18 May 1911
This time I won't spare you my letter as long as I did last time. The change in Stekel's behaviour is gratifying. The symbolism he has unearthed in his book is considerable, and it would be a pity if we lost his olfactory organ ...

I am extremely sorry to hear of your son's illness. Where the dickens did he get such an ailment?

All is well with us, except for the worry (another false alarm, fortunately) about the blessing of too many children. One tries every conceivable trick to stem the tide of these little blessings, but without much confidence. One scrapes along, one might say, from one menstruation to the next. The life of civilized man certainly does have its quaint side.

As for your preface to *The Interpretation of Dreams*, I can well understand Deuticke's agonizings. Honesty carried to those lengths is too much; it is rewarded only in heaven and not on earth. The latter consideration might seem the more pertinent to you, too.

Ever sincerely yours, JUNG

259J

1003 Seestrasse, Küsnacht–Zürich,

Dear Professor Freud,   12 June 1911

Since last writing to you (too long ago, alas!) I have made good use of my time. I was at the Meeting of Swiss Psychiatrists in Lausanne and spoke on 'forms of unconscious fantasy'. These things are contributions to, and elaborations of, my paper in the current *Jahrbuch*, which, incidentally, is taking shape terribly slowly (because of the wealth of material). Everything I am doing now revolves round the contents and forms of unconscious fantasies. I think I've already got some really fine results ...

My evenings are taken up very largely with astrology. I made horoscopic calculations in order to find a clue to the core of psychological truth. Some remarkable things have turned up which will certainly appear incredible to you. In the case of one lady, the calculation of the position of the stars at her nativity produced a quite definite character picture, with several biographical details which did not pertain to her but to her mother – and the characteristics fitted the mother to a T. The lady suffers from an extraordinary mother complex. I dare say that we shall one day discover in astrology a good deal of knowledge that has been intuitively projected into the heavens. For instance, it appears that the signs of the zodiac are character pictures, in other words libido symbols which depict the typical qualities of the libido at a given moment ...

I hope all is as well with you as with us ...

With kindest regards,

Most sincerely yours, JUNG

260F

Dear friend,   15 June 1911, Vienna, IX. Berggasse 19
I cannot like you report interesting work and startling findings; I am
tired and count the days. That is why I have not taken the trouble to
write letters and have made no claims on you . . .

I have finally got rid of Adler. After I had pressed Bergmann to
dismiss him from the *Zentralblatt*, he twisted and turned and finally
came up with a strangely worded statement which can only be taken
as his resignation. At least, this interpretation is supported by his
announcement that he is leaving the ΨA Society. And then he came
out with what he had been holding back: 'Despite its unprecedented
resolution at one time to that effect, the society has not had sufficient
moral influence on you to make you desist from your old personal
fight (!!) against me. Since I have no desire to carry on such a personal fight with my former teacher, I hereby announce my resignation.' The damage is not very great. Paranoid intelligences are not
rare and are more dangerous than useful. As a paranoiac of course
he is right about many things, though wrong about everything. A few
rather useless members will probably follow his example . . .

In matters of occultism I have grown humble since the great lesson
Ferenczi's experiences gave me. I promise to believe anything that
can be made to look reasonable. I shall not do so gladly, that you
know. But my hubris has been shattered. I should be glad to know
that you are in harmony with F. when one of you decides to take the
dangerous step into publication. I believe that is compatible with
perfect independence during the work process . . .

Kind regards to you and your beautiful house.

Yours ever, FREUD

261J

1003 Seestrasse, Küsnacht–Zürich,
23 June 1911

Dear Professor Freud,

... Have you seen Havelock Ellis's book on dreams? Won't you do a critical review for the *Jahrbuch*? What a watery brew Ellis has concocted! Just what is needed to make everything unclear.

You are probably right about Honegger. Although it may be true that the fantasy systems in D. pr. exhibit parallels with the daydreams of hysterical patients, it is certain from the start that by no means all cases possess such a system, or at least they do not have it *at their disposal*. That it is *not* of great therapeutic importance to get patients to produce their latent fantasies seems to me a very dubious proposition. The unconscious fantasies contain a whole lot of relevant material, and bring the inside to the outside as nothing else can, so that I see a faint hope of getting at even the 'inaccessible' cases by this means. These days my interest turns more and more to ucs. fantasy, and it is quite possible that I'm attaching too great hopes to these excavations. Ucs. fantasy is an amazing witches' cauldron:

Formation, transformation,
Eternal Mind's eternal recreation.
Thronged round with images of things to be,
They see you not, shadows are all they see.[90]

This is the matrix of the mind, as the little great-grandfather correctly saw. I hope something good comes out of it.

Kindest regards, JUNG

[90] Goethe, *Faust*, *II*, (tr Philip Wayne, Penguin Classics).

262F

Dear friend,   27 June 1911, Vienna, IX. Berggasse 19
My wife is touched by the repetition of your kind invitation and
promises to reconsider. Since I know all the factors, I think she will
stick to her earlier decision and that I shall come *before* the congress.

I enclose the draft of the invitation to the congress, without comment. It is agreed, I presume, that you are to chair the congress.
I also think you ought to use the mornings for papers as you did last
year, which raises the spirits, and leave business matters for the afternoon. One afternoon will probably not be enough, because time will
be needed for the members to make practical suggestions regarding
the organization of the international association. Whether it is necessary on this occasion to hold elections as provided for in our statutes,
I do not know. I believe you will have to sift the papers to make sure
that nothing of inferior quality is served up.

In respect to ucs. fantasies, I share your assumptions as well as
your expectations. Incidentally, if the old gentleman was not referring to these things in his verses, I should be glad to know what they
do apply to.

I trust that we are now rid of Adler. He has resigned from the
society and, after a 'declaration',[91] from the *Zentralblatt* as well. But
the battle had its nasty and embarrassing episodes . . .

I shall review Stekel and Havelock Ellis for the *Jahrbuch*,
With kind regards to you all

Yours, FREUD

[91] Adler's name as editor disappears from the masthead in *Zentralblatt*, I: 10/11
(July/Aug 1911), which opens with this 'Declaration': 'I hereby notify the
readers of this journal that as of today I am resigning as editor. The director
of this journal, Prof Freud, was of the opinion that there exist such strong
scientific disagreements between him and myself which [sic] make further
collaboration in editing the journal seem inopportune. I therefore decided to
resign as editor of the journal of my own free will. Dr Alfred Adler.'

263J

1003 Seestrasse, Küsnacht–Zürich

Dear Professor Freud,   11 July [1911]

I'm sick of work myself and longing for the holidays. Lately I have
made the mistake of letting myself be swamped by my practice, my
scientific work has fallen badly in arrears, and this is not at all good
for me. My libido protests vigorously against any kind of one-sided
occupation . . .

I received the enclosed letter from Adler. He seems to be extending
his delusional ideas to me, since he refers to a rumour allegedly
circulating in Vienna to the effect that *I have demanded his removal
from the society*. Of course I wrote immediately saying that this was
quite out of the question, that on the contrary I would find his loss
most regrettable, etc. Who is it starts this kind of rumour? . . .

Many kind regards,

Most sincerely yours, JUNG

264F

Dear friend,   13 July 1911, Karlsbad, Haus Columbus

Yes, I am on holiday now, torturing myself 'in obedience to the laws'
in the hope of recovering my so-called health. If my irritation in the
following seems excessive, do please consider my abnormal body
chemistry.

I know who manufactures these rumours. It's not hard to guess.
Adler in person, and I also know why. In writing you things which he
knew you could easily refute, he was counting on the automatism of
good manners. He knew you would say: no, on the contrary, sorry to
hear it. And you let yourself be taken in, which puts me in a difficult
situation.

Adler concocted his 'rumour' from two private though not

confidential remarks of mine: 1) that the journal suffered from the fact that he as editor had no personal contact with you and the other foreign contributors; and 2) that I ought to have taken steps long ago, at the time when he penned his inadmissible observation to the effect that the 'Little Anna' material was 'consistently slanted' and therefore its mythologies were inconclusive. His rumour has no other basis. And now he hears from you that you regret his resignation, regard it as a loss, etc. From this he will now draw capital; he has obtained a statement of your disapproval of my treatment of him, he has brought us into conflict with one another, etc. Now that the harm is done, I can only request that in future you handle Adler, who undoubtedly has more tricks up his sleeve, with psychiatric caution.

His saying that the better element is resigning from the society with him is of course nonsense, as you will see for yourself . . .

I wish you all enjoyment of your well deserved holiday and am delighted with your decision not to let yourself be enslaved by your practice in the future. If I do so, I must be forgiven because of my age, my complexes, and the numerous offspring I have to provide for.

If it is agreeable to you, I shall come on September 16th – alone.

With kind regards to you, your wife, and children.

Yours ever, FREUD

265J

1003 Seestrasse, Küsnacht–Zürich,
Dear Professor Freud,   19 July 1911

I am very annoyed that I have been taken in by Adler. Later he will find that I am much farther away from him than he now thinks. I did, in fact, act to some extent on the psychiatric principle of never arguing with a paranoiac, and simply issued soothing official denials. Bleuler is very much of the same kidney and there is only a few degrees' difference between them (though it's an important one) in practice. He has all but severed personal relations with me; I attribute this solely to the alcohol question.

I have a terrible lot to do and must make heroic efforts to hold my practice at arm's length. Now I have got to the point where I can set aside one day for myself each week, in addition to Sunday, so that I can at last get down to some scientific work. All the hours that used to be free are now completely taken up with lecture courses, seminars, and correspondence (at present also with the perennial visitors). Things are so bad that to my consternation I can no longer enjoy my Sundays since I have to spend all of them resting. This deplorable state of affairs will cease on August 1st. On the 9th I go to Brussels for a week and then, on the 19th, to the mountains with my wife. At the beginning of September I'll be back in Zürich and shall look forward to seeing you on the 15th and harbouring you under my roof as a most welcome guest. My address during this time remains the same.

With many kind regards and best wishes for the success of your pleasure cure.

Most sincerely yours, JUNG

266F

Dear friend,   Karlsbad, 21 July 1911

Your letter has appeased my irritation but at the same time aroused my anxiety. You must not take me as a model; on the contrary, you must arm yourself, before it is too late, against the dragon Practice. Give your charming, clever, and ambitious wife the pleasure of saving you from losing yourself in the business of money making. My wife often says she would be only too proud if she were able to do the same for me ... Your taste for money making already worried me in connection with your American dealings. On the whole, it will prove to be good business if you forgo ordinary pursuits. Then, I am sure, extraordinary rewards will come your way ...

I have received the invitations to the congress. My cure in Karls-bad is not an unmingled pleasure. I have decided to endow a votive tablet if only I get rid of all the ailments I have acquired here. However, it looks as if I were going to come off with some benefit.

With kind regards to you and your family,

Yours ever, FREUD

267J

                              1003 Seestrasse, Küsnacht–Zürich
Dear Professor Freud,   26 July 1911
It's not all that bad with my money making; nevertheless I grant you are right. The feeling of inferiority that often overcomes me when I measure myself against you has always to be compensated by increased emulation. I need a large practice in order to gain experience, for I do not imagine that I know too much. Also, I have had to demonstrate to myself that I am able to make money in order to rid myself of the thought that I am non-viable. These are all frightful stupidities which can only be overcome by acting them out. I think I am now over the mountain so far as my practice is concerned. During the winter semester I shall be merciless with myself. This stage has to be overcome too. It is, as you know, no light matter to suffer financial success. I have never thrived on it. Scientific work does me far more good.

... I am so looking forward to the time we shall have together. There are all sorts of things I want to show you. I hope, too, that you won't find it a bore to be present at the seminars along with Putnam, etc. We could have a very pleasant colloquy of considerable importance to the future of psychoanalysis.

Meanwhile with many kind regards.

Most sincerely yours, JUNG

268F

Dear friend,   Hotel Post, 20 August 1911
... I am greatly looking forward to our meeting. This place has a
very special kind of beauty. I am planning to stay here until 14
September and then go directly to Zürich.

Since my mental powers revived, I have been working in a field
where you will be surprised to meet me. I have unearthed strange and
uncanny things and will almost feel obliged *not* to discuss them with
you. But you are too shrewd not to guess what I am up to when I add
that I am dying to read your 'Transformations and Symb. of the
Lib.'.

It goes without saying that I should be glad to hear from you, how
you all are, how it went in Brussels, and what further plans you have
for the holidays.

I am expecting Ferenczi today for a prolonged visit.

With kind regards in friendship from a happy heart,

Yours, FREUD

269J

1003 Seestrasse, Küsnacht–Zürich,
Dear Professor Freud,   29 August 1911
I was overjoyed by your letter, being, as you know, very receptive to
any recognition the father sees fit to bestow. It is more pleasing than
the loud recognition conferred on us by the unremitting malevolence
of our opponents. At the same time, your letter has got me on tenterhooks because, for all my 'shrewdness', I can't quite make out
what is going on so enigmatically behind the scenes. Together with
my wife I have tried to unriddle your words, and we have reached
surmises which, for the time being at any rate, I would rather keep to

myself. I can only hope that your embargo on discussion will be lifted during your stay here. I, too, have the feeling that this is a time full of marvels, and, if the auguries do not deceive us, it may very well be that, thanks to your discoveries, we are on the threshold of something really sensational, which I scarcely know how to describe except with the Gnostic concept of 'Sophia', an Alexandrian term particularly suited to the reincarnation of ancient wisdom in the shape of ΨA. I daren't say too much, but would only counsel you (very immodestly) to let my 'Transf. and Symb. of the Lib.' unleash your associations and/or fantasies: I am sure you will hit upon strange things if you do. (Provided, of course, that the mysterious hint in your letter has not already done so in anagrammatic form. With that letter anything seems possible.)

Well then – I was in Brussels from 11–16 August. The congress and its proceedings were so idiotic that I played truant most of the time. I was present, so to speak, only at my own lecture. It was a colossal piece of cheek. I knew that after all those longueurs the public would fall like rabbits. The speaking time was limited to twenty minutes. I took almost an hour, one can't do a decent report on ΨA in twenty minutes. I felt sure the chairman (van Schuyten, who has his knife into ΨA anyway) was going to cut me short. And he did. I told him I would willingly stop at once but would like to leave the decision to the congress (c 200 people). The congress granted me further time by acclamation. The same thing happened a *second time*. The chairman was hopping mad but had to swallow his rage. My lecture had the effect of a bombshell. Afterwards one heard mutterings like 'Vous avez déchainé un orage,' 'Oh, c'est un homme odieux,' etc. A few people left the hall in mute protest. One Danish doctor flew into a rage with me; I didn't deign to answer him and that made him more furious than ever, for the rabble likes to be answered in kind. But a few of the brighter heads and a few good ones had noticed something and from now on can be counted among our silent collaborators . . .

So far I have only four announcements of lectures for Weimar (Sadger, Abraham, Körber, Jung). I have asked Bleuler, Sachs, and Rank, and will also try Pfister. I am counting on you absolutely;

would you please let me know the title of your lecture *as soon as possible* ... This time the feminine element will have conspicuous representatives from Zürich: Sister Moltzer, Dr Hinkle-Eastwick (an American charmer), Frl Dr Spielrein (!), then a new discovery of mine, Frl Antonia Wolff[92], a remarkable intellect with an excellent feeling for religion and philosophy, and last but not least my wife ...

I look forward very much to seeing you here again in the near future. I'm expecting Putman next week.

Many kind regards,

Most sincerely yours, JUNG

270F

Dear friend,   Klobenstein, 1 September 1911

I am glad to release you as well as your dear wife, well known to me as a solver of riddles, from the darkness by informing you that my work in these last few weeks has dealt with the same theme as yours, to wit, the origin of religion. I wasn't going to speak of it for fear of confusing you. But since I can see from a first reading of your article in the *Jahrbuch* (I shall have to reread it; for the moment Ferenczi has made off with the volume) that my conclusions are known to you, I find, much to my relief, that there is no need for secrecy. So you too are aware that the Oedipus complex is at the root of religious feeling. Bravo! What evidence I have to contribute can be told in five minutes.

Your letter came on a beautiful happy day and has further raised my spirits. Your Brussels experiences are very amusing. It seems to me that we have had enough congresses for a while ...

We Viennese have nothing to compare with the charming ladies you are bringing from Zürich. Our only lady doctor is participating like a true masochist in the Adler revolt and is unlikely to be present.

92 Toni Wolff (1888–1953) – the name she used throughout her later career as an analytical psychologist in Zürich – was Jung's close friend and collaborator for more than forty years.

We are indeed disintegrating. As you know, this shift to the West is not entirely contrary to my wishes ...

I shall surely write you again before leaving. For now I send my kindest regards to you all. Auf Wiedersehen!

Yours ever, FREUD

The Weimar Congress

Freud travelled alone from his vacation spot near Bozen (Bolzano) to Zürich, where Jung met him upon his arrival early in the morning of 16 September. He stayed in the Jungs' house at Küsnacht for four days.

The Third Psychoanalytic Congress was held at the best hotel of Weimar, the Erbprinz, beginning at 8am on 21 September and continuing on the next day. Karl Abraham was in charge of arrangements. The official report names 55 in attendance, of whom 46 posed for a group photograph. Twelve papers were read – 'of a high order', writes Jones, including 'several classics of psychoanalytic literature'.

271F

[Barracks, St Gallen],
Dear Professor Freud,   4 October 1911
At last I can settle down to write to you. I have now been in barracks for a week doing my duty as a medical jack of all trades, anointing feet, cutting out corns, treating diarrhoea, and am beginning to feel squat and ugly again. Luckily I have some time for myself, so I am not entirely pulverized by the constant spectacle of odious corporeality ...

The congress in Munich must have been a frightfully stupid affair. I have heard reports of it from various quarters. Frank perpetrated the following pronouncement: 'It is enormously important in ΨA that not only the lady patient should repose comfortably on the couch but the doctor as well.' Jones and Seif stood up for us. With what result I don't know ...

For our interpretation of the Utnapishtim episode in Gilgamesh I have found some rather weird parallels which shed light on Utna-pishtim's gnomic utterances. I won't reveal anything yet, but must mull them over first.

Two boring things will be included in the next *Jahrbuch*, but because of their scientific veneer they will impress the kind of public that likes indirect statements. We must do a bit more infiltrating in scientific circles.

I hope you got back to Vienna safe and sound and took home with you many good impressions of Switzerland so that you will wish to come again another year.

With kindest regards and my compliments to your wife.

Yours very sincerely, JUNG

273F

Dear friend,   12 October 1911, Vienna, IX. Berggasse 19
Rather tired after battle and victory, I hereby inform you that yesterday I forced the whole Adler gang (six of them) to resign from the society. I was harsh but I don't think unfair. They have founded a new society for 'free' ΨA as opposed to our own unfree variety, and are planning to put out a journal of their own, etc: nevertheless they insisted on their right to stay with us, naturally in order to provide themselves parasitically with ideas and with material to misrepresent. I have rendered such a symbiosis impossible. The same evening we enrolled three new members, Stärcke and Emden in Holland and Fräulein Dr Spielrein who turned up unexpectedly. She said I didn't look malicious, as she had imagined I would ...

Eder[93] in London has just sent me the first ΨA paper to have been read before the British Medical Association (*British Medical Journal*, 30 Sept 1911) ...

Bleuler is a genius at misunderstanding, rather like a prickly eel, if there is such a thing.

---

[93] M. D Eder, charter member of the London society, 1913; translated writings of Jung. Prominent champion of Zionism.

The days in Zürich and Weimar seem even more splendid in retrospect. Toothache and strain sink into oblivion, the exchange of ideas, the hopes and satisfactions that were the substance of those days stand out in all their purity.

I wish you full enjoyment of your military rest, which I hope will not be disturbed by the war in the Mediterranean, and send you, your wife and children my kind regards.

Yours ever, FREUD

274F

Dear friend, 13 October 1911, Vienna, IX. Berggasse 19
To you in your military solitude I send the following contribution to our conversations on the Gilgamesh material.

Though I do not contest the interpretation of Gilgamesh and Eabani as man and crude sensuality, it nevertheless occurs to me that such pairs consisting of a noble and base part (usually brothers) are a motif running through all legend and literature. The last great offshoot of the type is Don Quijote with his Sancho Panza (literally: paunch). Of mythological figures, the first that come to mind are the Dioskuroi (one mortal, the other immortal) and various pairs of brothers or twins of the Romulus and Remus type. One is always weaker than the other and dies sooner. In Gilgamesh this age-old motif of the unequal pair of brothers served to represent the relationship between a man and his libido.

These ancient motifs are always being reinterpreted (even, I concede, in terms of astronomy); but what is their original source?

In regard to the motif under discussion it is not hard to say. The weaker twin, who dies first, is the placenta, or afterbirth, simply because it is regularly born along with the child by the same mother. We found this interpretation some months ago in the work of a modern mythologist totally ignorant of ΨA, who for once forgot his science and consequently had a good idea. But in Fraser's *Golden Bough*, Volume 1, one can read that among many primitive peoples the afterbirth is called *brother* (sister) or *twin*, and treated accordingly, that is, fed and taken care of, which of course cannot go on for very long. If there is such a thing as a phylogenetic memory in the individual, which unfortunately will soon be undeniable, this is also the source of the *uncanny* aspect of the 'doppelgänger'.

I just wanted to surprise you with the news that basically Eabani is Gilgamesh's 'afterbirth'. All sorts of ideas and connections still remain to be unearthed in this material. It's a pity we can only work together in such technical matters.

Very cordially yours, FREUD

275J

Barracks, St Gallen (until Oct 31),
17 October 1911

Dear Professor Freud,

Many thanks for your two letters and all their news. I was interested in the goings-on in Vienna. May we know the names of the dissidents soon? In my view this purge is a blessing . . .

Your contribution to the symbolism of the brothers, which you hinted at in Zürich, is extraordinarily interesting and very valuable. As I have discovered since then, symbolism is widely disseminated and age-old. I am most grateful for this contribution since it fits in very well with certain other observations which have forced me to conclude that the so-called 'early memories of childhood' are not individual memories at all but phylogenetic ones. I mean of course the *very early* memories like birth, sucking, etc. There are things whose only explanation is *intrauterine*: much of the water symbolism, then the enwrappings and encoilings which seem to be accompanied by strange skin sensations (umbilical cord and amnion). Just now my Agathli is having dreams like this; they are closely related to certain Negro birth myths, where these envelopments in slimy stuff also occur. I think we shall find that infinitely many more things than we now suppose are phylogenetic memories . . .

I hope your cold has long since disappeared. Many kind regards,

Most sincerely yours, JUNG

From Emma Jung

Dear Professor Freud,   Küsnacht, 30 October [1911]
I don't really know how I am summoning the courage to write you
this letter, but am certain it is not from presumption; rather I am
following the voice of my unconscious, which I have so often found
was right and which I hope will not lead me astray this time.

Since your visit I have been tormented by the idea that your relation with my husband is not altogether as it should be, and since it
definitely ought not to be like this I want to try to do whatever is in
my power. I do not know whether I am deceiving myself when I
think you are somehow not quite in agreement with 'Transformations of Libido'. You didn't speak of it at all and yet I think it
would do you both so much good if you got down to a thorough
discussion of it. Or is it something else? If so, please tell me what,
dear Herr Professor; for I cannot bear to see you so resigned and I
even believe that your resignation relates not only to your real children (it made a quite special impression on me when you spoke of it)
but also to your spiritual sons; otherwise you would have so little
need to be resigned.

Please do not take my action as officiousness and do not count me
among the women who, you once told me, always spoil your friend-
ships. My husband naturally knows nothing of this letter and I beg
you not to hold him responsible for it or to let any kind of unpleasant effects it may have on you glance off on him.

I hope nevertheless that you will not be angry with your very
admiring

EMMA JUNG

278F

Dear friend,   2 November 1911, Vienna, IX. Berggasse 19
I am glad you are home again and no longer playing soldiers, which
is after all a silly occupation. Let this letter welcome you home . . .

Four publishers have now turned down the new journal (Deuticke,

Bergmann, J. A. Barth, Urban & Schwarzenberg). I am hoping to make arrangements next week with H. Heller, the art publisher, who is a member of our group. But it's not so good; this and various other things make a pitiful impression that leaves me depressed. In addition, I have not been fully employed this month; the nestlings are opening hungry mouths, the ones outside my house at least; those at home are still getting enough to eat. My psychology of religion is giving me a good deal of trouble; I have little pleasure in working and constant *douleurs d'enfantement*;[94] in short, I feel rather gloomy and I am not quite well physically either. Old age is not an empty delusion. A morose senex deserves to be shot without remorse ...

My son Ernst is well. My daughter Sophie is better but nothing has been decided yet. The rest of them are fine. I hope to hear the same of you and your little barnyard.

Very cordially yours, FREUD

From Emma Jung

My dear Professor Freud,   Küsnacht, 6 November [1911]
Your nice kind letter has relieved me of anxious doubts, for I was afraid that in the end I had done something stupid. Now I am naturally very glad and thank you with all my heart for your friendly reception of my letter, and particularly for the goodwill you show to all of us.

In explanation of my conjecture I would like to tell you, first, that it is not a question at all of things consciously perceived; you didn't even let us sympathize with your toothache, which ordinarily is a perfect justification for even the worst mood. If I talked about 'Symbols' it was chiefly because I knew how eagerly Carl was waiting for your opinion; he had often said he was sure you would not approve of it, and for that reason was awaiting your verdict with some trepidation. Of course this was only a residue of the father (or mother) complex which is probably being resolved in this book; for actually Carl, if he holds something to be right, would have no need

[94] = 'labour pains'.

to worry about anybody else's opinion. So perhaps it is all to the good that you did not react at once so as not to reinforce this father-son relationship.

The second reason was provided by the conversation on the first morning after your arrival, when you told me about your family. You said then that your marriage had long been 'amortized', now there was nothing more to do except – die. And the children were growing up and then they become a real worry, and yet this is the only true joy. This made such an impression on me and seemed to me so significant that I had to think of it again and again, and I fancied it was intended just for me because it was meant symbolically at the same time and referred to my husband.

Please don't be angry if I venture to speak again about the 'manifest content' of your talk. I wanted to ask then if you are sure that your children would not be helped by analysis. One certainly cannot be the child of a great man with impunity, considering the trouble one has in getting away from ordinary fathers. And when this distinguished father also has a streak of paternalism in him, as you yourself said! Didn't the fracture of your son's leg fit in with this picture? When I asked you about it you said you didn't have time to analyse your children's dreams because you had to earn money so that they could go on dreaming. Do you think this attitude is right? I would prefer to think that one *should not* dream at all, one should live. I have found with Carl also that the imperative 'earn money' is only an evasion of something else to which he has resistances. Please forgive me this candour, it may strike you as brazen; but it disturbs my image of you because I somehow cannot bring it into harmony with the other side of your nature, and this matters so much to me. The thought also occurred to me that it was perhaps on our account that you didn't send your son to study in Zürich; you did speak about it at one time and for us it would naturally have been a great pleasure to see him now and then.

Another thing I must mention is your resignation in science, if one can call it that. You may imagine how pleased and honoured I am by the confidence you have in Carl, but it almost seems to me as though you were sometimes giving too much – do you not see in him the follower and fulfiller more than you need? Doesn't one often give much because one wants to keep much?

Why are you thinking of giving up already instead of enjoying your well earned fame and success? Perhaps for fear of letting the right moment for it pass you by? Surely this will never happen *to you*. After all, you are not so old that you could speak now of the 'way of regression', what with all these splendid and fruitful ideas you have in your head! Besides, the man who has discovered the living fountain of ps. a. (or don't you believe it is one?) will not grow old so quickly.

No, you should rejoice and drink to the full the happiness of victory after having struggled for so long. And do not think of Carl with a father's feeling: 'He will grow, but I must dwindle,' but rather as one human being thinks of another, who like you has his own law to fulfil.

Don't be angry with me.

With warm love and veneration, EMMA JUNG

280F

Dear friend,   12 November 1911, Vienna, IX. Berggasse 19
Thank you for your letter and parcel. I am busy enough again to have been able to put off answering until Sunday . . .

. . . The reading for my psychology of religion is going slowly. One of the nicest works I have read (again), is that of a well known author on the 'Transformations and Symbols of the Libido'. In it many things are so well expressed that they seem to have taken on definitive form and in this form impress themselves on the memory. Sometimes I have a feeling that his horizon has been too narrowed by Christianity. And sometimes he seems to be more above the material than in it. But it is the best thing this promising author has written, up to now, though he will do still better. In the section about the two modes of thought I deplore his wide reading. I should have liked him to say everything in his own words. Every thinker has his own jargon and all these translations are tedious.

Not least, I am delighted by the many points of agreement with things I have already said or would *like* to say. Since you yourself are this author, I shall continue more directly and make an admission: it is a torment to me to think, when I conceive an idea now and then, that I may be taking something away from you or appropriating something that might just as well have been acquired by you. When this happens, I feel at a loss; I have begun several letters offering you various ideas and observations for your own use, but I never finish them because this strikes me as even more indiscreet and undesirable than the contrary procedure. Why in God's name did I allow myself to follow you into this field? You must give me some suggestions. But probably my tunnels will be far more subterranean than your shafts and we shall pass each other by, but every time I rise to the surface I shall be able to greet you. 'Greetings' is a good cue on which to end this long letter. I need only add a 'heartfelt', addressed also to your wife and children.

Yours ever, FREUD

282J

1003 Seestrasse, Küsnacht–Zürich
Dear Professor Freud,   14 November 1911
Many thanks for your very nice letter which I have just received. However, the outlook for me is very gloomy if you too get into the psychology of religion. You are a dangerous rival – if one has to speak of rivalry. Yet I think it has to be this way, for a natural development cannot be halted, nor should one try to halt it. Our personal differences will make our work different. You dig up the precious stones, but I have the 'degree of extension'. As you know, I always have to proceed from the outside to the inside and from the whole to the part. I would find it too upsetting to let large tracts of human knowledge lie there neglected. And because of the difference

in our working methods we shall undoubtedly meet from time to time in unexpected places. Naturally you will be ahead of me in certain respects but this won't matter much since you have anticipated by far the greatest part already. It is difficult only at first to accustom oneself to this thought. Later one comes to accept it ...

All's well here except for the frightful cases that loom ahead: I am supposed to analyse *Pfister's wife*! I shall resist as long and as fiercely as I possibly can. These days I'm getting practically nothing but divorce cases. To hell with them!

On this note of imprecation, to which I can hardly add a 'heartfelt', I bid you adieu.

With best regards, JUNG

From Emma Jung
Dear Professor Freud,   Küsnacht, 14 November [1911]
You were really annoyed by my letter, weren't you? I was too, and now I am cured of my megalomania and am wondering why the devil the unconscious had to make you, of all people, the victim of this madness. And here I must confess, very reluctantly, that you are right: my last letter, specially the tone of it, was really directed to the father-image, which should of course be faced without fear. This thought never entered my head; I thought that, knowing the transference side of my father-attitude towards you, it would all be quite clear and do me no harm. After I had thought so long before writing to you and had, so I believed, fully understood my own motives, the unconscious has now played another trick on me, with particular finesse: for you can imagine how delighted I am to have made a fool of myself in front of you. I can only pray and hope that your judgement will not prove too severe.

There is one thing, however, I must vigorously defend myself against, and that is the way you take my 'amiable carpings', as you call them. Firstly I do not mean at all that Carl should set no store by your opinion; it goes without saying that one recognizes an authority, and if one cannot it is only a sign of overcompensated insecurity. So that is not what I mean, it was only the rest of it that made him anxious and uncertain which seemed superfluous to me. Truth to tell,

I must confess that I have missed the mark here too, without suspecting it. Lately Carl has been analysing his attitude to his work and has discovered some resistances to it. I had connected these misgivings about Part II with his constant worry over what you would say about it, etc. It seemed out of the question that he could have resistances to his own work; but now it appears that this fear of your opinion was only a pretext for not going on with the self-analysis which this work in fact means. I realize that I have thus projected something from my immediate neighbourhood into distant Vienna and am vexed that it is always the nearest thing that one sees worst.

You have also completely misunderstood my admittedly uncalled-for meddling in your family affairs. Truthfully I didn't mean to cast a shadow on your children. I know they have turned out well and have never doubted it in the least. I hope you don't seriously believe that I wanted to say they were 'doomed to be degenerate'. I have written nothing that could even remotely mean anything of the sort. I know that with your children it is a matter of physical illnesses, but just wanted to raise the question whether these physical symptoms might not be somehow psychically conditioned, so that there might for instance be a reduced power of resistance . . .

Please write nothing of this to Carl; things are going badly enough with me as it is.

EMMA JUNG

From Emma Jung
My dear Professor Freud,   Küsnacht, 24 November 1911
Heartfelt thanks for your letter. Please don't worry, I am not always as despondent as I was in my last letter. I was afraid you were angry with me or had a bad opinion of me; that was what made me so downhearted, especially because my main complex was hit. Usually I am quite at one with my fate and see very well how lucky I am, but from time to time I am tormented by the conflict about how I can hold my own against Carl. I find I have no friends, all the people who associate with us really only want to see Carl, except for a few boring and to me quite uninteresting persons.

Naturally the women are all in love with him, and with the men I am instantly cordoned off as the wife of the father or friend. Yet I have a strong need for people and Carl too says I should stop concentrating on him and the children, but what on earth am I to do? What with my strong tendency to autoerotism it is very difficult, but also objectively it is difficult because I can never compete with Carl. In order to emphasize this I usually have to talk extra stupidly when in company.

I do my best to get transferences and if they don't turn out as I wished I am always very depressed. You will now understand why I felt so bad at the thought that I had lost your favour, and I was also afraid Carl might notice something. At any rate he now knows about the exchange of letters, as he was astonished to see one of your letters addressed to me; but I have revealed only a little of their content. Will you advise me, dear Herr Professor, and if necessary dress me down a bit? I am ever so grateful to you for your sympathy.

With warmest greetings to you and yours,

EMMA JUNG

286F

Dear friend,   30 November 1911, Vienna, IX. Berggasse 19
Two days ago Bleuler notified me of his resignation and his reasons for it; his letter ends as follows: 'I venture to hope that in view of what has happened you will regard this resignation as a self-evident and necessary step, and above all that it will not affect our personal relations in any way.' This sentence authorized me to write a critical answer. My answer was already formulated yesterday and was sent off today – uninfluenced by your letter which came this morning.

I do not know whether I have handled the matter for the best, but the 'last trouser button of my patience had snapped'. It may have been impolitic, but one cannot put up with abuse for ever . . .

In my work on totemism I have run into all sorts of difficulties, rapids, waterfalls, sand-banks, etc; I don't know yet if I shall be able to float my craft again. In any event it is going very slowly and time alone will prevent us from colliding or clashing. I read between the lines of your last letter that you have no great desire for interim reports on my work, and you are probably right. But I had to make the offer.

I should be very much interested in knowing what you mean by an extension of the concept of the libido to make it applicable to Dem. pr. I am afraid there is a misunderstanding between us, the same sort of thing as when you once said in an article that to my way of thinking libido is identical with any kind of desire, whereas in reality I hold very simply that there are two basic drives and that only the power behind the sexual drive can be termed libido.

This letter must yield to pressure of time, though I could go on chatting with you about a good many things.

Amid all the vexation a cheerful greeting.

Yours cordially, FREUD

PS. A fourth edition of the *Everyday Life* is to appear this spring.

287J

Internationale Psychoanalytische Vereinigung
Dear Professor Freud,   Küsnacht–Zürich, 11 December 1911
Again I have kept you waiting because I am unable to get the better of my bad habits.

You will see from the letterhead in what manner I have replied to Bleuler's resignation. We won't let it dampen our spirits. We have accepted five new members in Bleuler's place. No one has followed his example. I suppose he said nothing to you about his co-directorship of the *Jahrbuch*. He knows how to keep his resistance to himself and is all affability with me ...

So far as possible I shall take note of your objections to my method of dealing with mythology. I should be grateful for some detailed remarks so that I can turn your criticism to account in my second part ...

If in my last letter I showed no (apparent) interest in your study of totemism, that is due solely to the Bleuler affair which left me no time to breathe. Naturally I am extremely interested in the progress of your work; it will be of extraordinary importance to me also, even though, unlike you, I am in the habit of proceeding from the outside in.

As for the libido problem, I must confess that your remark in the Schreber analysis, p 65, 3, has set up booming reverberations. This remark, or rather the doubt expressed therein, has resuscitated all the difficulties that have beset me throughout the years in my attempt to apply the libido theory to Dem. praec. The loss of the reality function in D. pr. cannot be reduced to repression of libido (defined as sexual hunger). Not by me, at any rate. Your doubt shows me that in your eyes as well the problem cannot be solved in this way. I have now put together all the thoughts on the libido concept that have come to me over the years, and devoted a chapter to them in my second part. I have got down to a fundamental discussion of the problem and arrived at a solution which I am afraid I cannot discuss *in extenso* here. The essential point is that I try to replace the descriptive concept of libido by a *genetic* one. Such a concept covers not only the recent-sexual libido but all those forms of it which have long since split off into organized activities. A wee bit of biology was unavoidable here. My motto to the first part will protect me. One must after all take *some* risks. I wanted to make up for my abstention from theory in my 'Psychic Conflicts in a Child'. You must let my interpretation work on you as a whole to feel its full impact. Mere fragments are barely intelligible.

Congratulations on the new edition of *Everyday Life*!

Mighty rumblings in Zürich over ΨA. The Keplerbund* is sponsoring a public lecture against this abomination. Protest meetings are afoot!

What other news I have from Germany is sickening . . .

All is well with us. Kindest regards,

Most sincerely yours, JUNG

* Papists!

288F

Dear friend,   17 December 1911, Vienna, IX. Berggasse 19
I am very much impressed by your stationery. Opposition is strengthening the ties between us. Maybe Bleuler will treat us better than before, now that he has become an outsider. That would be in keeping with his ambivalence, ie his compulsive character.

I am all in favour of your attacking the libido question and I myself am expecting much light from your efforts. Often, it seems, I can go for a long while without feeling the need to clarify an obscure point, and then one day I am compelled to by the pressure of facts or by the influence of someone else's ideas.

My study of totemism and other work are not going well. I have very little time, and to draw on books and reports is not at all the same as drawing on the richness of one's own experience. Besides, my interest is diminished by the conviction that I am already in possession of the truths I am trying to prove. Such truths, of course, are of no use to anyone else. I can see from the difficulties I encounter in this work that I was not cut out for inductive investigation, that my whole makeup is intuitive, and that in setting out to establish the purely empirical science of ΨA I subjected myself to an extraordinary discipline.

This and all sorts of random influences have quite prevented me from working this week; all I can do is wait for better days ...

You have asked for an example of my objections to the most obvious method of exploiting mythology. I shall give you the example I used in the debate. Fräulein Spielrein had cited the Genesis story of the apple as an instance of woman seducing man. But in all likelihood the myth of Genesis is a wretched, tendentious distortion devised by an apprentice priest, who as we now know stupidly wove two independent sources into a single narrative (as in a dream). It is not impossible that there are two sacred trees because he found *one* tree in each of the two sources. There is something very strange and singular about the creation of Eve. Rank recently called my attention to the fact that the Bible story may quite well have reversed the original myth. Then everything would be clear; Eve would be Adam's mother, and we should be dealing with the well known motif of mother-incest, the punishment for which, etc. Equally strange is the motif of the woman giving the man an agent of fruitfulness (pomegranate) to eat. But if the story is reversed, we again have something familiar. The man giving the woman a fruit to eat is an old marriage rite (cf the story of Proserpina condemned to remain in Hades as Pluto's wife). Consequently I hold that the surface versions of myths cannot be used uncritically for comparison with our ΨAtical findings. We must find our way back to their latent, original forms by a comparative method that eliminates the distortions they have undergone in the course of their history . . .

It can't be denied that our great cause looks rather pitiful at the moment.

So let us go on toiling. We too have a destiny to fulfil.

I greet you and your whole family most warmly,

Yours ever, FREUD

290F

Dear friend,   31 December 1911, Vienna, IX. Berggasse 19
I am writing to you once again this year, because I can't always wait for you to answer and prefer to write when I have time and am in the mood . . .

The last weeks of the year have brought me all sorts of vexations. All in all, when I stop to think of it, it has not been a brilliant year for our cause. The congress in Weimar was good, so were the days preceding it in Zürich; in Klobenstein I had a brief spell of productivity. The rest has been rather on the minus side. But I suppose there must be such periods . . .

Frau C— has told me all sorts of things about you and Pfister, if you can call the hints she drops 'telling'; I gather that neither of you has yet acquired the necessary objectivity in your practice, that you still get involved, giving a good deal of yourselves and expecting the patient to give something in return. Permit me, speaking as the venerable old master, to say that this technique is invariably ill advised and that it is best to remain reserved and purely receptive. We must never let our poor neurotics drive us crazy. I believe an article on 'counter-transference' is sorely needed; of course we could not publish it, we should have to circulate copies among ourselves.

If you really feel any resentment towards me, there is no need to use Frau C— as an occasion for venting it. If she asks you to tell me about your conversation with her, I beg you, don't let her influence you or browbeat you; just wait for my next misdeed and have it out with me directly. My last set-to of this sort was with Ferenczi, who thought me cold and reserved and complained bitterly about my lack of affection, but has since fully admitted that he was in the wrong and that my conduct had been well advised. I don't deny that I like to be right. All in all, that is a sad privilege, since it is conferred by age. The trouble with you younger men seems to be a lack of understanding in dealing with your father-complexes.

And now my very best wishes for the year 1912 to the house on the lake and all its inhabitants.

Yours ever, FREUD

291J

Villa Spelma,
Dear Professor Freud,   St Moritz, 2 January 1912
First of all, heartiest New Year wishes to you and yours! May the new year add many a leaf to the laurel crown of your undying fame and open new fields for our movement.

I have waited a long time for Frau C— to inform you, as arranged, about this awkward situation. It has been weighing on my mind. I don't know what she has told you. This is what happened: she asked me about her sister, and came to see me. Then she put the crucial question. Sensing a trap, I evaded it as long as I could. It seemed to

me that she was not in a fit condition to go back to Vienna. To make
things easier for her I told her how disagreeable it was for me to find
myself involved. I said she had given me the impression that she
expected some sign of encouragement from you, and this seemed like
a personal sacrifice on your part. I also told her that I did not pretend
my view was right, since I didn't know what was going on. As far as I
could make out, I said, all she wanted was a little bit of sympathy
which you, for very good reasons best known to yourself, may have
withheld. Such sympathy would ease things for the moment, but
whether it would lead to good results in the end seemed to me doubtful, to say the least. I myself was unable, often very much *malgré
moi*, to keep my distance, because sometimes I couldn't withhold my
sympathy, and since it was there anyway, I gladly offered it to the
patient, telling myself that as a human being he was entitled to as
much esteem and personal concern as the doctor saw fit to grant him.
I told her, further, that this was how it *seemed* to me; I might be
mistaken, since my experience could in no way be measured against
yours. Afterwards I felt very much annoyed at having allowed
myself to be dragged into this discussion. I would gladly have
avoided it had not my pity for her wretched condition seduced
me into giving her the advantage, even at the risk of sending her off
with a flea in her ear. I comforted myself with the thought that,
once she was with you she would soon be on the right track again.
My chief concern was to do the right thing and get her back to
Vienna, which has in fact been done. I only hope the end justifies the
means ...

Frau Lou Andreas-Salomé,[95] of Weimar fame, wants to send me
a paper on 'sublimation'. This, if it amounts to anything, would be a
step towards the 'secularization' of the *Jahrbuch*, a step to be taken

[95] Lou Andreas-Salomé (1861–1937), born in St Petersburg, daughter of the
Russian general Von Salomé (of German Huguenot extraction); studied
theology in Zürich; friend of Nietzsche (1882); married (1887) to F. C. Andreas,
professor of archaeology at Göttingen; 1896, friendship with Rilke, with whom
she travelled twice in Russia (1899, 1900); an intimate friend of the Swedish
psychotherapist P. C. Bjerre and, in 1912–13, of the psychoanalyst Victor
Tausk. 'Frau Lou', as she was often called, remained a psychoanalyst and a
close friend of Freud to the end.

with great caution but one which would widen the readership and mobilize the intellectual forces in Germany, where Frau Lou enjoys a considerable literary reputation because of her relations with Nietzsche. I would like to hear your views.

I am spending a few days in the Engadin to recuperate from hard work.

With many kind regards and wishes,

Most sincerely yours, JUNG

292J

1003 Seestrasse, Küsnach–Zürich

Dear Professor Freud,   9 January 1912

I hope you received my last letter from St Moritz safely. I have been a niggardly correspondent, having spent a few more days travelling rather breathlessly round Germany visiting various art galleries and improving my education. Today I went back to work . . .

Stekel has announced a paper on 'Religious Symbolism in Dreams'. I *urgently* request you to read it beforehand. Since going more deeply into his *Language of Dreams* I find that Stekel's ways rather horrify me. I have no wish to cause him any undiplomatic difficulties. He will accept correction more readily from you than from me. His superficiality in scientific matters causes difficulties enough as it is.

The 'venerable old master' need fear no resentment on my part, especially when he happens to be right. I don't feel in the least put out, nor do I complain of lack of affection like Ferenczi. In this respect you would have more right to complain about me. As regards the counter-transference I am merely a little bit 'refractory' and indulge in peculiar fantasies by way of experiment. Pfister's standpoint in this matter is by no means my own. I am fully convinced that the patient must play the passive part, and that the analyst need never extort anything by means of the counter-transference (on the Christian principle: look what I've done for you, what will you do for me?). *For me* the cardinal rule is that the analyst himself must possess the freedom which the patient has to acquire in his turn, otherwise the analyst will either have to play possum or, as you say, be driven crazy. I think it is far more a question of our different ways of living than of any disagreement in principle. I do not claim any general validity for my views, so there is no reason for 'resentment'.

With very best regards,

Most sincerely yours, JUNG

293F

Dear friend, 10 January 1912, Vienna, IX. Berggasse 19
I had been racking my brains for a fortnight, wondering why I had received no answer from you – Frau C— could not have been the reason. Then with happy surprise I found the long awaited word from you in an envelope from the Engadin. And today a letter from Pfister, who assumes that I know you were bitten by a dog and have been in great pain. But I didn't know. I can understand your not writing about it; in a similar situation I would behave in the same way; but now that I know of it, I should prefer to have known right away. The wound must have healed by now, since you yourself have written. I trust there is no reason to worry about the dog.

What you must write about the Frau C— incident almost makes me feel sorry. You mustn't feel guilty towards me; if anything, you might modify your technique a little and show more reserve towards the patient. What the poor thing wants most is an intellectual flirtation that would enable her to forget her illness for a while. I keep cruelly reminding her of it . . .

If you want my opinion of Frau Salomé's offer, here it is: we ought not in principle to decline, provided she contents herself with sublimation and leaves sublimates to the chemists. If it turns out to be idealistic chitchat, we can reject it politely but firmly . . .

With kind regards, good wishes and a request for news at an early date.

Yours FREUD

Many thanks to your dear wife for the fine article about the lecture at the Keplerbund.

295J

1003 Seestrasse, Küsnacht–Zürich,
Dear Professor Freud,   23 January 1912
This time the reason for my failure to write is more complicated. We have been the victims of 'blackmail' by the newspapers and were publicly reviled although no names were named. I have even consulted a good lawyer with a possible view to bringing a libel action. But there is little prospect of success because the attack was indirect. I have therefore confined myself to a public protest by the International ΨA Association, Zürich branch; it will appear shortly in the press. This whole rumpus was precipitated by my article in *Rascher's Jahrbuch*. The time is most inopportune, as I am overwhelmed with work and grappling with the endless proliferation of mythological fantasies. In order to master the overwhelming mass of material I have to work unceasingly and am feeling intellectually drained . . .

Bleuler's 'Autism' is very misleading and extremely unclear theoretically. 'Shallow' is probably the right word for it.

I'm told Stekel's paper is brief; it can then be tucked away in an inconspicuous place.

Our French professor from Poitiers has now joined the Zürich group, so we have a professor in our midst again. Since Bleuler's departure we have been having very pleasant evenings at the society. Perceptible harmony all round. Is it true that Adler has offered his services to Specht?

With best regards,

Most sincerely yours, JUNG

On 20th Jan I lectured to 600 teachers. For an hour and a half I had to thunder out ΨA like Roland sounding his horn.

This letter is quite vacuous. At the moment I am not giving out any libido, it's all going into my work.

297J

1003 Seestrasse, Küsnacht–Zürich,
Dear Professor Freud,   2 August 1912
A quick word to let you know I am still alive. I am having grisly fights with the hydra of mythological fantasy and not all its heads are cut off yet. Sometimes I feel like calling for help when I am too hard pressed by the welter of material. So far I have managed to suppress the urge. I hope to reach dry land in the not too distant future.

Maeder or Pfister will have told you all about Zürich and our public struggles. At the moment there's a lull in the feud. For autumn Forel has saddled us with his confounded Psychotherapeutic Society and is already threatening us with total annihilation. But so far we are not annihilated in the least and the society flourishes as never before. Now the pedagogues have begun to move in. The director of the teachers' college in Bern was with me recently and wanted to collaborate. Zürich is seething, ΨA the talk of the town. One can see here how worked up people can get. On Feb 21st I have to lecture on ΨA to the clinicians; even they are eager to taste the poison. I think all this is an earnest of things to come.

I hope all is well with you. With us everything is peaceful and serene and my wife is working conscientiously at etymology.

With many kind regards,

Most sincerely yours, JUNG

298F

Dear friend,　　　　　18 February 1912, Vienna, IX. Berggasse 19
I was very glad to receive a letter from you. I am not fond of breaking habits and find no triumph in it. Wrenched out of the habit, I no
longer remember what I have told you, and besides, I still want to be
considerate of your work.

　. . . I am enclosing a prospectus of *Imago* (there are still mistakes).
I should have been glad to see your name figure prominently in this
journal and the *Zentralblatt*, but instead you hide behind your religious libidinal cloud. It seems to me that you are still giving me too
much precedence. . . . I myself am busy with my study of Taboo. I
have not been consistently well, my daily practice has prevented me
from doing much good work . . .

　For once everything is all right at home. My kind regards to you,
your wife and children.

Yours, FREUD

300J

　　　　　　　　　　　　　1003 Seestrasse, Küsnacht–Zürich,
Dear Professor Freud,　　　　　　　　25 February 1912
Many thanks for your friendly letter. I am *most* interested in the
experimental confirmation of dream analysis. Where can one read
about it? . . .

　I think I am not wrong in suspecting that you rather resent my
remissness as a correspondent. In this regard my behaviour is indeed
a little irresponsible, as I have allowed all my libido to disappear into
my work. On the other hand I don't think you need have any appre-
hensions about my protracted and invisible sojourn in the 'religious-
libidinal cloud'. I would willingly tell you what is going on up there if
only I knew how to set it down in a letter. Essentially . . . what is
keeping me hidden is the *katabasis* to the realm of the Mothers,

where, as we know, Theseus and Peirithoos remained stuck, grown fast to the rocks. But in time I shall come up again. These last days I have clawed my way considerably nearer to the surface. So please do forbear with me a while longer. I shall bring all sorts of wonderful things with me *ad majorem gloriam* ΨA.

Most sincerely yours, JUNG

301F

Dear friend,   29 February 1912, Vienna, IX. Berggasse 19

... What you say about my resentment of your tendency to neglect our correspondence warrants more thorough ΨA elucidation. There can be no doubt that I was a demanding correspondent, nor can I deny that I awaited your letters with great impatience and answered them promptly. I disregarded your earlier signs of reluctance. This time it struck me as more serious; my suspicion was aroused by your refusal to inform me of the state of your health after the dog bite and by the C— episode. I took myself in hand and quickly turned off my excess libido. I was sorry to do so, yet glad to see how quickly I managed it. Since then I have become undemanding and not to be feared. As we know, irresponsibility is not a concept compatible with depth psychology.

But it would be a severe blow to all of us if you were to draw the libido you require for your work from the association. I have the impression that the organization is not functioning properly at present. The groups know nothing of each other, there is no contact between them. The reason is that the organ designed to promote such contact – the *Bulletin* – does nothing. It has appeared only once since the congress and, as the *Zentralblatt* goes to press a month in advance, the next *Bulletin* cannot come out until April at the earliest. Every month it should offer reports on the activity of the local groups and a message from the president; and it should provide information about the destinies of ΨA in the world at large.

I am told here that Riklin has not been answering letters or acknowledging receipt of manuscripts. The bond within the association has narrowed down to receiving the *Zentralblatt*. Yet we believed the organization to be necessary. We made sacrifices and alienated people in order to set it up. I am unable to withdraw from the day-to-day concerns of ΨA to the extent that I planned when we founded the association and I proposed Adler as chairman here. But I am less concerned with the present than with the future; I am determined to make all necessary preparations for it, so as to see everything safe in your hands when the time comes.

I should like also to remind you that you undertook at the last congress to make arrangements for the next one early in the year. I personally shall not mind if it is dropped this year; that would leave me free in September. But of course I shall attend if it is held ...

Let me assure you of my keen interest in your libido paper. With kind regards,

Yours ever, FREUD

303J

1003 Seestrasse, Küsnacht–Zürich

Dear Professor Freud,   3 March 1912
Your letter has made me very pensive. First of all I would like to tell you, with reference to the *Bulletin*, that Riklin had strict instructions which once again he has simply neglected. For the sake of my work I wanted to dispense with pure formalities for two months. Riklin has failed in a way I cannot permit to carry out my instructions. I have therefore issued an ultimatum: I shall relieve him of his post if he continues to neglect his duties. I shall accept his resignation at the next opportunity. The reports he received from the local groups should have been sent to the *Zentralblatt* every month.

I have by no means forgotten the arrangements to be made for the congress. On the contrary I have repeatedly requested the military authorities to let me know when my period of service falls due this year. So far I have not succeeded, because the tour of duty for the mountain troops, to which I am detailed, is not yet fixed. This should be known very shortly. It was for *this reason* that I was unable to set a date for the congress . . .

As for the other remarks in your letter, I must own that I have never been able to rid myself of the idea that what I have done and still am doing to promote the spread of ΨA must surely be of far greater moment to you than my personal awkwardness and nastiness. If ever anything serious had befallen me that might have imperilled our work, it goes without saying that I would have informed you. I have my work cut out to put up with my own personality without wishing to foist it on you and add to your burdens. Whenever I had anything important to communicate I have always done so. I have not kept up a lively correspondence during these last weeks because I wanted if possible to write *no letters at all*, simply in order to gain time for my work and not in order to give *you* a demonstration of ostentatious neglect. Or can it be that you mistrust me? Experience has shown how groundless this is. Of course I have opinions which are not yours about the ultimate truths of ΨA – though even this is not certain, for one cannot discuss everything under the sun by letter – but you won't, I suppose, take umbrage on that account. I am ready at any time to adapt my opinions to the judgement of someone who knows better, and always have been. I would never have sided with you in the first place had not heresy run in my blood. Since I have no professional ambitions I can afford to admit mistakes. Let Zarathustra speak for me:

One repays a teacher badly if one remains only a pupil.
And why, then, should you not pluck at my laurels?
You respect me; but how if one day your respect should tumble?
Take care that a falling statue does not strike you dead!
    You had not yet sought yourselves when you found me.
Thus do all believers – .
Now I bid you lose me and find yourselves;
and only when you have all denied me will I return to you.[96]

96 Tr R. J. Hollingdale, Penguin Classics.

This is what you have taught me through ΨA. As one who is truly your follower, I must be stout hearted, not least towards you.

With kindest regards,

Most sincerely yours, JUNG

304F

Dear friend,   5 March 1912, Vienna, IX. Berggasse 19

Why so 'pensive' when the situation is so simple? I have pointed out to you that the association cannot prosper when the president loses interest in it over a period of months, especially when he has so unreliable an assistant as our friend Riklin. You seem to recognize that I am right, which disposes of one point. You make it clear to me that you don't wish to write to me at present, and I reply that I am trying to make the privation easy for myself. Isn't that my right? Isn't it a necessary act of self-defence?

Otherwise we agree about everything. You write that you have always thought your past and prospective contributions to the cause should mean more to me than your 'personal nastiness and awkwardness' – (your friends would put it more mildly and speak of your 'moods'). I beg you to go on thinking so. The indestructible foundation of our personal relationship is our involvement in ΨA; but on this foundation it seemed tempting to build something finer though more labile, a reciprocal intimate friendship. Shouldn't we go on building?

You speak of the need for intellectual independence and quote Nietzsche in support of your view. I am in full agreement. But if a third party were to read this passage, he would ask me when I had tried to tyrannize you intellectually, and I should have to say: I don't know. I don't believe I ever did. Adler, it is true, made similar complaints, but I am convinced that his neurosis was speaking for him. Still, if you think you want greater freedom from me, what can I do but give up my feeling of urgency about our relationship, occupy my unemployed libido elsewhere, and bide my time until you discover that you can tolerate greater intimacy? When that happens, you will find me willing. During the transition to this attitude of reserve, I have complained very quietly. You would have thought me insincere if I had not reacted at all.

Why, I repeat, should you be so 'pensive'? Do you think I am looking for someone else capable of being at once my friend, my helper and my heir, or that I expect to find another so soon? If not, then we are at one again, and you are right in expending your pensiveness on your study of the libido. My question about the congress was only remotely connected with the affective theme of this letter. Thank you for your answer. About the new groups, I agree with you: they must spring up in response to a spontaneous need. Rest assured of my affective cathexis and continue to think of me in friendship, even if you do not write often.

With kindest regards,

Yours ever, FREUD

310J

Hotel Milan–Bahnhof,
Lugano, 2 April 1912

Dear Professor Freud,

At last I have got away from Zürich so as to be alone with myself for a few days before going to Florence with my wife. As you see I am in Lugano, where it is raining miserably. Nevertheless, I am on my own here and unknown, and that is the acme of pleasure.

... Strange things must be going on at Burghölzli. There is talk of Bleuler's retirement. They say he wants to seclude himself in his father's place in Zollikon. (All this is only hearsay, of course.) ...

Frau Lou's manuscript will be sent to you only after your holiday. There are 'tremendous' things in it.

I am eager to see *Imago*. I cannot, however, quite suppress the fear that it will drain valuable forces away from the *Jahrbuch*. We have in Zürich too scanty a stock of young blood. Perhaps I am being over-pessimistic because the mass of case material now piling up in the ΨA literature has begun to sicken me. Of course this is only a subjective feeling, no doubt induced by my patients. All the same, case material is unbelievably monotonous once you have got over the first shock of wonderment.

I hope you will have some fine and peaceful days on the Adriatic together with Ferenczi. I too must gather strength to produce the eight lectures, which are to be given in *English*. This forces me to take every word literally. A formidable task. This time I shall travel back via the West Indies.

Kind regards,

Most sincerely yours, JUNG

311F

Dear friend,   21 April 1912, Vienna, IX. Berggasse 19
I hope you are home again, refreshed by a pleasant holiday. Now perhaps you will be interested to hear about the rather uneventful interval.

... My correspondence with Binswanger has revived; what I had interpreted as flagging interest might better have been explained by illness and an operation.

Your news of Bleuler is of the greatest interest to me. If he receives an appointment elsewhere or resigns, you can imagine how glad I should be for you to exchange your house on the lake for Burghölzli. But I don't think he will leave unless he gets an appointment. His material circumstances would not allow it. On the other hand, I note to my regret that his withdrawal from the Zürich group seems to have done the group more harm than I could foresee, and I would greatly welcome the news that he had rejoined. I shall write to him again when I have an offprint of the *Imago* article, naturally making no mention of what I have just said. As you know, peacemakers are not usually very successful.

I attributed it to your *pre*-holiday mood that you regarded *Imago* as a rival of the *Jahrbuch*. Don't forget that it's the same company under three different names, with slight variations in function. I am looking forward with resignation to Lou Salomé's essay. But now I want to bring up a matter that may warrant intervention on your part. As you can see from the enclosure, Morton Prince has made use of ΨA for a personal attack on Roosevelt, which seems to be creating quite a stir over there. In my opinion such a thing is absolutely inadmissible, an infringement on privacy, which to be sure is not greatly respected in America. But I leave it entirely to you whether you regard a statement as expedient, especially since you will be seeing the American association in September . . .

I am eagerly looking forward to your second libido paper with its new concept of the libido, because I imagine that the 'Declaration of Independence' you announced a while ago is expressed in it and may indeed have related to nothing else. You will see that I am quite capable of listening and accepting, or of waiting until an idea becomes clearer to me.

I am satisfied with the work being done here and with the group . . . I am less pleased with the general world situation of the cause; but perhaps that is a mood brought on by overwork.

One learns little by little to renounce one's personality.

With kind regards,

Yours ever, FREUD

312J

1003 Seestrasse, Küsnacht–Zürich

Dear Professor Freud,   27 April 1912

It was good of you to have your letter waiting for me on my return. I spent some very pleasant days in Florence, Pisa, and Genoa and now feel quite rested . . .

Morton Prince is just a mudslinger. Nothing can be done directly, since one cannot start a fight with American newspapers. All they are interested in is sensationalism, bribery, and corruption. But in my American lectures I can slip in a parenthetical remark that will make our position clear ...

I would like to keep the article on Roosevelt a few days longer for further study, and then send it back to you.

Now and then I correspond 'amicably' with Bleuler on scientific matters. There seems to be a tacit agreement between us not to tread on one another's corns.

... Many thanks for your exceedingly interesting article in *Imago*. A pity the bulk of my manuscript is already with Deuticke; I could have made a number of improvements. Like you, I am absorbed in the incest problem and have come to conclusions which show incest primarily as a fantasy problem. Originally, morality was simply a ceremony of atonement, a substitutive prohibition, so that the ethnic prohibition of incest may not mean biological incest at all, but merely the utilization of infantile incest material for the construction of the first prohibitions. (I don't know whether I am expressing myself clearly!) If biological incest were meant, then father-daughter incest would have fallen under the prohibition much more readily than that between son-in-law and mother-in-law. The tremendous role of the mother in mythology has a significance far outweighing the biological incest problem – a significance that amounts to pure fantasy.

Kind regards,

Most sincerely yours, JUNG

313J

1003 Seestrasse, Küsnacht–Zürich,
Dear Professor Freud,   8 May 1912
I very much regret my inability to make myself intelligible at a distance without sending you the voluminous background material. What I mean is that the exclusion of the father-daughter relationship

from the incest prohibition, usually explained by the role of the father as (egoistic) lawgiver, must originate from the relatively late period of patriarchy, when culture was sufficiently far advanced for the formation of family ties. In the family the father was strong enough to keep the son in order with a thrashing, and without laying down the law, if in those tender years the son showed any incestuous inclinations. In riper years, on the other hand, when the son might really be a danger to the father, and laws were therefore needed to restrain him, the son no longer had any real incestuous desires for the mother, with her sagging belly and varicose veins. A far more genuine incest tendency is to be conjectured for the early, cultureless period of mother-right, ie in the matrilineal family. There the father was purely fortuitous and counted for nothing, so he would not have had the slightest interest (considering the general promiscuity) in enacting laws against the son. (In fact, there was no such thing as a father's son!) I therefore think that the incest prohibition (understood as primitive morality) was merely a formula or ceremony of atonement *in re vili*:[97] what was valuable for the child – the mother – and is so worthless for the adult that it is kicked into the bush, acquires an extraordinary value thanks to the incest prohibition, and is declared to be desirable and forbidden. (This is genuine primitive morality: any bit of fun may be prohibited, but it is just as likely to become a fetish.) Evidently the object of the prohibition is not to prevent incest but to consolidate the family (or piety, or the social structure).

With Bleuler I have had an apparently amicable but in reality painful to-do about a dissertation which he had given me on his own initiative for the *Jahrbuch*, but which I rejected as worthless. Maybe you will be called in as a super-expert. In my view the paper is too stupid and too bad. The female patient it deals with is imbecilic and hopelessly sterile, and the authoress is a goose. The whole thing is a complete bore.

Thank heavens Frau Lou Andreas-Salomé has suddenly been enlightened by a kindly spirit and has taken back her paper for an indefinite period. So we are rid of that worry.

97 = 'in worthless matters'.

Winterstein[98] has turned up, throbbing with the awe of an initiate admitted to the inner sanctum, who knows the mysteries and the hallowed rites of the *katabasion*. We welcomed him with the benevolent smile of augurs.

With best regards,

Most sincerely yours, JUNG

314F

Dear friend,   14 May 1912, Vienna, IX. Berggasse 19

It will surely come as no surprise to you that your conception of incest is still unclear to me. Sometimes I have the impression that it is not far removed from what we have thought up to now, but this can only be clarified by a more detailed discussion. As for your arguments, I have three observations to make; they are not refutations but should be taken merely as expressions of doubt.

1   Many authors regard a primordial state of promiscuity as highly unlikely. I myself, in all modesty, favour a different hypothesis in regard to the primordial period – Darwin's.

2   Mother right should not be confused with gynaecocracy. There is little to be said for the latter. Mother right is perfectly compatible with the polygamous abasement of woman.

3   It seems likely that there have been father's sons at all times. A father is one who possesses a mother sexually (and the children as property). The fact of having been engendered by a father has, after all, no psychological significance for a child . . .

Of course I am willing to express an opinion of the paper in dispute between you and Bleuler, but I should not like to make a decision, because his rights as a director are not inferior to mine.

I should welcome a postcard with your answer.

Sincerely yours, FREUD

[98] Alfred Baron von Winterstein, psychologist of Leipzig.

315J

1003 Seestrasse, Küsnacht–Zürich,
Dear Professor Freud,   17 May 1912

... As regards the question of incest, I am afraid of making a very
paradoxical impression on you. I only venture to throw a bold conjecture into the discussion: the large amount of free-floating anxiety
in primitive man, which led to the creation of taboo ceremonies in
the widest sense (totem, etc), produced among other things the *incest
taboo* as well (or rather: the mother and father taboo). The incest
taboo does not correspond with the specific value of incest *sensu
strictiori* any more than the sacredness of the totem corresponds with
its biological value. From this standpoint we must say that incest is
forbidden *not because it is desired* but because the free-floating
anxiety regressively reactivates infantile material and turns it into a
ceremony of atonement (as though incest had been, or might have
been, desired). Psychologically, the incest prohibition doesn't have
the significance which one must ascribe to it if one assumes the existence of a particularly strong incest wish. The aetiological significance
of the incest prohibition must be compared directly with the so-
called sexual trauma, which usually owes its aetiological role only to
regressive reactivation. The trauma is *seemingly important* or real,
and so is the incest prohibition or incest barrier, which from the
psychoanalytical point of view has taken the place of the sexual
trauma. Just as *cum grano salis* it doesn't matter whether a sexual
trauma really occurred or not, or was a mere fantasy, it is psychologically quite immaterial whether an incest barrier really existed or
not, since it is essentially a question of later development whether or
not the so-called problem of incest will become of apparent importance. Another comparison: the occasional cases of real incest are of
as little importance for the ethnic incest prohibitions as the occasional outbursts of bestiality among primitives are for the ancient
animal cults. In my opinion the incest barrier can no more be explained by reduction to the possibility of real incest than the animal
cult can be explained by reduction to real bestiality. The animal cult

is explained by an infinitely long psychological development which is of paramount importance and not by primitive bestial tendencies – these are nothing but the quarry that provides the material for building a temple. But the temple and its meaning have nothing whatever to do with the quality of the building stones. This applies also to the incest taboo, which as a special psychological institution has a much greater – and different – significance than the prevention of incest, even though it may look the same from outside. (The temple is white, yellow, or red according to the material used.) Like the stones of a temple, the incest taboo is the symbol or vehicle of a far wider and special meaning which has as little to do with real incest as hysteria with the sexual trauma, the animal cult with the bestial tendency and the temple with the stone (or better still, with the primitive dwelling from whose form it is derived).

I hope I have expressed myself a bit more clearly this time.

Bleuler has withdrawn the dissertation. By golly, it was really too stupid. And I won't have any stupidities in the *Jahrbuch*. As director, Bleuler should make better use of his critical faculties. I only hope you won't be bothered with it.

With many kind regards,

Most sincerely yours, JUNG

316F

Dear friend,   23 May 1912, Vienna, IX. Berggasse 19
Many thanks for your quick answer and explanations . . .
In the libido question, I finally see at what point your conception differs from mine. (I am referring of course to incest, but I am thinking of your heralded modifications in the concept of the libido.) What I still fail to understand is why you have abandoned the older view and what other origin and motivation the prohibition of incest can have. Naturally I don't expect you to explain this difficult matter more fully in letters; I shall be patient until you publish your ideas on the subject.

I value your letter for the warning it contains, and the reminder of my first big error, when I mistook fantasies for realities. I shall be careful and keep my eyes open every step of the way.

But if we now set reason aside and attune the machine to pleasure, I own to a strong antipathy towards your innovation. It has two sources. First the regressive character of the innovation. I believe we have held up to now that anxiety originated in the prohibition of incest; now you say on the contrary that the prohibition of incest originated in anxiety, which is very similar to what was said before the days of ΨA.

Secondly, because of a disastrous similarity to a theorem of Adler's, though of course I do not condemn all Adler's inventions. He said: the incest libido is 'arranged'; ie the neurotic has no desire at all for his mother, but wants to provide himself with a motive for scaring himself away from his libido; he therefore pretends to himself that his libido is so enormous that it does not even spare his mother. Now this still strikes me as fanciful, based on utter incomprehension of the unconscious. In the light of your hints, I have no doubt that your derivation of the incestuous libido will be different, But there is a certain resemblance.

But I repeat: I recognize that these objections are determined by the pleasure principle.

I shall be closer to you geographically during the Whitsun weekend. On the evening of the 24th I shall be leaving for Constance to see Binswanger. I am planning to be back on the following Tuesday. The time is so short that I shall not be able to do more.

With kind regards to you and your family,

Yours, FREUD

318J

1003 Seestrasse, Küsnacht–Zürich,
Dear Professor Freud,   8 June 1912
Many thanks for kindly sending me your offprint, 'Recommend-
ations', so excellent in content and worthy of emulation!

On the question of incest, I am grieved to see what powerful
affects you have mobilized for your counter offensive against my
suggestions. Since I think I have objective reasons on my side, I am
forced to stand by my interpretation of the incest concept, and see no
way out of the dilemma. It is not for frivolous reasons or from regressive prejudices that I have been led to this formulation, as will, I
hope, become clear to you when you read my painstaking and intri-
cate examination of the whole problem in my second part. The parallel with Adler is a bitter pill; I swallow it without a murmur.
Evidently this is my fate. There is nothing to be done about it, for my
reasons are overwhelming. I set out with the idea of corroborating
the old view of incest, but was obliged to see that things are different
from what I expected ...

The fact that you felt no need to see me during your visit to
Kreuzlingen must, I suppose, be attributed to your displeasure at my
development of the libido theory. I hope we shall be able to come to
an understanding on controversial points later on. It seems I shall
have to go my own way for some time to come. But you know how
obstinate we Swiss are.

With kind regards,

Most sincerely yours, JUNG

319F

Dear friend,   13 June 1912, Vienna, IX. Berggasse 12

About the libido question, we shall see. The nature of the change you have made is not quite clear to me and I know nothing of its motivation. Once I am better informed, I shall surely be able to switch to objectivity, precisely because I am well aware of my bias. Even if we cannot come to terms immediately, there is no reason to suppose that this scientific difference will detract from our personal relations. I can recall that there were profounder differences between us at the beginning of our relationship. In 1908 it was reported to me from various quarters that a 'negative fluctuation' had occurred in Burghölzli, that my views had been superseded. This did not deter me from visiting you in Zürich, in fact it was my reason for doing so, and I found everything quite different from what I had been led to expect. Consequently I cannot agree with you when you say that my failure to go to Zürich from Constance was motivated by my displeasure at your libido theory. A few months earlier you would probably have spared me this interpretation, all the more so because the circumstances do not warrant it. They are as follows: because of illness in my family my visit to Binswanger was definitely decided on only a few days in advance. When I saw it would be possible, I wrote to you, so that you must have known at the time of my arrival that I would be in Constance. I then spent two nights and one day on the train, so as to be able to spend two nights and two days in one place. After a period of gruelling work that was just about enough travelling. To go to Zürich I should have had to sacrifice one of the two days and so deprive my host of half the time allotted to him. I had a special reason unknown to you, for wanting to talk with Binswanger at that time.[99] But if you had come and spent half a day in Constance, it would have been a great pleasure for us all. I did not ask you to come, because it is an imposition to ask anyone to spend a holiday in such a way if he has something better to do or wants to

---

[99] Binswanger underwent surgery for a malignancy (Max Schurr, *Freud: Living and Dying*, 1972, p 262).

rest. But I should have been pleased if you yourself had thought of it. Binswanger would not have taken it amiss, because he phoned Häberlin asking him to come – as it happened, he was unable to, because his wife was on holiday. Your remark pains me because it shows that you do not feel sure of me . . .

Imago is thriving and already has 230 subscribers.

Adler's book *On the Nervous Character* appeared a few days ago. I am unlikely to read it but I have been made acquainted with parts of it. Perhaps he will capture the Viennese citadel that has resisted us so stubbornly. He can have it. Viennese interest in *Imago*, for instance, has been conspicuously small, whereas subscribers turn up in the unlikeliest small towns in Germany . . .

With kind regards,

Yours, FREUD

320J

1003 Seestrasse, Küsnacht–Zürich,
Dear Professor Freud,   18 July 1912
Until now I didn't know what to say to your last letter. Now I can only say: I understand the Kreuzlingen gesture. Whether your policy is the right one will become apparent from the success or failure of my future work. I have always kept my distance, and this will guard against any imitation of Adler's disloyalty.

Yours sincerely, JUNG

321J

1003 Seestrasse, Küsnacht–Zürich,

Dear Professor Freud, 2 August 1912

... Rank's book has arrived. It is a very distinguished piece of work and will make a big impression. But, as you know, I am not in agreement with his theoretical position on the incest problem. The salient fact is simply the regressive movement of libido and not the mother, otherwise people without parents would have no chance to develop an incest complex; whereas I know from experience that the contrary is true. In certain circumstances, indeed as a general rule, the fantasy object is *called* 'mother'. But it seems to me highly unlikely that primitive man ever passed through an era of incest. Rather, it would appear that the first manifestation of incestuous desire was the prohibition itself. Later I shall review Rank's book for the *Jahrbuch*. It contains some splendid material, and with the above proviso I fully subscribe to Rank's interpretation. I shall also subject Adler's book to critical scrutiny and take the occasion to underline its improprieties.

My American lectures are now finished and will put forward tentative suggestions for modifying certain theoretical formulations. I shall not, however, follow Adler's recipe for overcoming the father, as you seem to imagine. That cap doesn't fit.

I shall table my presidency for discussion at the next congress so as to let the association decide whether deviations are to be tolerated or not.

With best regards,

Most sincerely yours, JUNG

The Fordham Lectures; the Committee

After his Army service, Jung left Zürich for New York on Saturday, 7 September. Jung's foreword to the lectures, entitled The Theory of Psychoanalysis, *states that they were given in the extension course at Fordham University, Bronx, New York, in September. They set forth in detail Jung's chief departures from Freudian principles.*

It was also during this summer that Jones, who was in Vienna, conceived the idea of forming 'a small group of trustworthy analysts as a sort of "Old Guard" around Freud'. He was distressed, he writes, by the defections of Adler and Stekel, 'and it was disturbing to hear from Freud in July, 1912, that now his relations with Jung were beginning to be strained.' Ferenczi and Rank concurred with Jones, who on 30 July wrote to Freud about the idea and received an enthusiastic response. Sachs and Abraham were brought into the 'Committee', as the secret group was called, and in 1919 Freud proposed Eitingon as the sixth member. (See Jones, II, ch VI.)

323J

1003 Seestrasse, Küsnacht–Zürich,
Dear Professor Freud,   11 November 1912

I have just got back from America and hasten to give you my news. Of course I should have done so from America weeks ago but was so busy that I had neither the inclination nor the leisure to write.

I found the activities of the ΨA Society most satisfactory. There are some really bright people in it. Brill has gone to a lot of trouble and is now reaping the rewards of his labours. Altogether, the ΨA movement over there has enjoyed a tremendous upswing since we were last in America. Everywhere I met with great interest and was favourably received. Thus I had rich soil to work on and was able to do a very great deal for the spread of the movement. I gave nine lectures at the Jesuit (!) University of Fordham, New York – a critical account of the development of the theory of ΨA. I had an audience of c 90 psychiatrists and neurologists. The lectures were in English. Besides that, I held a two-hour seminar every day for a fortnight, for c 8 professors. Naturally I also made room for those of my views which deviate in places from the hitherto existing conceptions, particularly in regard to the libido theory. I found that my version of ΨA won over many people who until now had been put off by the problem of sexuality in neurosis.[100] As soon as I have an offprint, I shall take pleasure in sending you a copy of my lectures in the hope that you will gradually come to accept certain innovations already hinted at in my libido paper. I feel no need to let you down provided you can take an objective view of our common endeavours. I regret it very much if you think that the modifications in question have been prompted solely by resistances to you. Your Kreuzlingen gesture has dealt me a lasting wound. I prefer a direct confrontation. With me it is not a question of caprice but of fighting for what I hold to be true. In this matter no personal regard for you can restrain me. On the other hand, I hope this letter will make it plain that I feel no need at all to break off personal relations with you. I do not identify you with a point of doctrine. I have always tried to play fair with you and shall continue to do so no matter how our personal relations turn out. Obviously I would prefer to be on friendly terms with you, to whom I owe so much, but I want your objective judgement and no feelings of resentment. I think I deserve this much if only for reasons of expediency: I have done more to promote the ΨA movement than Rank, Stekel, Adler, etc put together. I can only assure you that there is no resistance on my side, unless it be my refusal to be treated like a fool riddled with complexes. I think I have objective reasons for my views.

I lectured in Chicago, Baltimore, and at the New York Academy of Medicine with apparent success. I also gave two clinical lectures on Dem. praec. in Bellevue Hospital, New York, and another on Ward's Island, and in Washington I analysed fifteen Negroes, with demonstrations. On the way back I stopped off in Amsterdam and got van Renterghem, van Emden, and van der Chijs to start a local group.

I hear difficulties have arisen with Stekel. I'd like to know a bit

100 This is apparently what Freud refers to in 'On the History of the Pyscho-Analytic Movement' (orig. 1914) SE XIV, p. 58: 'In 1912 Jung boasted, in a letter from [sic] America, that his modifications of psycho-analysis had overcome the resistances of many people who had hitherto refused to have anything to do with it. I replied [324 F para. 1] that this was nothing to boast of, and that the more he sacrificed of the hard-won truths of psycho-analysis the more would he see resistance vanishing.'

more about this since the *Zentralblatt* is the official organ. I can hardly conceive of your withdrawing as director. This would be a source of endless difficulties, also for the association, not to mention the loss of face. It is rather Stekel who should quit. Stekel has done enough damage as it is with his mania for indecent confessions bordering on exhibitionism. I am rather surprised that, as president, I have received no direct news.

With best regards,

Most sincerely, JUNG

324F

Dear Dr Jung,   14 November 1912, Vienna, IX. Berggasse 19
I greet you on your return from America, no longer as affectionately as on the last occasion in Nuremburg – you have successfully broken me of that habit – but still with considerable sympathy, interest, and satisfaction at your personal success. Many thanks for your news of the state of affairs in America. But we know that the battle will not be decided over there. You have reduced a good deal of resistance with your modifications, but I shouldn't advise you to enter this in the credit column because, as you know, the farther you remove yourself from what is new in ΨA, the more certain you will be of applause and the less resistance you will meet.

You can count on my objectivity and hence on the continuance of our relations; I still hold that personal variations are quite justified and I still feel the same need to continue our collaboration. I must remind you that we first made friends at a time when you had gone back to the toxic theory of Dem. pr.

I must own that I find your harping on the 'Kreuzlingen gesture' both incomprehensible and insulting, but there are things that cannot be straightened out in writing.

I am eagerly looking forward to an offprint of your lectures, because your long paper on the libido, part of which – not the whole – I liked very much, has not clarified your innovations for me as I might have wished.

My letter to Riklin, written before I could have known you were back, has given you the information you ask for about developments at the *Zentralblatt*. For the sake of completeness I shall tell you a little more. I presume that you know now why I withdrew as director, instead of changing the editor. I saw that I did not have the power, that the publisher sided with Stekel and would find some indirect way of forcing me out, which would have had grave disadvantages. For a whole year I should have had to take the responsibility for a journal which Stekel manipulated at will and on which I could exert no influence. And by next September we should have been left without an organ. That was intolerable. And so I jettisoned the journal along with the editor.

You ask not unreasonably: but what about the official character of the journal? Naturally this was the first point I made in my discussions with Stekel. I suggested that we settle our dispute by letting the local groups (or the Viennese alone) vote on it. I spoke of his obligations, but he was puffed up with possessive pride and my appeals had no effect. His only answer was: It's my journal and none of the association's business. At this point I should have taken the logical step of submitting the matter to the president for an official decision if – said president had been within reach. But you had left for America without delegating anyone to attend to your presidential business; we had not been informed either officially or privately when you would return, and rumour had it that you would be gone a long time. If I had known you would be back on 12 November, I should have been glad to wait, to leave the decision to you as my superior, and to let you convince yourself that Stekel was not living up to his contract, that nothing could be done with Bergmann, and that we needed a new organ. As it was, I had to attend to it myself. The only other central authority provided for in our statutes, the council of presidents of the branch societies, did not exist; you had not activated such a council – a point which we ought perhaps to press at the next congress.

If I had waited indefinitely for your return, precious time would have been lost. With all the negotiations between Vienna, Zürich and Wiesbaden it would have been impossible to launch the new organ at the beginning of 1913; we should have had to wait until the middle of the year.

Thanks to my prompt action, we shall have an organ of our own again as of 15 January, with a new name and a different publisher, but otherwise, I trust, no worse for being edited by Ferenczi and Rank. I shall soon send you all the details concerning this new journal. But please don't forget that if I am to put your name on the masthead I need a formal statement from you renouncing the *Zentralblatt* and endorsing the new journal . . .

It may interest you to hear about a letter which was shown around at the Vienna society, in which Adler describes his impressions at the Zürich congress. He writes that he found the Zürich people in a state of panic flight from sexuality, but is unable to prevent them from making use of his ideas. Maybe that will be a lesson to Riklin, who praised him quite unnecessarily in his report on the congress.

Requesting your prompt attention to the matters here mentioned and wishing you well in your work, I remain

Sincerely,

Your colleague, FREUD

325J

Internationale Psychoanalytische Vereinigung

Dear Mr President,　　　　　　　Küsnacht–Zürich, 14 November 1912
In consequence of the latest developments in Vienna a situation has arisen which is in urgent need of discussion. I therefore invite the presidents of the various European branch societies to a conference in Munich on Sunday, November 24th. Kindly inform me *by return* whether you accept this invitation in principle. Further details concerning the place and date of the conference will be communicated later.

Very truly yours,
For C. G. Jung:
　　F. RIKLIN

326J

1003 Seestrasse, Küsnacht–Zürich,
15 November 1912

Dear Professor Freud,

Your letter, just arrived, has evoked in me a ΨA attitude which seems to be the only right one at the moment. I shall continue to go my own way undaunted. I shall take leave of Stekel's journal because I refuse to go on working with him. I dare not offer you my name for your journal; since you have disavowed me so thoroughly, my collaboration can hardly be acceptable. I should prefer to meet you on the neutral territory of the *Jahrbuch*, which I hope you will enable me to go on editing by not imposing too strict a regimen. I propose to let tolerance prevail in the *Jahrbuch* so that everyone can develop in his own way. Only when granted freedom do people give of their best. We should not forget that the history of human truths is also the history of human errors. So let us give the well meant error its rightful place.

Whether my liberalism is compatible with the further conduct of the association's affairs is a question to be discussed by the association itself at the next congress.

Adler's letter is stupid chatter and can safely be ignored. We aren't children here. If Adler ever says anything sensible or worth listening to I shall take notice of it, even though I don't think much of him as a person. As in my work heretofore, so now and in the future I shall keep away from petty complexes and do unflinchingly what I hold to be true and right.

With best regards,

Most sincerely yours, JUNG

The Munich Conference

Jung had called the meeting in Munich in order to discuss and settle formally Freud's plan of leaving the Zentralblatt *to Stekel and founding a new journal, the* Internationale Zeitschrift, *in place of it. The colleagues present were Freud, Jones (who had been in Italy), Abraham, Seif (of Munich), and from Zürich Jung, Riklin, and J. H.*

W. van Ophuijsen, then secretary of the Zürich society. All agreed with Freud's course of action.

The conference also settled the theme for the next congress, which would be in Munich in September 1913: 'The Function of Dream'. Maeder was to introduce it, and Rank would be his co-speaker.

Then, during a two-hour walk before lunch, Freud and Jung discussed the 'gesture of Kreuzlingen'; Jung admitted an oversight and made an apology, and a reconciliation was effected. Towards the end of a high-spirited lunch, Freud began to criticize the Swiss for omitting his name from their psychoanalytic publications. Suddenly, he had a fainting attack. Jung has described and analysed the episode in Memories.

Of the conference, Freud wrote to Putnam, 28 Nov 1912: 'Everybody was charming to me, including Jung. A talk between us swept away a number of unnecessary personal irritations. I hope for further successful cooperation. Theoretical differences need not interfere. However, I shall hardly be able to accept his modification of the libido theory since all my experience contradicts his position' (Putnam and Psychoanalysis).

328J

1003 Seestrasse, Küsnacht–Zürich,
Dear Professor Freud,   26 November 1912

I am glad we were able to meet in Munich, as this was the first time I have really understood you. I realized how different I am from you. This realization will be enough to effect a radical change in my whole attitude. Now you can rest assured that I shall not give up our personal relationship. Please forgive the mistakes which I will not try to excuse or extenuate. I hope the insight I have at last gained will guide my conduct from now on. I am most distressed that I did not gain this insight much earlier. It could have spared you so many disappointments.

I have been very worried about how you got back to Vienna, and whether the night journey may not have been too much of a strain for you. Please let me know how you are, if only a few words on a postcard.

May I ask you to be so kind as to make room for me among the contributors to your new journal? I shall try to send you something if the occasion arises. You know, of course, how limited my resources are, and how I am squeezed dry by the *Jahrbuch* and my teaching activities. However, I am counting on your patience . . .

I hope all is well with you personally and with your family.

With kind regards,

Yours sincerely, JUNG

329F

Dear Dr Jung,   29 November 1912, Vienna, IX. Berggasse 19

Many thanks for your friendly letter, which shows me that you have dispelled various misconceptions about my conduct and encourages me to entertain the best of hopes for our future collaboration. Believe me, it was not easy for me to moderate my demands on you; but once I had succeeded in doing so, the swing in the other direction was not too severe, and for me our relationship will always retain an echo of our past intimacy. I believe we shall have to lay by a fresh store of benevolence towards one another, for it is easy to see that there will be controversies between us and one always finds it rather irritating when the other party insists on having an opinion of his own.

Now I shall be glad to answer your questions. My attack in Munich was no more serious than the similar one at the Essighaus in Bremen; my condition improved in the evening and I had an excellent night's sleep. According to my private diagnosis, it was migraine (of the M. ophthalm. type), not without a psychic factor which unfortunately I haven't time to track down now. The dining room of the Park Hotel seems to hold a fatality for me. Six years ago I had a first attack of the same kind there, and four years ago a second. A bit of neurosis that I ought really to look into . . .

In the second number Ferenczi will probably publish a study of your libido paper, which, it is hoped, will do justice both to the author and to his work. I am gradually coming to terms with this paper (yours, I mean) and I now believe that in it you have brought us a great revelation, though not the one you intended. You seem to have solved the riddle of all mysticism, showing it to be based on the symbolic utilization of complexes that have outlived their function . . .

In the family all are well and looking forward to the wedding which is to take place at the end of January. My daughter is going to Hamburg.

With kind regards to you and your wife,

Your untransformed FREUD

330J

Internationale Psychoanalytische Vereinigung

Küsnacht–Zürich, 3 December 1912

This letter is a brazen attempt to accustom you to my style. So look out!

Dear Professor Freud,

My very best thanks for one passage in your letter, where you speak of a 'bit of neurosis' you haven't got rid of. This 'bit' should, in my opinion, be taken very seriously indeed because, as experience shows, it leads 'to the semblance of a voluntary death'. I have suffered from this bit in my dealings with you, though you haven't seen it and didn't understand me properly when I tried to make my position clear. If these blinkers were removed you would, I am sure, see my work in a very different light. As evidence that you – if I may be permitted so disrespectful an expression – *underestimate* my work by a very wide margin, I would cite your remark that 'Without intending it, I have solved the riddle of all mysticism, showing it to be based on the symbolic utilization of complexes that have outlived their function.'

My dear Professor, forgive me again, but this sentence shows me that you deprive yourself of the possibility of understanding my work by your underestimation of it. You speak of this insight as though it were some kind of pinnacle, whereas actually it is at the very bottom of the mountain. This insight has been self-evident to us for years. Again please excuse my frankness. It is only occasionally that I am afflicted with the purely human desire to be understood *intellectually* and not be measured by the yardstick of neurosis.

As for this bit of neurosis, may I draw your attention to the fact that you open *The Interpretation of Dreams* with the mournful admission of your own neurosis – the dream of Irma's injection – identification with the neurotic in need of treatment. Very significant.

Our analysis, you may remember, came to a stop with your remark that you 'could not submit to analysis *without losing your authority*'.[101] These words are engraved on my memory as a symbol of everything to come. I haven't eaten *my* words, however.

I am writing to you now as I would write *to a friend* – this is *our* style. I therefore hope you will not be offended by my Helvetic bluntness. One thing I beg of you: take these statements as an *effort to be honest* and do not apply the depreciatory Viennese criterion of egoistic striving for power or heaven knows what other insinuations from the world of the father complex. This is just what I have been hearing on all sides these days, with the result that I am forced to the painful conclusion that the majority of ΨAsts misuse ΨA for the purpose of devaluing others and their progress by insinuations about

101 In *Memories* (p 158/154), Jung writes of an occurrence during the trip to America in 1909, when he and Freud analysed one another's dreams every day. 'Freud had a dream – I would not think it right to air the problem it involved. I interpreted it as best I could, but added that a great deal more could be said about it if he would supply me with some additional details from his private life. Freud's response was . . . "But I cannot risk my authority!" ' Jung had recounted this experience previously in his Seminar in Analytical Psychology, Zürich, March–July 1925, concluding with 'This experience with Freud . . . is the most important factor in my relation to him.'

complexes (as though that explained anything. A wretched theory!). A particularly preposterous bit of nonsense now going the rounds is that my libido theory is the product of anal erotism. When I consider *who* cooked up this 'theory' I fear for the future of analysis.

I want no infantile outpourings of libidinal appreciation or admiration from ΨAsts, merely an understanding of my ideas. The pity of it is that ΨAsts are just as supinely dependent on ΨA as our opponents are on their belief in authority. Anything that might make them think is written off as a complex. This protective function of ΨA badly needed unmasking.

Now for Bergmann. He was quite disoriented and we have yet to ascertain whether you have in fact given up the directorship without breach of contract. He told me that he did not relieve you of your post in his letter. Also, the contract stipulates one year's notice. Naturally I was flabbergasted. So was B., because he had never really thought about it until then. The withdrawal of the International Association took him completely by surprise. He is only now beginning to realize the situation. You will hear from him shortly. I don't know what he is planning. For him it is a serious matter – a loss of over ten thousand marks ... On one point I had to admit B. was right. The founding of *Imago* has cost him a lot of subscribers. It goes against my feeling for sound business to start a new journal before either of the old ones is properly under way. This affair makes an unpleasant impression. Such is the general view. Bergmann is offering Volume III at half price, 4.50M, from No 3 to the end. Better terms could be negotiated (sum total: 652.50M). This can in part be furnished from our fund.

With kind regards, JUNG

332F

Dear Dr Jung,   5 [December] 1912 Vienna, IX. Berggasse 19
You mustn't fear that I take your 'new style' amiss. I hold that in
relations between analysts as in analysis itself every form of frankness is permissible. I too have been disturbed for some time by the
abuse of ΨA to which you refer, that is, in polemics, especially
against new ideas. I do not know if there is any way of preventing
this entirely; for the present I can only suggest a household remedy:
let each of us pay more attention to his own than to his neighbour's
neurosis.

Forgive me if I reverse the ratio observed in your letter and devote
more space to practical matters, which at least are easier to deal with
in a letter. I am referring to the Bergmann matter, in regard to which
I cannot conceal a certain dissatisfaction. Your information sounds
as if it came from another planet; I cannot fit the pieces together or
draw any inference about the situation of the new *Zeitschrift*. Nor
can I make a proposal for defraying any loss to the association
wholly or in part, until I know for what I should be making re-
paration. Finally, it is hard for me to understand or justify your own
bias in the matter.

You yourself have no doubt become familiar while in America
with the principle that a man who is out for profit must take a good
look at the persons and conditions on which his chances of profit
depend. And similarly in Europe ignorance is no excuse for a
businessman. I have less sympathy than you with Bergmann; if he
has been misled by Stekel, that is his affair. I too have suffered
enough at his hands.

If Bergmann believes he did not release me from my position in
his letter, he has a very low opinion of his own statements. I am
enclosing this letter as well as his previous one. He definitely accepts
my notice of resignation and promises to announce it in the next
issue of the *Zentralblatt*. And now he denies that he has let me out! If
he thought I was bound by contract to stay on until the end of the
year, that was the time to call it to my attention, instead of agreeing
to publish a notice. So you see there is no question of any 'breach of

contract' on my part. After this answer from B. I had every reason to consider myself free, whether I was before or not . . .

Now to the *Imago* question, in which to my regret you take sides against me. I cannot help recalling that when *Imago* was founded you reacted not as president of the international association but as editor of the *Jahrbuch*. I am unable to look at this matter from the standpoint of the publisher or of the editor, I can only respond to your reproaches from the standpoint of the ΨAtical cause. The *Zentralblatt* was unequal to our non-medical tasks, we needed another organ, which I conceived of as an appendage to the *Zentralblatt* and offered first to Bergmann for that reason. He declined, so it had to be published by someone else. As for the risk that the publisher might in one year acquire a certain number of subscribers, I did not take it very seriously. The two journals definitely have a greater appeal than only one, and in the end one helps the other. Stekel has agitated against *Imago* from the start.

I am sorry not to be able to discuss your remark on the neuroses of analysts at greater length, but this should not be interpreted as a dismissal. In one point, however, I venture to disagree most emphatically: you have not, as you suppose, been injured by my neurosis.

. . . Looking forward to further word from you, I send you my regards,

Very cordially yours, FREUD

333J

1003 Seestrasse, Küsnacht–Zürich,
7 December 1912

Dear Professor Freud,

Since you have taken so badly to my 'new style', I will tune my lyre a few tones lower, for the present.

Meanwhile, the Bergmann affair has settled itself. He has effectively discharged you, and has been sufficiently punished for it. In view of the fact that *the contract between the I. ΨA A. and Bergmann does not stipulate that your directorship is the indispensable precondition for our connection with the Zentralblatt*, we are committed by the wording of the contract to the subscription. I am convinced that we are not legally in a position to default on our obligations. In these circumstances our *provisional* contract strikes me as extremely favourable: we can withdraw the *Bulletin* forthwith, and the price for the remaining issues will be reduced by half. Bergmann could easily have insisted on more rigorous conditions. As I said, the agreement is provisional and can still be modified on our side. But this would involve a court of arbitration, and in the end we might get a worse deal for lack of the above formula. I therefore plead for acceptance ...

I won't bother you with other things just now. With kind regards,

Yours sincerely, JUNG

334F

Dear Dr Jung,   9 December 1912, Vienna, IX. Berggasse 19
I 'heard' from Bergmann today. Only a few sentences but I am quite satisfied. He tells me the *Zentralblatt* will no longer bear the official title. We all thank you for your successful handling of the matter. I incline to your argument that we have no proper contract on which to base our demands and will have your circular approved by our society on Wednesday (11 Dec). I repeat the offer I made in my telegram to pay half the ransom, so as not to bother our members.

At last I am done with this business and able to get back to work ... I dare say no more about your libido innovation now that you have made such fun of me for my discovery that it contained the solution to the riddle of mysticism. But I am very eager to read your English lectures. I hope they will meet with vigorous opposition on the part of our fellow analysts; my own opposition, even if it outlives my reading of the lectures, would be too self-evident to make an impression.

Your intention of attacking Adler's book has my entire approval.

Apart from the scientific aspect, such a step will also make for political clarity by putting an end to the rumours current here that you are 'swinging over' to him. I myself have not read the book; he has not sent me a copy and I am too stingy to spend my good money on such a product. Are you planning to put your criticism on ice (in the *Jahrbuch*) or to serve it hot (in the *Intern. Zeitsch.*)?

I follow you with interest through all the variations of the lyre that you play with such virtuosity.

With kind regards,

Yours sincerely, FREUD

335J

1003 Seestrasse, Küsnacht–Zürich,

Dear Professor Freud, [written between 11 and 14 December 1912]
I should be glad to make an occasional contribution to the new journal, provided of course that I have anything worthwhile, which is not always the case. The Zürich group proposes the following title:

'Internationale Zeitschrift für *therapeutische* Psychoanalyse'.

This suggestion comes from the *theologians*. They don't want to be left out. The pedagogues are also complaining. Perhaps you will lend a willing ear.

I see from Furtmüller's[102] forthcoming critique in the *Zentralblatt* that the Viennese prophets are wrong about a 'swing over' to Adler. Even Adler's cronies do not regard me as one of theirs.[103]

It is deplorable that science should still be treated like a profession of faith.

With kind regards,

Most sincerely yours, JUNG

[102] Carl Furtmüller, Viennese educator, originally a follower of Freud and at this time of Adler.
[103] Holograph: *Ihrigen* 'yours', instead of *ihrigen* 'theirs'.

337F

Dear Dr Jung,   16 December 1912, Vienna, IX. Berggasse 19
I shall submit your suggestion for changing the name of the *Zeitschrift* both to the society and to the two editors, and report to you on the outcome.

The habit of taking objective statements personally is not only a (regressive) human trait, but also a very specific Viennese failing. I shall be very glad if such claims are not made on you. But are you 'objective' enough to consider the following slip without anger?

'Even Adler's cronies do not regard me as one of *yours*.'

Yours nevertheless, FREUD

338J

                                1003 Seestrasse, Küsnacht–Zürich,
Dear Professor Freud,   18 December 1912
May I say a few words to you in earnest? I admit the ambivalence of my feelings towards you, but am inclined to take an honest and absolutely straightforward view of the situation. If you doubt my word, so much the worse for you. I would, however, point out that your technique of treating your pupils like patients is a *blunder*. In that way you produce either slavish sons or impudent puppies (Adler–Stekel and the whole insolent gang now throwing their weight about in Vienna). I am objective enough to see through your little trick. You go around sniffing out all the symptomatic actions in your vicinity, thus reducing everyone to the level of sons and daughters who blushingly admit the existence of their faults. Meanwhile you remain on top as the father, sitting pretty. For sheer obsequiousness nobody dares to pluck the prophet by the beard and inquire for once what you would say to a patient with a tendency to analyse the analyst instead of himself. You would certainly ask him: '*Who's* got the neurosis?'

You see, my dear Professor, so long as you hand out this stuff I don't give a damn for my symptomatic actions; they shrink to nothing in comparison with the formidable beam in my brother Freud's eye. I am not in the least neurotic – touch wood! I have submitted *lege artis et tout humblement* to analysis and am much the better for it. You know, of course, how far a patient gets with self-analysis: *not* out of his neurosis – just like you. If ever you should rid yourself entirely of your complexes and stop playing the father to your sons and instead of aiming continually at their weak spots took a good look at your own for a change, then I will mend my ways and at one stroke uproot the vice of being in two minds about you. Do you *love neurotics* enough to be always at one with yourself? But perhaps you *hate* neurotics. In that case how can you expect your efforts to treat your patients leniently and lovingly *not* to be accompanied by somewhat mixed feelings? Adler and Stekel were taken in by your little tricks and reacted with childish insolence. I shall continue to stand by you publicly while maintaining my own views, but privately shall start telling you in my letters what I really think of you. I consider this procedure only decent.

No doubt you will be outraged by this peculiar token of friendship, but it may do you good all the same.

With best regards,

Most sincerely yours, JUNG

340F

Dear Dr Jung   22 December 1912,[104] Vienna, IX. Berggasse 19
The main reason why the Vienna local branch rejected the proposed change of title was that the announcements, flyers, and so on, had already been printed or mailed, so that consideration for the publisher made it hard to envisage a change. It was really too late. The matter is of no great importance and will cause no trouble, I trust. I

[104] This letter, apparently not sent, was found among Freud's papers. (Some of its contents is repeated in 342 F.) It was published in *Letters*, ed E. L. Freud, no 160, in a different translation.

do not think 'therapeutic' was a good substitution; the pedagogues will soon find that the new journal will be just as receptive to their contributions as the old one was.

I am sorry my reference to your slip annoyed you so; your reaction seems out of all proportion to the occasion. In regard to your allegation that since I misuse psychoanalysis to keep my students in a state of infantile dependency I myself am responsible for their infantile behaviour, and to the inferences you draw from this contention, I prefer not to judge, because it is hard to judge in matters concerning oneself and such judgements convince no one. I wish merely to provide you with certain facts concerning the foundations of your theory, and leave you to revise it. In Vienna I have become accustomed to the opposite reproach, to wit, that I concern myself too little with the analysis of my 'students'. And it is quite true that since Stekel, for example, discontinued his treatment with me some ten years ago, I have never said one word to him about the analysis of his own person. In Adler's case I have been even more careful to do nothing of the kind. Whatever analytical remarks I have made about either were made to others and for the most part after our relations had broken off. Consequently I fail to see why you feel so sure of the contrary.

With cordial regards,

Yours, FREUD

342F *Internationale Zeitschrift für Ärtzliche Psychoanalyse*

Dear Doctor,   Vienna, 3 January 1913
... I can answer only one point in your previous letter in any detail. Your allegation that I treat my followers like patients is demonstrably untrue. In Vienna I am reproached for the exact opposite. I am held responsible for the misconduct of Stekel and Adler; in reality I have not said one word to Stekel about his analysis since it was concluded some ten years ago, nor have I made any use of analysis

with Adler, who was never my patient. Any analytical remarks I have made about them were addressed to others and for the most part at a time when we had ceased to associate with one another. In building your construction on this foundation you have made matters as easy for yourself as with your famous 'Kreuzlingen gesture'.

Otherwise your letter cannot be answered. It creates a situation that would be difficult to deal with in a personal talk and totally impossible in correspondence. It is a convention among us analysts that none of us need feel ashamed of his own bit of neurosis. But one who while behaving abnormally keeps shouting that he is normal gives ground for the suspicion that he lacks insight into his illness. Accordingly, I propose that we abandon our personal relations entirely. I shall lose nothing by it, for my only emotional tie with you has long been a thin thread – the lingering effect of past disappointments – and you have everything to gain, in view of the remark you recently made in Munich, to the effect that an intimate relationship with a man inhibited your scientific freedom. I therefore say, take your full freedom and spare me your supposed 'tokens of friendship'. We are agreed that a man should subordinate his personal feelings to the general interests of his branch of endeavour. You will never have reason to complain cf any lack of correctness on my part where our common undertaking and the pursuit of scientific aims are concerned; I may say, no more reason in the future than in the past. On the other hand, I am entitled to expect the same from you.

Regards,

Yours sincerely, FREUD

343J

Dear Professor Freud,   3 January 1913

Although you have evidently taken my first secret letter very much to heart or very much amiss, I cannot refrain, while avoiding that topic, from offering you my friendly wishes for the New Year. It is my hope that the ΨAtic movement will continue to advance, its vitality unimpaired and indeed heightened by internal conflicts and crosscurrents. Without them there is no life. When everything goes smoothly petrifaction sets in. 'I seek salvation not in rigid forms.'

Don't hesitate to tell me if you want no more of my secret letters. I too can get along without them. Needless to say I have no desire to torment you. But if you profess a friendly attitude towards me, I must insist on my right to reciprocate, and shall treat you with the same analytical consideration which you extend to me from time to time. You surely know that the understanding of ΨA truths is in direct proportion to the progress one has made in oneself. If one has neurotic symptoms there will be a failure of understanding somewhere. Where, past events have already shown. So if I offer you the unvarnished truth it is meant for your good, even though it may hurt.

I think my honourable intentions are perfectly clear, so I need say no more. The rest is up to you.

From the drift of this letter you will be able to guess what my wishes are for the New Year.

With best regards,

Most sincerely yours, JUNG

344J
Internationale Psychoanalytische Vereinigung

Dear Professor Freud,   Küsnacht–Zürich, 6 January 1913
I accede to your wish that we abandon our personal relations, for I
never thrust my friendship on anyone. You yourself are the best
judge of what this moment means to you. 'The rest is silence.'

Thank you for accepting Burrow's paper.

Yours sincerely, JUNG

346F *Internationale Zeitschrift für*
       Ärtzliche Psychoanalyse

Dear Mr President,   Vienna, 27 January 1913[105]
Dear Doctor,
I have the first number of our new *Zeitschrift* before me. I avail
myself of this opportunity to thank you for the friendly support
which you as president have given the undertaking. It has enabled
us from the very start to embark on a policy which we hope to pursue
to the satisfaction of all.

Both the editors and the director will be thankful to you for any
suggestion as to changes and improvements. The review of the *Jahrbuch* will be continued in the next issue, which will also carry a
study of your libido paper by one of the editors. The third number
will carry contributions by our American colleagues.

It now appears that a secret contract was concluded a year and a
half ago between Stekel and the publisher, providing for my dismissal in the event of a conflict between director and editor. A pretty
piece of treachery.

I hope that we shall arrive at a satisfactory understanding on the
basis of our common undertakings.

Regards,

Yours very sincerely, FREUD

PS. I am looking forward to your draft contract and to your decision
concerning my contribution to the compensation for Bergmann.

[105] Freud's last surviving letter to Jung.

350J

Internationale Psychoanalytische Vereinigung

Dear Professor Freud,   Küsnacht–Zürich, 3 March 1913

This is to let you know that tomorrow I have to go to America for five weeks. All the necessary arrangements have been made with Deuticke for the *Jahrbuch.* I have referred him to you should anything out of the ordinary happen. The last manuscripts to be sent to the printer are 'New Dream Experiments' by Dr J. Stärcke, Amsterdam, and my American lectures. These are really quite tame and in no way deserve the hullabaloo they have created. I have expressed in them only a few divergent opinions.

Pfister informs me that Adler has sidled up to him with the proposition that they make common cause against you. This manoeuvre has been rebuffed with indignation here.

I have talked with Maeder again and we have come to the conclusion that we don't want to push ourselves forward in any way. We are quite willing to fall in with another, better suggestion . . .

I have also received the paper from Graz. It would seem that dawn is gradually breaking in psychiatry.

With best regards,

Most sincerely yours, JUNG

355J

Internationale Psychoanalytische Vereinigung

Dear Professor Freud,   Küsnacht–Zürich, 29 July 1913

I am still waiting for the announcement of a lecture from your side. As I would like to have the programme printed soon, I should be grateful for an early reply.

Many thanks for sending me your offprints. I must, however, point out that in your paper 'An Evidential Dream', which in other respects shows the fine qualities I have always admired in your writings, you put forward a conception of our views which rests on a misunderstanding. This misunderstanding turns on the conception of the actual conflict, which for us is *not the petty vexation of the moment* but the problem of adaptation. A second misunderstanding seems to be that you think we deny the wish-fulfilment theory of dreams. We fully admit the soundness of the wish-fulfilment theory, but we maintain that this way of interpreting dreams touches only the surface, that it stops at the symbol, and that further interpretation is possible. When, for instance, a coitus wish appears in a dream, this wish can be analysed further, since this archaic expression with its tiresome monotony of meaning needs retranslating into another medium. We recognize the soundness of the wish-fulfilment theory up to a certain point, but we go beyond it. In our view it does not exhaust the meaning of the dream.

With best regards,

Yours sincerely, JUNG

The Munich Congress

Jung paid a visit to England in early August in order to read papers to two professional bodies. On 5 August he appeared before the Psycho-Medical Society, London, with a paper entitled merely 'Psycho-Analysis' (in CW 4, 'General Aspects of Psychoanalysis'), in which he applied the name 'analytical psychology' to the 'new psychological science'. On dream theory 'I find myself in entire agreement with the views of Adler' (para. 553). At the 17th International Congress of Medicine, London, 6–12 August, his subject was 'On Psycho-Analysis' (in CW 4, 'Psychoanalysis and Neurosis') the same paper he had read at the New York Academy of Medicine ten months earlier, proposing that 'psychoanalytic theory be freed from the purely sexual standpoint'.

Freud had gone to Marienbad in mid July for treatment, with 'his three womenfolk', as Jones states (II, p 112/99): 'His daughter tells me it was the only time she ever remembers her father being depressed.' In August the Freud family went to a resort in the Dolomites, where Ferenczi joined them. The two men travelled together to Munich, arriving there on 5 September.

The congress went on in an atmosphere Jones has described as 'disagreeable', and Freud as 'fatiguing and unedifying'. When Jung

*stood for re-election as president, twenty-two out of fifty-two of the
participants abstained from voting, in order that his election should
not be unanimous.*

357J

1003 Seestrasse, Küsnacht–Zürich,
27 October 1913

Dear Professor Freud,

It has come to my ears through Dr Maeder that you doubt my *bona
fides*. I would have expected you to communicate with me directly on
so weighty a matter. Since this is the gravest reproach that can be
levelled at anybody, you have made further collaboration impossible. I therefore lay down the editorship of the *Jahrbuch* with which
you entrusted me. I have also notified Bleuler and Deuticke of my
decision.

Very truly yours, DR C. G. JUNG

The end of the Jahrbuch

*Subsequently, the following announcements appeared in the Ja-
hrbuch, V:2 (1913):*

Statement by Prof Bleuler, Director

*After the termination of this volume I am resigning as director, but
shall of course maintain my interest in the journal as before.*
Bleuler

Statement by the Editor

I have found myself obliged to resign as editor of the Jahrbuch. *The
reasons for my resignation are of a personal nature, on which account I disdain to discuss them in public.*
C. G. Jung

Statement by the Publisher

After the secession of Prof Dr Bleuler and Dr Jung, Prof Dr Freud

will continue this Jahrbuch. *The next volume will appear in the
middle of 1914 under the title:* Jahrbuch der Psychoanalyse, *Edited
by Dr K. Abraham (Berlin) and Dr E. Hitschmann (Vienna).*
Fr Deuticke

So reconstituted, the Jahrbuch *continued publication for one more
year. The first issue (VI:1) contained the two works in which Freud
first published an account of the differences between his views and
those of Jung and Adler: 'On the History of the Psycho-Analytic
Movement' and 'On Narcissism: An Introduction' (both in SE
XIV), written in the early months of 1914.*

358J

Internationale Psychoanalytische Vereinigung

Dear Mr President,   Küsnacht–Zürich, 20 April 1914[106]
The latest developments have convinced me that my views are in
such sharp contrast to the views of the majority of the members of
our association that I can no longer consider myself a suitable personality to be president. I therefore tender my resignation to the
council of the presidents of the branch societies, with many thanks
for the confidence I have enjoyed hitherto.[107]

Very truly yours, DR C. G. JUNG[108]

[106] Typewritten and signed, with three *x*s at the end, written by pen. A circular
letter to the presidents of the branch societies. Its text was published subsequently
in the *Zeitschrift*, II: 3 (1914), 297.

[107] On 30 April, Jung submitted his resignation as privatdocent in the medical
faculty of Zürich University. It was accepted by the cantonal education
authorities on 3 June. (Extract from the official records, courtesy of Mr Franz
Jung.)

[108] In *Memories*, Jung recounts a thrice-repeated dream in April, May, and June
1914: 'In the middle of summer an Arctic cold wave descended and froze the
land to ice . . . All living green things were killed by frost . . . The third dream,
however, had an unexpected end. There stood a leaf-bearing tree, but without
fruit (my tree of life, I thought), whose leaves had been transformed by the
effects of the frost into sweet grapes full of healing juices. I plucked the grapes
and gave them to a large, waiting crowd' (pp 176/170).

The Final Break

In a letter of 30 April 1914 to the presidents of the six European branch societies – Berlin, Budapest, London, Munich, Vienna, and Zürich – Freud suggested that the presidents' council forgo a meeting and elect a provisional president of the association by correspondence. He proposed Karl Abraham, since he would be in the most advantageous position to make preparations for the congress at Dresden in the autumn of 1914.

Accordingly, the branch presidents agreed through correspondence that Abraham serve as provisional president until the next congress. He edited the Bulletin *in the next issue of the* Zeitschrift; *Dresden was proposed for the fifth congress in September 1914. But Abraham's* Bulletin *in the issue after that (I:5), a mere page in length, contained only three items of information: on 10 July, the Zürich society had voted to withdraw from the International Psychoanalytic Association; the* Zeitschrift *and* Imago *would continue to publish, but probably not the* Jahrbuch; *and, owing to 'events in the great world . . . our congress, like many other scientific arrangements, must be postponed for an unspecified time.'*

At the end of July, Jung was invited by the British Medical Association to lecture at its annual meeting, in Aberdeen 'On the Importance of the Unconscious in Psychopathology' (CW 3). He referred briefly to Freud ('To Freud we owe thanks . . . for having called attention to the importance of dreams') but did not mention the word psychoanalysis.

359J

228 Seestrasse,[109] Küsnacht–Zürich

Dear Professor Freud,   [day and month?] 1923

The purpose of this letter is to refer the following case to your medical authority:

Herr J—, who will shortly have the honour of introducing himself to you personally, is suffering from an obsessional neurosis. He has been treated by me for two years, but the illness brought many interruptions the reason for which will become apparent from the report drawn up by the patient himself. In the course of treatment he acquired a more intimate knowledge of his sexual fantasies and also of your scientific writings. The insights they afforded alleviated his symptoms so much that he even began dreaming about you. The wish to be treated by you personally was so unmistakable that I felt it my duty to do everything in my power to support his recuperative efforts and to facilitate his treatment at your hands. The unquestioned help which your views afforded him have prepared him for further progress in this direction.

Herr J— is by profession a diplomat, very intelligent and very well-to-do. His neurosis is certainly severe, and in addition he is no longer young, but at the same time he is sufficiently flexible for me to refer him to you with a good conscience. Moreover his decision to turn to you for help as a result of the treatment was so logical and convincing that I never doubted its rightness for a moment. For the symptomatology of the case I must refer you to the patient's own report, to which I have nothing to add.[110]

109 The same house as '1003', renumbered.
110 The following information was supplied by Aniela Jaffé: 'The case involved a Jew who could not or would not acknowledge his Jewishness. The analysis with Freud did not help him and he turned back to Jung. He then had a dream in which he found himself at an impassable place, beyond which a light shined. At the impasse sat an old woman, who said to him: "Only he who is a Jew can get through!" This was the beginning of the cure of his neurosis.'

In the sincere hope, dear Professor, that you will favour the patient with your help, I remain,

With respectful regards,

Very truly yours, DR JUNG

Appendix

The Collected Editions in English
The standard edition of the *Complete Psychological Works*
of Sigmund Freud. Translated from the German under the general
editorship of James Strachey, in collaboration with Anna Freud,
assisted by Alix Strachey, Alan Tyson, and Angela Richards.
London: The Hogarth Press and the Institute of Psycho-
Analysis. / New York: Macmillan.

The *Collected Works* of C. G. Jung. Editors: Sir Herbert Read, Michael Fordham, Gerhard Adler; William McGuire, executive editor. Translated from the German by R. F. C. Hull (except Vol 2). Princeton, NJ: Princeton University Press (Bollingen Series). / London: Routledge & Kegan Paul.

Index

309

Index

Index